ENDING DENIAL

Understanding Aboriginal Issues

WAYNE WARRY

University of Toronto Press

LIBRARY AND ARCHIVES CANADA CATALOGUING IN PUBLICATION

Warry, Wayne
Ending denial : understanding Aboriginal issues / Wayne Warry.
ISBN 978-1-44260-005-8
1. Native peoples—Canada.   2. Racism—Canada.   I. Title.
E78.C2W38 2007   971.004'97   C2007-900164-5

We welcome comments and suggestions regarding any aspect of our publications — please feel free to contact us at news@utphighereducation.com or visit our internet site at www. utphighereducation.com.

North America
5201 Dufferin Street
Toronto, Ontario, Canada, M3H 5T8

2250 Military Road
Tonawanda, New York, USA, 14150

ORDERS PHONE: 1-800-565-9523
ORDERS FAX: 1-800-221-9985
ORDERS EMAIL: utpbooks@utpress.utoronto.ca

UK, Ireland, and
Continental Europe
NBN International
Estover Road, Plymouth,
PL6 7PY, UK
FAX ORDER LINE: 44 (0) 1752 202333
TEL: 44 (0) 1752 202301
orders@nbninternational.com

This book is printed on paper containing 100% post-consumer fibre.

University of Toronto Press acknowledges the financial support for its publishing activities of the Government of Canada through the Book Publishing Industry Development Program (BPIDP).

Cover & Interior Design by Grace Cheong, Black Eye Design

Printed in Canada

ENDING DENIAL

We should study how Indians do off the reserve, because the great weight of evidence to date indicates nothing would better serve our Indian population than to integrate with Canadian society as a whole.

...

Tom Flanagan

The irony of the Information Age is that it has given new respectability to uninformed opinion.

...

John Lawton

The opposite of love is not hate, it is indifference.

...

Elie Wiesel

The Two Row wampum captures the original values that governed our relationship — equality, respect, dignity, and a sharing of the river we travel on.

...

Ovid Mercredi and Mary Ellen Turpel

Culture is a verb, not a noun, a process, not a thing in itself.

...

Ronald Niezen

CONTENTS

ACKNOWLEDGEMENTS

The inspiration for this book came from the students I meet each year who arrive at university ignorant of Aboriginal issues and who, through various courses, come to see Canada's treatment of Aboriginal peoples as appalling by any stretch of the moral imagination. Many individuals have helped me clarify my thoughts or pointed me to information about Aboriginal issues during the course of writing. My special thanks to Megan Corbiere, Pamela Cushing, Eleanor Debassige, Tracy Farmer, Barbara Erskine, Glenn Hallet, Douglas Graham, Dawn Martin-Hill, Carmen Jones, Phyllis Kinoshameg, Agnes Mandamin, Rick Montour, Harriett MacMillan, Bruce Minore, Valerie O'Brien, Brenda Roy, Marjory Shawande, Christina Taibossigai, and Kue Young. I wish to acknowledge the work of many graduate students whose research has deepened my understanding of Aboriginal issues, among them Kathleen Buddle-Crowe, Ed Koenig, Darrel Manitowabi, Jennifer Ranford, Craig Proulx, and Jairus Skye. I also acknowledge the many frontline health workers in Wikwemikong First Nation, M'Chigeeng First Nation, Noojmowin Teg, and Mnaamodzawin Health Services with whom I have had the opportunity to speak over the past decade and whose hard work and dedication demonstrates the capacity building that is occurring every day. Michael Asch reviewed the draft; I thank him for his insightful comments which greatly assisted me in my revisions to the book. I would also thank the second anonymous reviewer and my editors, Anne Brackenbury and Keely Winnitoy at Broadview Press, for their advice. I also gratefully acknowledge the help of Betsy Struthers who copy-edited the book, and Tara Trueman.

I wish to thank my parents and family for their encouragement and support throughout the many changes that occurred during this project. Special thanks to Adam and Andrew Warry for reminding me how esoteric academic writing can be. Don Jaffray, Craig Jackson, Christopher Justice, Marion Maar, Greg Mayne, and Patricia Seymour helped me think through various issues while I was drafting the book. Kristen Jacklin read the draft manuscript and identified a number of important sources. Her love and friendship, as well as her dedication to various health research projects, afforded me the opportunity and peace of mind to complete the book. Finally, I wish to acknowledge David, who provides me with an education each and every day.

A NOTE ON TERMINOLOGY

Words have power. A writer's choice of words indicates political orientation and potential bias. The era of political correctness may be gone, but we have been left with the awareness that we should strive for language that is non-offensive and accurate. Briefly, here are my thoughts on some of the key terminology in this book.

The terms Indian (non-status and status), Aboriginal, Indigenous, Native, Métis, and Inuit are all labels that appear in media and in everyday conversation. Students often ask whether Indian is still an appropriate word. The answer is that it depends on how it is used. Some Native people find the word Indian offensive because they feel it is a colonial word, a term commonly associated with India and Columbus—a lost white man who didn't have the sense to know where he was! But this is bad etymology. As the Aboriginal author Taiaiake Alfred notes, "India, was at the time, known as Hindustan, and the word 'Indian' most probably derives from Columbus's use of the phrase 'una gente *in Dios*' ('a people in/of God') to refer to the Taino people, early inhabitants of what is now known as the Dominican Republic" (Alfred 1999: xxv-xxvi). Indian is also a term that is used by Native people themselves, often with a special political meaning, so we should not reject it out of hand. In common conversation we still refer to reserve land as Indian country and to Indian time or Indian summer. However, we should recognize that the word sometimes is used pejoratively by mainstream writers—indeed, the use of the word Indian in media reports commonly signals a right-of-centre political orientation. Because Indian is used by some Canadians in a derogatory way, it is often considered offensive by Native Canadians when used by non-Natives. In sum, Indian is a word that is easily avoided by using the more politically correct word, Aboriginal, and I use it infrequently in the book.

In Canada, Indian is also a legal term—it used to signify those people the government recognizes as having Indian status; that is, those people who have an identifiable Band, who live or were born on reserve, who are recognized under the Indian Act. The term "non-status Indians" is formally used to refer to Native people who are not recognized by the government because their parents or ancestors enfranchised or lost their Indian status for a variety of reasons. Non-status Indians may identify themselves as Aboriginal, yet they are not considered status Indians by the government and so do not have many of the same rights under law.

Safer and correct terms are Native or Aboriginal peoples. When lecturing or writing I use the word Native, which rolls off the tongue a little easier than Aboriginal, in opposition to mainstream or other Canadians; for example, "Native and non-Natives agree that policy must change." Today the term Aboriginal is the most appropriate word and has formal standing in the 1982 Constitution Act. For me, the term Aboriginal connotes a *unique* status, a status that is different from other Canadians and from other ethnic or racial groups.

Throughout the text I use the terms Aboriginal and Indigenous as synonyms (see also Asch 2001). However, it should be noted that the latter word — literally meaning "originating in an area" — is sometimes used to connote aspects of Aboriginal culture that are specifically tied to peoples' spiritual connection to the land or environment, such as Indigenous medicine or Indigenous knowledge. Prior to the 1970s, the word had limited application in anthropology as a term for tribal peoples; its widespread use began in the 1980s. As Ronald Niezen notes, "The interesting thing about the relative newness of the concept is that it refers to primordial identity, to people with primary attachments to land and culture, 'traditional' people with lasting connections to ways of life that have survived from time immemorial" (Niezen 2003: 3). The increasing use of the word, and its associated meaning "original peoples," is testimony to the success of the worldwide Indigenous rights movement. Because there are Indigenous peoples throughout the world (there are, for example, over 40 million Indigenous peoples in China) the term also has an international connotation.

I use the term First Nation to describe the various communities of Aboriginal peoples in Canada who are not of Inuit or Métis descent (the term settlement is often used in the latter cases). First Nations' peoples are represented by the Assembly of First Nations (AFN). The term is also now used instead of the more dated "Indian Band" and has a decidedly political connotation, often being used with the term Council, as in First Nations Councils, to describe the political representatives or organization of communities.

Increasingly, Aboriginal peoples are returning to their languages to describe themselves and their communities. Aboriginal words are replacing European ones — we hear Anishnabek, rather than Ojibway, Haudenausaunee rather than Iroquois (the latter is an Algonkian term meaning rattlesnake and long used by Europeans). In this way, the community formally known as the "Ojibways of Spanish River" become the Sagamok Anishnabek First Nation. Taiaiake Alfred claims these Indigenous words help Aboriginal people to "free their minds" from definitions imposed by Europeans (Alfred 1999: xxv). For non-Natives these Aboriginal words are often difficult to pronounce, but to master them is to make an important statement about respecting Aboriginal cultures.

The use of the plural Aboriginal peoples is important because it also signals political orientation. Conservative writers refer to Native people. While the use of

Aboriginal *people* can be grammatically correct in specific contexts, this characterization homogenizes; it turns all Aboriginal persons into a "type," a generalized category. The use of Aboriginal *peoples* immediately recognizes the diversity of Aboriginal cultures — and there are many, many distinct Aboriginal cultures in Canada. Another indicator of political orientation is whether to capitalize terms. Indian, like Caucasian (and other racial or ethnic designations) is capitalized. The Nelson Canadian Dictionary (1997) capitalizes the adjective Aboriginal. But Aboriginal denotes more than race, it signals a special political status, as do the adjectives Canadian or American. Conservative writers refuse to capitalize the term, precisely because they do not wish to acknowledge the special political status of Aboriginal peoples. Indeed, the use of the lower-case aboriginal along with the singular people, the patronizing use of Indian, or phrases like "*our* Native people" are quick reality checks on a writer's political orientation.

Finally, a note on two other terms: mainstream Canadians and dominant society. These terms are increasingly problematic as the Canadian population becomes more diverse. Both connote for me the historical, European, and Eurocentric value system, which was introduced to Canada and which, over time, became the foundation of Canada's central institutions. The phrase dominant society is particularly important as it signals those people in power who have made policy that effects minority and marginalized groups. As the population becomes increasingly diverse, immigrants and persons of colour comprise an increasing percentage of mainstream Canada. How, if at all, members of these cultures influence and eventually change dominant society values remains to be seen.

INTRODUCTION

Canadians remain remarkably insulated from the misery in the world. We know, but have not fully experienced, terrorism, modern epidemics, natural disasters, and extreme poverty. We know that we are privileged. Every United Nations survey ranks us among the elite nations on this earth. By any standard—wealth, natural resources, acceptance of diversity—we are immeasurably fortunate. Yet, there remains within Canada an almost unspeakable reality, which, like a cancer, slowly sickens the body politic. This is the reality of life for Aboriginal peoples, who in many parts of the country experience chronic illness, who live in poverty in Third World conditions, and who do not have the opportunities available to the majority of mainstream Canadians.

This book tackles the vexing questions of why Canadians have been unable to come to grips with Aboriginal issues and why we have created a country not fully inclusive of Aboriginal peoples. The irony of our society is that the values of tolerance and multicultural diversity are accepted and heralded as part of a national ethic even as Aboriginal peoples are marginalized and their cultures denigrated. This book explores some of the more obvious reasons why this should be so—our fear of change, our ignorance of Aboriginal peoples, our feelings of guilt, and our denial of history.

Aboriginal affairs in Canada are in disarray. We need a way out of the morass, a set of signposts, a rationale, a guide—not a liberal or neo-conservative "road map," but an Aboriginal guide that is both pragmatic and visionary at the same time.[1] We need new ideas and new dialogue that will take us not only to a workable union between Aboriginal and mainstream Canadians, but also to an understanding of Aboriginal rights that is both satisfying to Aboriginal peoples and unthreatening to the rest of us.[2] The simple fact is that this guide exists but is ignored; it can be found in the successive policies developed in the aftermath of the report of the Royal Commission on Aboriginal Peoples (RCAP) and advocated by national Aboriginal organizations such as the Assembly of First Nations (AFN).

RCAP argues that reconciliation between mainstream Canada and Aboriginal peoples requires an understanding of the history of European-Aboriginal relations and of contemporary Aboriginal cultures. What Canadians should want is reconciliation in a country where Aboriginal peoples have a standard of living equal to that of mainstream Canadians and where the anger and acrimony that exists around Aboriginal issues has been ended. These are obtainable goals. The revitalization of Aboriginal cultures and the reconstitution of sustainable Aboriginal economies are possible within the next several generations, that is to say, within this century.

The resolution of Aboriginal affairs also requires an understanding of culture that is absent in most public discourse, including media reports and political debate. Culture is one of the most central social science concepts for understanding the human condition. Anthropology, more than any other social science, has advanced our knowledge of it. As an anthropologist, I believe that an appreciation of culture is one of the preconditions required to formulate a new direction in Aboriginal affairs.

In terms of population size or percentage of dollars spent by governments, Aboriginal peoples represent only a small part of contemporary Canada. However, in our definition of Canada and our identity as Canadians, Aboriginal issues occupy a geographic and psychic space that is inordinately large. Any representation of Canada — for example, the promotional video for Vancouver's 2010 Olympic bid — is unthinkable without reference to Aboriginal peoples and images. Already, Aboriginal beliefs about the environment, justice, social well-being, and political life have informed national and regional policy and programs. These contributions, unfortunately, often go unrecognized by the media.

But, despite the significance of Aboriginal issues for our country's past and future, Canadians are remarkably ignorant of Aboriginal peoples. I routinely lecture to second- and third-year undergraduate students on Aboriginal cultures and contemporary conditions. The vast majority invariably admit to being surprised, if not shocked, when they learn about the social and economic conditions on reserve. Put simply, upon entering university, students know little or nothing of Aboriginal issues and are ill-equipped to filter the many conflicting perspectives and arguments they hear about the challenges facing Aboriginal communities. When they learn more, most are baffled by the government's inability or unwillingness to place Aboriginal issues higher on the political agenda.

This ignorance is widespread. I recently developed training sessions on Aboriginal history, culture, and health for delivery in Cancer Care sites in Ontario. The majority of participants — nurses, radiologists, and administrators — frankly admitted to being embarrassed at their lack of knowledge of Aboriginal peoples and issues. In session after session, they asked, "Why didn't we know this?" They commented on the failing of an educational system that continues to ignore Aboriginal peoples' history and place in contemporary society. These and other experiences have convinced me that the "average" Canadian lacks the knowledge of Aboriginal peoples necessary for an informed public debate about self-government or other Aboriginal issues. Moreover, I believe this ignorance makes Canadians susceptible to supporting misinformed and misguided social policy. Our belief in the superiority of European values and our ignorance of Aboriginal cultures sustain the structural racism that marginalizes and impoverishes Aboriginal peoples.

Ending Denial is aimed at undergraduate students and other Canadians who wish to develop a perspective on the complexity of Aboriginal rights arguments. I disentangle the different political positions taken on Aboriginal affairs and confront a number of misinformed arguments about Aboriginal issues that prevent us from developing social policy that could end the internal colonialism that still exists in this country.

An adequate understanding of Aboriginality is essential to a reformulation of the Canadian identity. Canada is a young country, but we will remain in adolescence, not fully mature to act in the world, until we resolve Aboriginal issues. It is difficult for Canada to be taken seriously on matters of human rights when we continue to turn a blind eye to the social, political, and economic status of First Nations. Nonetheless, Canada's approach to Aboriginal rights is seen in countries such as Australia as progressive and is sometimes hailed as a model to follow, in part because Aboriginal rights are entrenched in the Constitution. Canadian leadership in this arena could potentially influence the development of progressive policies concerning Indigenous rights that could affect hundreds of millions of people around the world.

For this reason, I occasionally cite examples from other countries where Indigenous rights debates occur. In particular, I use Australian examples in order to highlight issues, intentions, and motivations of those who write from the neo-conservative right. Australia and Canada have much in common: both are Commonwealth nations with parliamentary systems and a complex mixture of federal and state (provincial) jurisdictions. In Canada the Aboriginal population is around 3 per cent (and growing), while in Australia it is slightly less than 2 per cent of its 19 million people. Aboriginal history and identity are critical elements in the national identity of both countries. But there are important differences. Aboriginal Australians have, at least as yet, no constitutional recognition or protection of their rights, and there is no specific history of treaty relations.[3] Political and intellectual debates in Australia are more sharply polarized between left and right, between Labour and Liberal parties,[4] often resulting in vehement, dramatic, and at times ugly differences expressed about the truth and interpretation of past and present policies.

The title of this book is reminiscent of Robert Manne's *In Denial* (2001). Manne is an Australian academic, columnist, and political commentator, and his book confronts how Australians have tried to deny the evidence associated with the mistreatment of Australian Aboriginals, especially the removal of Aboriginal children from their families. The Australian case bears many resemblances to the residential school and child welfare experiences of Aboriginal families in Canada (see Chapter 3). Manne suggests that many Australians, particularly members of the neo-conservative right, actively deny the consequences of colonialism. I believe many Canadians are also in denial about their past and, significantly, deny the continuing impacts of colonial practices that discriminate against Aboriginal peoples in what is, supposedly, a post-colonial era.

Ending denial is also important from the perspective of Aboriginal peoples (Warry 1998: 138, 209). Individuals and entire communities are confronting many difficult issues — alcohol abuse, family violence, mental illness, and sexual abuse — which are often linked to residential schools and other forms of colonialism. Through this confrontation, Aboriginal peoples are able to examine the roots of current problems and to grapple with their own cultural solutions to these issues. Canadians need to better understand that, despite the many challenges that lie ahead, Aboriginal communities have turned the corner; there are hopeful signs that current government policies, however inadequate, are having a positive impact on Aboriginal health and economic well-being. At the heart of these improvements is the enhanced capacity related to Aboriginal political control over their communities.

There is, I believe, in Canada both an indifference about Aboriginal issues and a denial of colonial actions that create a kind of accidental racism. My use of this term is not meant to sugar-coat, but rather to signal that many, if not the majority, of Canadians are not only ignorant of Aboriginal culture, they are also ignorant of their ignorance. Aboriginal readers may well object to the idea that racism is in any way accidental — most, if not all, have felt the sting of racism and discrimination in their daily lives, and some mainstream Canadians have clearly expressed racist views. Mathew Coon Come, Ovid Mercredi, and other Aboriginal leaders have long charged that Canadians tolerate systemic racism (Stackhouse 2001). However, I have refrained from characterizing even the most conservative political positions on Aboriginal peoples as racist because, at least as stated, these views express a desire to improve the health and well-being of Aboriginal peoples.[5]

Manne argues that there is a "culture war" between the left and right in Australia with Aboriginal peoples and immigrants as the focus.[6] There are faint and not so faint echoes of these Australian political battles in academic and media writing about Aboriginal rights in Canada. Canadian party politics have been less polarized than in Australia, with mainstream values holding sway to a liberal-conservative "middle course." But the rise of the Reform and Alliance parties, with their culmination in the new Conservative Party of Canada, has brought neo-conservative values to the centre stage of Canadian politics. The discourse about Aboriginal peoples in Canada is perhaps less polemic, and more polite, than in Australia, but the debates about Aboriginal issues are inherently ideological.

My reading of media reports and key academic and public policy commentary suggests that a common sense discourse exists that undermines Aboriginal rights and promotes assimilationist attitudes and values. This discourse appeals to many Canadians who do not think of themselves as neo-conservative or right wing but who do believe that Aboriginal peoples should integrate into the mainstream or that they should be treated the same as other Canadians. Thus, when it comes to Aboriginal issues, the neo-conservative view *is* the mainstream. The neo-conservative right argues, at times convincingly, that the continuing problems associated with alcohol abuse, family violence, poverty, and ill health in Aboriginal communities are the result of state-created dependency and the failure of ill-conceived government policies. It also argues, without evidence, that the idea of self-determination is flawed and that the solution to Aboriginal issues is to treat Aboriginal peoples equally with other Canadians, that is, as ordinary citizens. These views are dangerous — they undermine an Indigenous social and political agenda that is central to the very fabric of our national identity. If followed, they will ensure a future colonialism that will produce policies as dark and damaging as those of the past.

While what surveys we have of public opinion about Aboriginal issues indicate considerable division about key issues like self-government and land claims, they do not even begin to troll the depths of mainstream Canadians' understanding of Aboriginal peoples. In short, they are often surveys of uninformed citizens (Simpson 2002). There is a lot to learn. We need to make decisions about Aboriginal issues on the basis of a sound understanding of their cultures and aspirations. We need to understand the diversity of Aboriginal culture, the history of colonialism and treaty relations, and the nature of contemporary Aboriginal communities, including those in cities. We must recognize that some Aboriginal people drive SUVs; marry non-Natives; attend university and church; and still remain distinctly Aboriginal in mind, body, emotion, and spirit. Aboriginal cultures remain vibrant and individual, with their leaders asserting the collective rights of their peoples on reserve and in urban centres.

Misinformed views of Aboriginal peoples are everywhere; they are not constrained by class or education. I have met many university-educated people who believe that Aboriginal peoples are somehow privileged because they have special access to land or who think that rights should not be extended on the basis of race. I wrote this book because, as a Canadian citizen and as an anthropologist, I feel compelled to "do something" to raise awareness about Aboriginal peoples and the rights that they are guaranteed under the Constitution. Social scientists like myself must confront the biases, misunderstandings, and misinformed political positions concerning Aboriginal issues that so frequently appear in the media and in public discourse. I am very concerned by arguments that pit mainstream Canadians against Native people, that present Aboriginal communities as somehow "in the way" of economic progress,[7] and that openly advocate for the assimilation or integration of Aboriginal peoples into the mainstream of society.

I use key social science concepts in this book without bogging the reader down in the esoteric details of academic argument. The short but related chapters allow readers to pick and choose specific topics of interest. Key academic articles and texts, government reports, and newspaper articles are cited. Basic and well-established facts that are easily verified through census or other statistical reports are also referenced, even when they may be slightly contentious (for example, figures pertaining to program costs or population). I have used my own best judgement and have chosen conservative or median estimates wherever possible.

Aboriginal peoples are poised to make a significant contribution to new national and international political processes. I draw on anthropologists, human rights scholars, and Indigenous authors who have participated in the emerging discourse on the nature of Aboriginal identity in contemporary society and Indigenous rights around the globe. One of these authors, Ronald Niezen, has been particularly influential in my thinking. He and others claim that in the course of mapping out a modern hybridized identity, Aboriginal peoples have asserted their citizenship rights in a unique way that raises challenges for the development of nation-states within the context of global political processes (Niezen 2003). In other words, the future of Aboriginal peoples is tied to the reinvention of the nation-state.

As part of this book is concerned with political debates about the proper course of action for Aboriginal issues, I should briefly detail my political orientation and research experience. Although I am on the left of any standard political spectrum and guided by principles of social justice, I share many values with those who might easily be characterized as neo-conservative: I believe in limiting government involvement in the everyday lives of families and in limiting government bureaucracy; I want to see my tax dollars spent wisely and not wastefully; and I believe that social programs need to be effectively and efficiently delivered. I am part of what Tom Flanagan would describe as the "new orthodoxy" in that I ascribe to the need for a liberal interpretation of Aboriginal rights.

Why should the reader trust my judgement or interpretations of the arguments that follow? I am an applied medical anthropologist who has worked in a variety of urban and reserve communities and organizations for over 20 years. Most of my work concerns the direct application of cultural knowledge and interpretation to real life problems, and most of my publications have been for First Nation or government readers rather than for academics. Often these reports provide evidence for a specific policy or program change. In university lectures and cross-cultural awareness training, I spend considerable time informing people about Aboriginal history, health, and culture. My research has been funded directly by the government and Aboriginal organizations and indirectly through federal government agencies such as the Social Science and Humanities Research Council or the Canadian Institutes of Health Research. I have worked closely with Aboriginal communities and assisted them in designing and evaluating culturally appropriate health systems. Far from being in an ivory tower, I am intimately connected to the real world of Aboriginal peoples.

Because I am an expert in the field of Aboriginal health and lecture broadly on Aboriginal issues, I rely on a critical analysis of the literature available in the areas of constitutional law, treaty research, and economic development. As well as mainstream social scientists, educators, and lawyers, I also cite a number of Aboriginal leaders, academics, and researchers. Elsewhere I have written about issues of voice and representation in Aboriginal research (Warry 1998: 9-11); Aboriginal leaders and academics are quite capable of speaking on their own behalf. Yet, I have not seen a book such as this written by an Aboriginal person — and if it were, it would be a very different book. I believe the challenges faced by Aboriginal peoples require action and advocacy by mainstream Canadians, like myself; these challenges cannot, and will not, be met by Aboriginal peoples alone.

Sadly, the type of first-hand experience I have is all too often lacking in our politics and media. Too often commentators with little or no practical experience in Aboriginal communities are prepared to voice their opinions about Aboriginal issues. I have met career bureaucrats who have considerable authority for a particular niche of Aboriginal policy but who have never ventured onto a reserve or remote First Nation. Even today, it is common for columnists in Toronto, Vancouver, Edmonton, or Ottawa to write about solutions for Aboriginal peoples without ever experiencing Aboriginal life.

Where Canadians stand on Aboriginal issues indicates a choice about fundamental values that will shape the future of our country. Should Aboriginal peoples be allowed to pursue a separate course of social, economic, and political action, or is the best option for them integration into mainstream society? Such questions revolve around the issue of whether we should recognize or deny the significance of culture as a core concept of citizenship, that is, whether we should accept and promote Aboriginal cultures or continue to force Aboriginal peoples, through policy and practice, into the Canadian mainstream. These debates are not simply about the best way to improve Aboriginal social conditions but are concerned with the very nature of Aboriginal rights and fundamental issues of justice. They are not just about tolerance of diversity but about whether mainstream values and institutions must be changed in order to accommodate Aboriginal aspirations. The challenge of Aboriginal issues is that they require social policy that supports both the pursuit of alternatives and, at times, contradictory belief systems. We cannot solve the "Aboriginal question" without deciding what kind of country we want Canada to be.

NOTES

1 See Brody 1981 for a wonderful account of the differences between Native and non-Native conceptions of space and mapping.

2 "Aboriginal rights are commonly understood to be the rights of the original peoples of a region
   that continue to exist notwithstanding the imposition of power over them by other peoples"
   (Asch 2001: 1). He notes that the definition of Aboriginal (or Indigenous) rights, "while seem-
   ingly straightforward ... is complex and contested."

3 The political climate facing Australian Aboriginals is different from that in Canada: Aboriginal
   Australians have, at least as yet, no constitutional recognition or protection of their rights, and
   there is also no specific history of treaty relations in Australia. The 1992 Australian High Court
   decision in the Mabo case recognized Aboriginal title to land and resulted in the Native Title Act
   1993. This act instituted a specific program of "land title" claims, which has allowed Aboriginal
   peoples to lay claim to specific territories. Many anthropologists and historians are engaged in
   this research. The Act has been actively opposed by farmers, fishing, and mining interests.

4 The Liberal Party of Australia is a right-of-centre party, equivalent to the Conservative Party of
   Canada.

5 In the strict sense of the word, racism implies the superiority of one group over another on the
   basis of biological attributes or abilities. The arguments put forward by conservatives are more
   accurately described as Eurocentric in asserting the superiority of European culture.

6 In a more specific context, Adelson (2004: 105) has used "culture wars" to characterize the dis-
   agreements between the Eastern Cree and Quebec government over land and natural resources.

7 See Blaser et al. 2004. I return to this subject in Chapter 9.

PART I
....

TRUTH AND DENIAL

CHAPTER 1 Truth, Advocacy, and Aboriginal Issues

Speaking to the American Association of Broadcast Journalists in 1995, just as the age of the Internet and globalized communication dawned, veteran reporter John Lawton suggested that "the irony of the Information Age is that it has given new respectability to uninformed opinion."[1] Today, the Internet offers incredible access to information, much of it of questionable reliability and validity. Columnists and commentators offer opinions on a range of topics, with little research or hard evidence to back their positions. Reality shows abound; the line between news and entertainment, between fiction and reality, has been blurred. Politicians present issues in terms of black and white, often simplifying complex realities into ten-second sound bites. In such a world, how do we differentiate truthful explanations from political rhetoric and propaganda? This question must be confronted before turning to specific questions about Aboriginal issues in Canada.

Information used in public debate needs to be subject to rigorous standards of truth. We must first distinguish the message from the messenger by determining who has the authority to speak to issues and on what basis they have such expertise. However entertaining I may find the opinions of newspaper columnists such as Rex Murphy or Margaret Wente, I would not consider their views as expert assessments and certainly do not think they should form the basis for public policy. Nor do academic credentials ensure credibility. Too often, academics who are experts in one intellectual area construe this expertise as licence to speak on issues in a completely different area. To deal with this, McMaster University has instituted a policy that prohibits faculty from making reference to their university positions if they express opinions that are "unrelated to [their] area of academic and professional expertise" (CAUT 2003). This has been criticized as an attempt to limit freedom of academic speech in the name of protecting the university from liability for potentially slanderous remarks and to avoid negative publicity. But however heavy-handed the policy, its intent is admirable.[2] It may be that the public is interested, for example, in hearing what David Suzuki thinks of American foreign policy. But do Dr. Suzuki's background and his expertise in environmental science provide him with the credentials to speak about such political issues? Perhaps. But we should know when academics are speaking from their positions as experts and when they are voicing their personal opinions, however well-informed they may be. Expertise can be gained in numerous ways — through formal education, experience, and/or familiarity with particular issues in the public and private sectors. First-hand experience in Aboriginal affairs, including knowledge of Aboriginal community life and culture, is essential to the formulation of Aboriginal policy. However, this experience is often all too lacking among the academic experts who offer opinions about Aboriginal issues.

The nature of truth and the degree of objectivity that is possible in research are much debated in the social sciences.[3] The social science equivalent of Heisenberg's uncertainty principle is that truth is situated and that objective facts are relative. Indeed, this is one of the distinguishing features of postmodernism — that values, truth, and reality are socially constructed and contextualized. If five people see an accident, their accounts of the event will differ slightly — or greatly — according to a number of factors, such as location. Even two people standing side by side will offer slightly different interpretations of what happened ("the light was red" or "the light was turning from yellow to red"). Some witnesses will read in to the event's motivations or pass judgement on individuals ("the car was going too fast" or "the driver looked drunk"). If the account is given by the drivers, we might naturally question their interpretation and wonder if they are changing their stories in order to make themselves appear less responsible. We might suggest the shock of the accident has made them unreliable or unable to accurately recall what occurred. Such is the nature of bias, a condition that, for whatever reason, inhibits impartial assessment of events.

Police are trained to assemble different versions of events into the most reliable account of an accident. Truth is assembled, commonly by stressing those points that witnesses (or informants) agree on. This truth can later by questioned — for example, by lawyers — and the questioning will often revolve around points of disagreement. Lawyers are often seen as advocates, a role that requires a person to act on behalf of, or plead the case of, another. Advocates are trained to rigorously challenge versions of the truth presented by their opposition and to present facts in a manner that represents their clients in the best possible light. In the end, judges and juries pass sentence after weighing evidence about points that are agreed upon and the degree of disagreement about finely shaded observations.

This type of legal advocacy is different from that which occurs in social science, because lawyers are driven by the need to ensure the best possible defence of their clients rather than by adherence to consensual and objective truth. Social scientists often assume a role that combines characteristics of the police, lawyers, and judges. The witnesses to the events are key informants or consultants, the participants in research. Objectivity is sustained, first and foremost, through adherence to rigorous methodology. It is derived from the questions asked (they should be neutral and not leading) and from analysis where all data (answers to questions, observations) or points of view are considered. Objectivity in research, analysis, and writing — and here is a major difference between commentary and social science — is obtained by carefully and critically evaluating information, understanding the potential biases of studies, carefully weighing evidence, and giving expression to conflicting points of view or ideas.

This book is an example of advocacy anthropology. It is possible to be objective and an advocate at the same time. In some social sciences, especially anthropology, personal contact and involvement in a situation are essential to understanding and interpretation. The central method of anthropology, participant observation, requires its practitioners to participate in a variety of social situations in the life ways of individuals and communities in order to gain an in-depth understanding of events, along with people's values and motivations.[4] This intensity of interaction has been misinterpreted by some commentators, including other social scientists, as producing bias: anthropologists are sometimes seen as too close to the communities in which they work and so are considered to be biased when they act as advocates.[5]

However, many anthropologists believe that their methods do produce objective findings. They feel that good analysis is similar to a judge's search for truth when sorting through the different perspectives of witnesses to an event. Thus, the role of good advocate is closer to that of judge than lawyer. Anthropologists base their advocacy on solid, objective research methods and make politically positioned arguments only after an impartial reading of recent research literature. The very nature of generalization requires them to sum up the general or collective point of view on a certain issue in order to establish the most reliable representation of reality even while recognizing individual diversity of opinion and action.

Geoffrey Bagshaw, an Australian anthropologist who has conducted land claims research and testified in court, suggests that the key to sound advocacy is to separate the "rigorous and intellectually impartial conduct of anthropological research" from personal choices and any form of "deliberately partisan" approach (see Bagshaw 2001 and Rigsby 2001). He is clear that the first responsibility of the anthropologist who serves as expert witness is not to his clients, be they Aboriginal peoples or the state, but to "professionally constituted truth" and to the court. Although he recognizes both the need for interpretation in social science and the fact that recent postmodern understandings mean that the very nature of objectivity can be seriously contested, Bagshaw is adamant that "fearless and impartial application of intellectual rigor" is necessary:

> Leaving aside philosophical considerations concerning the very existence and nature of objectivity *per se*, most of us are, I suspect, likely to agree with the view that, at least as a rule of thumb, the practical measure of anthropological objectivity must

(and can only be) the degree to which observations and analysis are shown to have an index in empirical (including historical) reality. (Bagshaw 2001: 2)

Advocacy, then, is the result of objective research. Once the facts are known, anthropologist advocates are obliged to act politically and morally to use their research to change the world in some small way (Warry 1992). This is what the applied anthropologist, Richard Price, of York University, referred to as "*informed* advocacy," an advocacy based on the objective assessment of a wide range of data or evidence and that, in the end, offers recommendations that are of a political nature.[6]

Price differentiated this informed advocacy from propaganda, which is usually associated with political campaigns and, ultimately, with warfare. For instance, the Bush Administration's justification for invading Iraq—that Saddam Hussein was stockpiling weapons of mass destruction there—is a prime example of propaganda, since it was known at the time, and has since been proven, to be untrue. Propaganda involves the purposeful and disingenuous ignoring of facts or data that are inconvenient to counter opposing arguments; it ignores reliable information to make a political case. Informed advocacy, in contrast, makes an argument that has political implications but that is based on solid information.

Make no mistake: propaganda is central to the cultural debates involving Aboriginal peoples in Canada. In assessing the arguments about Aboriginal issues, it is important to evaluate the bias or underlying rationale for political positions that lead commentators to ignore alternative facts, interpretations, and explanations. A great deal of influential media commentary on the subject is not only unreliable and invalid but also can be judged as propaganda by the criteria shown above. Political rhetoric and positions on Aboriginal rights are even more polemical. Truth, facts, and objective evaluation are often casualties in these debates.

If truth is situated, it is also shaped by history and different systems of perception and belief, especially in cross-cultural contexts. If members of different cultures wish to agree on policy or common courses of action, they must seek a consensus truth that gets around their different or incommensurable beliefs. The alternative is to assert the superiority of one system of beliefs or ideology over another.

As Ronald Niezen (2003: 100-01) notes, most anthropologists assume a relativistic position that denies the possibility of universal or dominant paradigms of truth. Immersing themselves in other cultures to understand their value systems, they come to admit that many Western or European beliefs are arbitrary and contestable. That is, rather than suggest that one cultural practice or value is somehow better than another, anthropologists tend to see cultures as offering different and unique ways of adapting to similar environments. This relativism creates problems when evaluating claims to universal human rights or assessing whether fundamental Western values (for example, freedom, individual choice, gender equality) should be encouraged in other cultures. Because meaning is always contextual and culturally constructed, even the most severe behaviours — torture, cruelty, and other forms of violence — can always be explained (or rationalized) by appealing to a culture's own internal logic or ideology.

Let us consider an extreme case to illustrate this issue — the practice in some cultures of surgically removing parts of the female genitalia (labia majora and minora and, more rarely, the clitoris) as a rite of passage. A relativist may call this "female circumcision," while a universalist names it "female genital mutilation." A human rights perspective argues that it should not be tolerated or needs to be changed. The label indicates the degree to which the practice is understood in its own cultural terms or is regarded as offensive according to European values.

Thus, the merits of other cultural practices — democracy, child labour, capital punishment, marriage forms — and their implications for the human rights of individuals or societies can be debated at every turn. The search for consensus truth includes balancing the need for universal standards of behaviour against the right of peoples and cultures to choose their own values and practices even when they are offensive to Western morals. It is also about recognizing when cultural traditions or beliefs are outmoded and must be abandoned in order to build more inclusive and humane cultural and social practices.

In short, cross-cultural contexts, at least ideally, require us to appreciate cultural diversity but to guard against embracing other cultures uncritically. A recurrent theme in this book is the need to revitalize Indigenous knowledge to create culturally appropriate institutions that can help address the economic, health, and social conditions of Aboriginal peoples.[7] Identifying and reclaiming Indigenous forms of knowledge are central to the rejection of colonialism and the affirmation of Aboriginal culture. For example, my research brings me into contact with many Aboriginal people who strongly believe in the healing power of Indigenous medicine. Indigenous knowledge of ethnobotany is central to healing traditions that can be used to cure a variety of ailments. Western science has accepted such knowledge, and pharmaceutical companies have patented synthetic drugs based on Indigenous natural remedies. However, there is little good research on the efficacy of many Indigenous healing practices, which have only recently come under close scrutiny. Over the past decade, Indigenous healers have come forward to embrace the idea of Western research, including randomized control trials, in order to demonstrate the efficacy of their treatments. So, should an Aboriginal cancer patient reject chemotherapy and instead turn to a traditional healer?[8] No. Most healers would suggest that Indigenous and biomedical therapies be pursued sequentially. Many Aboriginal people continue to rely on Western physicians while seeking out Indigenous medicine for a variety of ailments in much the same way that mainstream Canadians pursue herbal or other complementary treatments. Social and health research must continue to assess the efficacy of Indigenous and Western medicine objectively, so that more culturally appropriate and effective health care systems, inclusive of different cultural traditions, can be built.

Niezen notes that applied anthropologists, too, are often relativists — they are interested in diverse solutions to social problems and in ensuring that culture is understood so that policy, or other interventions, succeed.[9] This means finding a consensus truth between members of the dominant society and minority cultures. For example, traditional forms of hereditary leadership cannot be approved if they are shown to trounce on the rights of Aboriginal women, but the development of culturally specific practices and institutions shown to be useful in solving social problems and sustaining cultural diversity should be encouraged. This may mean the development of specific alternative justice programs for ethnic minorities, support for language programs or religious forms of education, and much more.

What this requires is an openness to other cultures and ways of seeing the world. All too often those who write on Aboriginal cultures — or, rather, write against Aboriginal cultures — are stuck in their own European frame of reference and, assuming that mainstream or European values are always right or best, are unable to see the value in culturally specific alternatives. For example, European laws and court procedures have proven horribly ineffective in dealing with Native conflict with the law, particularly among youth. As a result, circle courts based on Indigenous social and legal norms have been developed and have proven so effective that they have now been adopted by the mainstream legal system for use with non-Native young offenders. Similarly, there are many forms of democracy and many good reasons why Aboriginal political forms might be created as alternatives to the one person/one vote system used in Canada. Ideas about representational democracy, the appropriate age to vote, and ways of representing minority voices are constantly being debated; for example, there is now some consideration being given to lowering the current voting age to 16. So, there is no reason why social institutions and political forms cannot be opened to allow greater expression of Aboriginal values.

We must confront misinformation and cultural blindness in our own culture and in the culture of others. Aboriginal peoples' collective right to justice or to democratic institutions must be respected, but in creating alternatives, basic human rights must be protected. Dialogue and consensus-building are necessary to find this balance between respect for culture and the protection of common human and humane values. The critical consensus that the following debates speak to concerns how collective Aboriginal rights to self-determination can be reconciled with mainstream rights.

There is a marked anti-intellectualism in some neo-conservative commentary, which views academics as members of an elite and privileged class with their heads in the clouds, too far removed from the real world to understand it. Anti-intellectual claims, like the appeal to common sense as opposed to evidence-based arguments, are familiar strategies of the propagandist. The book jacket promotion of Gary Johns's *Waking Up to Dreamtime*, a well-known collection of conservative commentary opposing Aboriginal self-determination in Australia states:

> White leaders support Aboriginal self-determination because it is fashionable in intellectual circles. Black leaders like self-determination because it brings them power and prestige. (Johns 2001a)

As well as denigrating all Aboriginal leaders as self-interested and power-hungry, this statement implies that political support for Aboriginal causes comes not from well-thought-out analysis, but from some desire to be liked or perhaps affirmed by intellectuals. Elsewhere Johns says:

> Political opportunists, vested interests, cause-seeking lawyers, ivory-tower anthropologists and hopelessly misguided do-gooders, have, for years, been charting the destiny of Australia's Aboriginal community. What a disaster they've made of it! *Waking Up to Dreamtime* examines the outrageous policies that have inflicted such harm and demands these be replaced by enlightened self-realism.[10]

This passage promotes "enlightened self-realism" (common sense) as an alternative to research and suggests that those arguing for Aboriginal self-determination are biased, self-interested, or simply misguided.

In Canada, Melvin Smith, Tom Flanagan, and many others associated with the former Reform, Alliance, and now the Conservative Party of Canada rail against the "Indian Industry," which Smith states is comprised of "the national Native leadership, the many lawyers, consultants, advisers, and academics — all government funded" who are supposedly behind many of the current federal policies and who profit from the federal money directed at First Nations. Dave Chatters, a former Reform Party critic of Aboriginal affairs, blames the "insidious parasitic Indian industry" for current initiatives in Aboriginal land claims and suggests that "lawyers, consultants, bureaucrats, and Indian leaders year after year swallow up the vast majority of money designated to solve the problems of poverty, illiteracy, substance abuse and suffering among our (sic) Native people" (Smith 1995: xii; 42, passim). Jonathan Kay writes of the need to assimilate Aboriginal peoples and suggests that it is impossible for them to sustain their economy and culture in the modern era. This idea, he argues, is a fiction of left-leaning advocates. He concludes his article by stating that it is "tragic that so many hundreds of thousands of aboriginals must pay with their livelihoods, and often their lives, for the self-loathing of our country's intellectual class" (Kay 2001).

These views are founded on the accusation of biased academic argument and a deep anti-intellectualism that attempts to deny the weight of empirical research about Aboriginal issues. Academics are often the target of public criticism — and sometimes for good reason. Tenured academics are extraordinarily privileged; they are under no obligation to explain their research to the public.[11] But the intellectual-bashing of Smith and Johns is misplaced. There is no "Indian industry," at least not in the organized or conspiratorial sense proposed above. While it is true that there is waste, the amount of money spent on Aboriginal research is infinitesimally small compared to the total research pie in Canada. It can be argued, as I have elsewhere, that in order to solve the many problems confronting Aboriginal communities, what is needed is more, not less, research and more applied research controlled by Aboriginal peoples themselves (Warry 1998: 244-49).

By attacking academics and aligning intellectuals with Aboriginal leaders, Smith, Johns, and other commentators hope to deflect attention from the reality: there is already a huge and objective body of social science research literature that demonstrates that the solution to Aboriginal poverty, ill health, and marginalization — all the legacy of colonialism — lies in Aboriginal self-determination. Many neo-conservatives would have Canadians ignore this research in favour of common sense approaches to Aboriginal problems, in the style of the former Progressive Conservative government of Ontario. Centre-left political stances are labeled impractical, unrealistic, and, more often than not, expensive. As we will see, neo-conservatives often criticize long-term approaches to social problems as a waste of taxpayers' money, as putting the prosperity of the majority at risk. What are the consequences of this practical wisdom? The answer may be discrimination against specific individuals and reduced public services. All too often common sense solutions are the obvious, the mainstream, the status quo. They appear attractive in the short term, but make questionable social policy in the long term. Common sense can be very short-sighted.

Yet, common sense solutions are appealing because they imply simple understandings of the world. And simple, so the saying goes, is better than complex at every turn. In mathematics, the concept of parsimony suggests that where two explanations are equally valid, the simpler of the two should rule. But people are not, fortunately, numbers, and in social science, which deals with human interaction, we rarely, if ever, find simple understandings of any situation. Social science has come to value the kind of complexity necessary to understand Aboriginal culture and community. We need policies that acknowledge the role of history and colonialism in the production of Aboriginal problems, and we need to appreciate that the solutions to these problems are long term.

NOTES

1 Lawton 1995. Speech, American Association of Broadcast Journalists, available at <http://mary laine.com/exlibris/xlib124.html>.

2 In 2006, after faculty criticism, the McMaster Senate revised the policy to state that the policy is not meant to restrict academic freedom; however, the policy continues to state the need for an individual to distinguish between personal and professional opinion when communicating with the media.

3 See, for example, the exchange and commentary between Roy D'Andrade and Nancy Scheper-Hughes (1995).

4 There are many books and articles on social science methodology. The following discussion owes much to Barnard 1998.

5 And by judges who assess anthropological research in court cases. See Waldram, Berringer, and Warry 1992.

6 This view acknowledges that even "pure" research that at first glance seems to have no political purpose, comes with biases and is politically positioned in some way. It is important to acknowledge any potential sources of bias first; this includes, for example, one's own political orientation, who has funded the research, and who might benefit from reports or conclusions resulting from the research.

7 For two seminal works on Indigenous knowledge, see Battiste and Youngblood Henderson 2000 and Tuhiwai Smith 2001. See also Brascoupe and Mann 2001 and Simpson 2004. For a discussion of Indigenous health knowledge and translation, see Smylie et al. 2003. Dawn Martin-Hill (2003) has reviewed recent thinking on Indigenous medicine or traditional healing.

8 If opposed to "contemporary" or "modern," the term "traditional" can be problematic in implying "out of date" ideas or values. But as used by Aboriginal peoples it conveys practices that sustain cultural values and are constantly updated and renovated. See Martin-Hill 2003.

9 This is a restatement of the discussion in Niezen 2003: 109.

10 This quote was obtained from the promotional website from the publisher of *Waking Up to Dreamtime*. See <http://www.mediamasters.com.sg/>. See also the promotional material for the book at <http://www.bennelong.com.au/books/waking.php>.

11 For an excellent critique of the contemporary university system in Canada, including the tenure system and the relationship between teaching and research, see Pocklington and Tupper 2002.

CHAPTER 2 The New Assimilation Arguments

Assimilation is a word that is used all too casually by Native and non-Native peoples alike. A non-Native person might say that Aboriginal peoples have been assimilated, so suggesting that they have lost their culture. It is also relatively common to hear an Aboriginal person say that their people have been assimilated or that they can't go back to the old ways or traditions of their culture. Yet, in the same breath, Aboriginal speakers talk of belonging to two cultures or of the significance of their Aboriginal identity.

Assimilation — literally the process by which a minority population is absorbed into a prevailing or dominant culture — is a loaded word. Have Aboriginal people been absorbed into mainstream Canada? Clearly not. Many Canadians, however, continue to believe that Aboriginal peoples should be so assimilated or integrated. A starting point for understanding contemporary Aboriginal issues is to recognize how past and current government policies have tried to promote assimilation and why many Canadians think of assimilation as desirable.

For the first hundred years or more after contact, Aboriginal and European cultures coexisted on equal footing. Early settlers, whalers, and traders relied on Indigenous knowledge of the environment for their subsistence and livelihood, sometimes for their very survival. Once settlements were firmly established, however, the colonists considered it their duty to convert Aboriginal peoples to European and Christian ways. Assimilation meant that they would become "civilized" by adopting European customs. Where Aboriginal peoples were in the way of settlements, as in Upper Canada, plans were made for them to relocate to reserves. Many of these were envisioned as temporary places where the people would learn farming and obtain European skills and values. In the nineteenth century, it was assumed that Aboriginal peoples would naturally join mainstream society if given the opportunity.

Many government policies and practices were aimed at encouraging, or forcing, Aboriginal peoples to assimilate. The Indian Act (1876) consolidated many prior pieces of legislation and still governs the state's relationship to Aboriginal peoples today. Despite many changes, it remains a notoriously antiquated piece of legislation that has assimilation as its aim. For example, it declares that appropriate political structures for Aboriginal peoples are democratically elected councils, thus denying them the right to practice their own political forms. It ignores such complex political structures that existed, for example, in the West Coast hereditary leadership systems and the Iroquoian chief and council system, which provided early American leaders with ideas for their own democracy. Such systems were seen as uncivilized and therefore inappropriate. If they were taught the advantages of voting, it was believed that Aboriginal peoples could one day fully participate in a democratic society.

The most obvious assimilationist policy was enfranchisement: the process whereby individuals were endowed with the rights of citizenship. Until late into the last century, status Indians were not considered citizens. Under the Indian Act, there were a number of ways they could become enfranchised, but in so doing they were required by law to relinquish their Indian status. Indeed, from a European perspective, this was logical, because to be an Indian was to be uncivilized. The classic example of enfranchisement was the requirement that when an Indian woman married a white man, she automatically lost her status and became a citizen, as did her children. An Indian man who married a white woman, however, retained his status, and his European wife and their children became status Indians as well. Of course, given the logic of the day, it was rare for a white woman to marry an Indian man — why would a civilized woman wish to join the ranks of a savage society? In contrast, the desire and practicality of Indian women to "elevate" their status by marrying into white society was considered self-evident. This Indian Act provision was not successfully contested until the 1970s and was amended through Bill C-31 in 1986, in part because it was by then recognized that it was contrary to the equality provisions of the Charter of Rights and Freedoms. The legacy of this colonial mentality is the division we find today between non-status and status Indians and the identity politics of contemporary Indian affairs (see Chapter 6).

Other ways of enfranchisement existed under the Indian Act. Indians were not allowed to drink alcohol in a public place, to vote in elections, or to obtain a university education without relinquishing their status. Aboriginal people became full citizens, with the right to vote, only in 1960. Until then, it was impossible to be an Indian and a full member of society. Thus, even though Indians fought for Canada in both world wars, as veterans they did not receive the same pensions or compensations as other Canadians. Many other examples of differential treatment, racism, and discrimination resulting from the Indian Act could be cited. Here, I wish only to note that the enfranchisement provisions of the Act were clearly designed to force Indians to assimilate, that is, to relinquish their identity as members of a culture in order to join European society.

But the politics of enfranchisement were fatally flawed. The vast majority of status Indians, from the nineteenth century onwards, never chose to become citizens, despite the opportunities enfranchisement afforded. Instead, they retained their independence and separate identity and status as Indians. And many of those thàt did lose their status, as recognized under legislation by the federal government, continued to practice their culture and eventually, regained their status under Bill C-31.

Education, literacy, Christianity, and the assumption of Western technology (the use of snowmobiles rather than dogsleds, for example) have all been taken as signs of gradual assimilation whereby Aboriginal peoples have chosen to abandon their culture and assume European behaviours. Well into the 1960s, many social scientists, anthropologists chief among them, framed their understanding of Aboriginal culture in terms of the gradual loss of traditional ways and adoption of European values and customs. However, it has become apparent that Aboriginal people, rather than *adopting* Western practices and ideas, were *adapting* them to suit their own cultural purposes. This distinction is critically important and greatly misunderstood in mainstream discourse. The use of snowmobiles and ATVs allowed Aboriginal people to hunt in new and more efficient ways but did not result in fundamental changes in their relationship to the land or to animals. When children were trained in Western educational institutions, including residential schools, it did not necessarily lead them to embrace mainstream values; in some cases, it produced a generation of Aboriginal leaders who were radical in defending the need for Aboriginal rights and protecting Indigenous cultures. Thus, anthropologists began to look more closely at how Aboriginal peoples resisted the influence of the dominant society and how their culture was sustained; participation in the dominant society, or even acceptance of European values, did not necessarily imply that assimilation had occurred.

By the late 1960s, the idea of assimilation began to lose favour in academic circles, but it remained entrenched in government policies. In 1969 the federal government, under Prime Minister Pierre Trudeau and Indian Affairs Minister Jean Chrétien, produced the White Paper on Indian Affairs. It argued for the elimination of the Indian Act, recognized the need for special educational and social welfare programs to assist Aboriginal people to achieve the same standard of living as other Canadians, and asserted that Aboriginal peoples should share in the same rights and responsibilities as all Canadians. From a European perspective, the White Paper was yet another well-intentioned policy aimed at providing Aboriginal peoples with equal opportunity to participate as equal Canadian citizens, that is, to assimilate.

The Aboriginal reaction was immediate and dramatic, leading to collective action that marked the formation of the contemporary Aboriginal rights movement. Aboriginal political organizations successfully opposed the White Paper, which the government withdrew. Over time, Aboriginal leaders, including the late Harold Cardinal, argued for a view of Aboriginal status as unique — a status as "Citizens Plus." This view, which has since been entrenched in the 1982 Constitution, argues that Aboriginal peoples have all the rights of other Canadians plus additional rights that derive from treaties and their historical status as First Peoples who inhabited the country prior to European arrival.

But even though the special status of Aboriginal peoples is entrenched in the Canadian Constitution, assimilationist thinking continues. Most Canadians, like their government, seem incapable of conceiving of a society in which Aboriginal values and practices are promoted and placed on equal footing with European ones. One of the clearest examples of assimilationist thinking is the promotion of the indigenization of government services. Throughout the 1980s and 1990s and into the present, Aboriginal people have been encouraged to assume roles in parallel programs, which have created a separate space for them while duplicating European social and political practices, thus protecting and ensuring the continuance of mainstream institutions. Such Aboriginal-specific services include, for example, child welfare agencies, educational institutions, health services, and police forces. The phrase "brown faces in white roles" aptly sums up this strategy.

In each case, as with previous attempts to assimilate, the unexpected — from the government's perspective — has happened. Aboriginal peoples find that when they try to apply European practices to their own culture, they are opposed or rejected by their communities. Given local beliefs and traditions, European systems simply make no sense. The participation of Aboriginal people in Western institutions and programs naturally transforms their very nature, so that they begin to take on a distinctly Aboriginal quality. Practice patterns in Native child welfare agencies or addiction centres, for example, are very different than in their European counterparts. Lawyers in remote communities, recognizing that European courts are ineffective and inappropriate, have adopted circle courts more suited to Aboriginal ways of discussing community problems.[1] Alternative courts or healing circles have emerged. Aboriginal constables assume roles more akin to mediators or peacemakers than mainstream police officers. And Aboriginal health centres include both biomedical and Indigenous medical practices.[2]

These transformations have led Aboriginal advocates to call for greater freedom to create culturally specific forms of self-government that would allow for Aboriginal alternatives to mainstream institutions. In the long run, policies of indigenization, rather than encouraging Aboriginal participation in mainstream institutions, have afforded Aboriginal peoples the opportunity to develop culturally appropriate institutions. Indigenous forms of governance, medical practice, and legal processes are now emerging across the country.

The word assimilation is now politically incorrect as it is associated with such colonial policies as residential schools, which deliberately attempted to erase all vestiges of Aboriginal culture. Consequently, the word is often avoided in public discourse. However, assimilationist thinking remains pervasive. Canadians assume that Aboriginal peoples wish to participate in mainstream life and that, once they do so, they will choose to adopt mainstream culture and leave their own culture behind. A common belief is that Aboriginal peoples would be "better off" if they became part of the mainstream or that the number of Aboriginal people who have left the reserve for the city is "proof" that they have adopted Western ways.

Current neo-conservative discourse speaks occasionally of the benefits of assimilation. As late as 2001, Jonathan Kay, writing on "A Case for Native Assimilation" for the *National Post*, suggested that protecting Aboriginal culture is impossible if Aboriginal economic development is to be achieved. For him, the solution to Aboriginal poverty is for Aboriginal people to abandon their culture and assimilate into mainstream society (Kay 2001).

I return to this argument in Chapters 5, 7, and 9, for it illustrates a naïve understanding of contemporary Aboriginal culture and colonialism. Here I note only that neo-conservative writers commonly suggest that the integration rather than assimilation of Aboriginal peoples into mainstream society should be encouraged. The difference between these two words is at times infinitesimally small. Integration implies equal participation and equality under the law and competing for opportunities on equal terms.[3] It is also still frequently used to connote the close working relationship between different parts of a social system as, for example, in the integration of traditional and Western medicine. The problem is that integration often implies co-optation or gradual absorption by the dominant institution or culture. For this reason, careful academic analysis increasingly avoids using this word. Aboriginal academics, for example, speak of the harmonization, rather than integration, of their systems of healing with Western biomedicine. This language allows for the continued integrity of Aboriginal healing while recognizing that interfacing mechanisms and collaboration between medical systems can exist.

All too often the word integration is used to deny difference and, therefore, to undermine the unique Aboriginal status entrenched in the Constitution. The most common misuse of the term comes in the assumption that Aboriginal people choose to integrate into the mainstream when they leave the reserve, a view that masks more insidious assimilationist thinking. The practice of one's culture or language is seen as somehow inappropriate to or incompatible with the exercise of shared citizenship rights. Much of the public discourse on Aboriginal issues, in fact, is embedded with assimilationist ideas that are signaled by appeals to the idea of equal rights and equal treatment under the law.

The starting point for the new assimilation arguments is the poverty and marginalization of Aboriginal peoples. Neo-conservatives suggest that federal policies of self-determination have failed to produce economic well-being for Native communities. In order to solve the "Indian Problem," Aboriginal people must be allowed to compete equally "on the same footing" with other Canadians and to fully participate in the Canadian economy. The idea is summed up succinctly in

the words of Tom Flanagan: "Aboriginal self-government will likely solve nothing. Joining Canada's mainstream will" (1998: 1).

These new assimilation arguments are most evident in the works of a small
number of political commentators, social scientists, conservative politicians, and
think tanks such as the Fraser Institute. Many were institutionally embedded in the
platform of the Alliance Party and are now entrenched in the Conservative Party of
Canada under the leadership of Stephen Harper. They continue to be found in the
national news media, particularly the *National Post* and the *Globe and Mail*. The
idea that assimilation is the solution to the current marginalization of Aboriginal
peoples is not simply right wing but a predominant mainstream view.

The argument for the assimilation or integration of Aboriginal peoples is appealing to many Canadians for several reasons. First, it seems to offer a well-intentioned and common sense solution to the continuing poverty of Aboriginal
communities and the non-participation of Aboriginal people in the economy,
both caused by poor government policies. Second, it presents a "no cost" solution
to Aboriginal poverty. Aboriginal people can abandon their culture, move from
their reserves, and enter urban life at no cost to the taxpayer. Indeed, neo-conservatives suggest that Aboriginal migration to cities is evidence that assimilation
is occurring. Third, since Canadians believe in justice and social equality, we inherently reject policies that separate a minority population on the basis of race,
particularly if we believe that this separation creates dependency and marginalization. Thus, the race-based arguments that underlie the rights of Aboriginal
peoples should be rejected as unreasonable in a democratic society that values
equal rights.[4]

Let us look at the work of three well-known writers — Melvin Smith, Tom
Flanagan, and Alan C. Cairns — in order to fully explore neo-conservative attitudes and arguments about Aboriginal rights. These critics explicitly put forward
clear statements of an assimilationist or integrationist ideology, and their books
have since influenced media reports and extensive commentary about Aboriginal
affairs. For this reason, their ideas need to be confronted before we can build a
more complex understanding of Aboriginal cultures.

Some might argue that Smith's book[5] is best ignored, but the fact that his views
have been embraced and repeated by neo-conservative commentators makes
them an apt starting point for a discussion of Canadian attitudes to Aboriginal
issues. At the heart of his thesis is an illogical but pervasive fear that Aboriginal
peoples pose a threat to Canadian values.

As Cairns notes, Smith writes from a position analogous to the former Reform
Party and is committed to the assimilationist 1969 White Paper policy (Cairns
2000: 72).[6] For Smith, the White Paper was — and is — "a bold government initiative" and a "revolutionary approach" to Indian policy (Smith 1996: 1-4). This is
understandable: the 1960s was the era in which Smith made his finest contribu-

tions to public life. However, this is tantamount to thinking that 1960s public policy, which allowed smoking in the workplace and discrimination on the basis of sexual orientation, should be followed 40 years later. Smith not only fails to see the fundamentally misguided design of the White Paper, but blames the Trudeau government for "mistakenly" sowing the seeds of the "Indian Industry" by funding Aboriginal political organizations and creating a comprehensive land claims process, which he notes has been expanded to include the "special rights Aboriginal peoples will have in the future with respect to land and resources" (Smith 1996: 7-8).[7]

The book was lauded as a "wake-up call" for Canadians by right-wing political commentators such as Gordon Gibson and Diane Francis, whose remarks grace the book jacket (see Chapter 4). Smith's work was quickly picked up by anti-Native organizations and writers, particularly on the Internet. For example, in an on-line C-FAR newsletter, Doug Collins reviewed the book as follows:

> ... Our Home or Native Land offers some valuable debunking of the notion that Canadian aboriginals, Indians, native people, or whatever the politically correct moniker is, are a victimized minority. Far from it they enjoy privileges the majority does not. Worse, if the current orgy of guilt and secretive lands claims settlements continue apace, we may find ourselves stripped of much of our country.[8]

As a form of political commentary, the book relies on personal opinion rather than on first-hand knowledge of Aboriginal communities or the examination of actual historical events and contemporary communities.[9] That is to say, it is political propaganda. It is poorly researched; its evidence and arguments, if presented by an undergraduate student, would be evaluated as inconsistent, biased, and unsubstantiated. Smith ignores contemporary political and social science literature on Aboriginal issues and instead cites as sources his friends and political commentators of the right.[10] In the Preface, he suggests that "the book will anger some readers" and that "those with a vested interest in the Indian Industry will condemn" his arguments. This is a pre-emptive attack suggesting the bias of potential critics, a common tactic in the propaganda game.

Our Home OR Native Land is a litany of complaints about Aboriginal policy. In separate chapters, Smith rails against the creation of Nunavut, self-determination, the *Delgamuukw* case,[11] and the cost and work of the Royal Commission on Aboriginal Peoples (not yet completed when his book was written). In perhaps his best documented chapter, "The Aboriginal Commercial Fishery in BC," Smith anticipates the race-based argument concerning access to fisheries which received new impetus in 2003 when Judge Kitchen of the British Columbia Provincial Court ruled that Aboriginal-specific fisheries should be eliminated because they violate the Charter of Rights and Freedoms equality provisions. Indeed, one suspects that Judge Kitchen has read Smith, for his decision mirrors much of Smith's argument, which suggests that the courts have privileged Aboriginal peoples' special access to land and water resources, an argument I return to in Chapter 8.

Smith also claims that Aboriginal peoples control huge tracts of land and are therefore privileged; in fact, most Aboriginal people live in poverty and ill health and control little land. Since reserves comprise 10,021 square miles, Smith characterizes this as "one of the largest land holdings in the free world" (Smith 1996: 271). As the Canadian Human Rights Commission has noted, Aboriginal people comprise less than 3 per cent of the population, and yet reserve lands south of the 60th parallel make up less than one-half of 1 per cent of the Canadian land mass.[12]

Smith espouses the idea of reverse racism (Smith 1996: 249-57). He points to Canada's opposition to South African apartheid to argue that Canadian policies have also divided Canada on the basis of race. He suggests that "we are well on the way to establishing that system [apartheid] in Canada through native self-governments based on the ill-found concept of the inherent right." A clearer statement of the neo-conservative view of reserves is found in the Forward to the book, written by Rafe Mair:

> Tiny communities are given enormous tracts of land while the majority of Canadians is [sic] not only ignored but kept in the dark ... We have committed ourselves to a land full of native homelands, the very notion which revolted the civilized world when they were created in South Africa. How ironic it is that Mel Smith, in pointing out the folly of states within the state, where rights are determined by the colour of one's skin, must fight off the claim that *he* is a racist. (Smith 1996: viii)

The characterization of Aboriginal reserves as African homelands, often repeated in public discourse, is simplistic and inappropriate. It is axiomatic that those who are oppressed should best understand the nature of their oppression and be capable of pointing the way to their liberation. Blacks in South Africa were denied the right to vote or to participate in central democratic processes. In Canada these rights were achieved in the 1960s. Blacks in South Africa demanded the end to apartheid but did not necessarily call for the end to a territorial base or the security of homelands. Aboriginal leaders in Canada call for the end of discriminatory policies and the expansion of the reserve system to create a viable land base. Despite failed government policy and the marginal economic status of reserves, land is essential to Aboriginal identity, and a sustainable land base is an essential component of Aboriginal self-government. The suggestion that recognizing historical claims to land and moving toward self-governing Aboriginal communities is tantamount to "going backward" toward the kind of segregated society epitomized by the South African policy of apartheid is illogical.

Smith believes that governments have "allowed themselves to be overwhelmed with a collective sense of guilt over past dealings with native peoples" (Smith 1996: 251), a sentiment expressed by other neo-conservative writers.[13] This guilt, he suggests, is "reinforced at every opportunity by the national native leadership." The guilt concerning Aboriginal peoples is real. Many Canadians are disappointed with the government's inability to address Aboriginal poverty. Many feel angry or ashamed when they learn of the social conditions on reserve, and, at least for some, this emotional response compels them to want to do something to assist Aboriginal people. But Smith believes this guilt (if, indeed, that is the correct label for what we feel when we think of Aboriginal people) is misplaced. As a result, he denies the impact of colonialism and asserts that Aboriginal-specific policies somehow privilege Aboriginal peoples over other Canadians.

Our Home OR Native Land reflects the thinking of many Canadians who oppose Aboriginal rights and who feel threatened by specific policies or programs that may benefit Aboriginal peoples. As his title suggests, Smith's book is narrow in outlook and mentality; it is framed without tolerance of diversity and is explicit in its pronouncement of out-moded assimilationist ideas, which have long been rejected by Aboriginal people but which continue to colour right-wing political arguments.

Tom Flanagan is a well-known guru of the neo-conservative right, a media commentator, and political consultant to Prime Minister Stephen Harper. The arguments in *First Nations? Second Thoughts* (2000)[14] are founded on neo-conservative values and evoke the language of equal opportunity and equal rights.[15] Flanagan is a political scientist and historian who denies the cumulative weight of colonialism and the oppression of Aboriginal peoples.[16] His ideas are Eurocentric and come wrapped in a set of out-dated cultural assumptions. But his work is widely read. Conservative writers in Australia, for example, routinely cite him as proof that Australia should not engage Aboriginal peoples in discussions concerning self-determination and as evidence that the constitutional recognition of Aboriginal rights is a serious error for modern nation-states (see Johns 2001).

Flanagan argues that for Canadians to accept Aboriginal self-government, current First Nations councils must demonstrate effective management practices: Aboriginal governments must be held accountable to their own community members, and such accountability can be achieved through self-taxation (Flanagan 2000: 197). By tracing the legal history that has given rise to the modern liberal interpretation of Aboriginal rights, he questions the validity of government policies and the recommendations of RCAP, which he argues represents the "new aboriginal orthodoxy," that is, the established or liberal-left view of Aboriginal rights.

Colin Scott, a McGill anthropologist, has documented how Flanagan's views are founded on European notions of progress, civilization, private property, and the rejection of any notion of special rights. Scott sees Flanagan's arguments as "one of the most closely reasoned positions on the political right — a rare one from a person with scholarly expertise on Indigenous topics." He states:

> One suspects, in fact, that the old orthodoxy, nicely articulated by Flanagan in his rebuttal of RCAP recommendations, is well entrenched among federal and provincial politicians, and remains powerfully influential in the worldview of the Canadian public. (Scott 2004: 302)[17]

The old orthodoxy Scott refers to is the neo-conservative position on Aboriginal issues, one which remains popular and populist, reflecting the thinking of many mainstream Canadians.

Flanagan is interested in confronting the "emerging consensus on fundamental issues" which "is widely shared among aboriginal leaders, government officials and academics" (Flanagan 2000: 4). He admits that there is no central authoritative voice for what he calls this new orthodoxy, but he insists that it is represented in RCAP reports and in examples of important and widely referenced social science texts such as Michael Asch's *Aboriginal and Treaty Rights* (1997), Menno Boldt's *Surviving as Indians* (1993), and Rick Ponting's *First Nations in Canada* (1997). Thus, in one small passage, Flanagan dismisses a wide range of social science research, offering instead his more common sense view of Aboriginal affairs.

Flanagan is fearful of the long-term impact of the RCAP reports (Flanagan 2000: 4-5). Even though many specific recommendations have been ignored by the government for political expediency, they constitute a social policy platform that cannot be entirely disregarded by bureaucrats and decision-makers (see Warry 1998: 250-53). Indeed, the RCAP recommendations have already been renovated to become part of significant proposals by the AFN and other Aboriginal organizations — and this is precisely what Flanagan fears:

> Unless there is serious debate, sooner or later we are likely to end up where the RCAP wanted us to go. Canada will be redefined as a multinational state embracing an archipelago of aboriginal nations that own a third of Canada's land mass, are immune from federal and provincial taxation, are supported by transfer payments from citizens who do pay taxes, are able to opt out of federal and provincial legislation, and engage in "nation to nation" diplomacy with whatever is left of Canada. That is certainly not the vision of Canada I had when I immigrated in 1968 and decided to become a Canadian citizen in 1973; I doubt it's what most Canadians want for themselves and their children. (Flanagan 2000: 5)

Flanagan's vision must have included a homogeneity based on what he clearly thinks are superior European values. He is angry that status Indians escape taxation and that government monies go toward transfer payments in an effort to improve the lives of Canada's most marginalized population.

Flanagan's archipelago analogy misstates the RCAP view of self-government. RCAP suggests that, because of the economies of scale and the small size of First Nations, larger self-governing collectivities should be recognized and sufficient land bases established for them through treaty renovation or comprehensive claims. In Ontario, for example, the Anishnabek Nation (Union of Ontario Indians) and Nishnabe Aski Nation represent over 40 individual First Nations who share a common history of treaty relations and regional political interests. It is such political unions that RCAP envisions as serving as the basis for self-government, not, as Flanagan suggests, small individual First Nations.

Flanagan's characterization makes it appear that RCAP's recommendations call for revolutionary changes that would transform the Canadian political landscape and threaten Canadian unity. He acknowledges that, unlike Quebec nationalism, Aboriginal self-government does not pose any major threat to Canada as it is currently constituted. However, he does see self-government as "troubling" because it would be "a constant irritant" to the status quo and because "it would be a standing invitation to other racial and/or ethnic communities to demand similar corporate status" (Flanagan 2000: 194).[18] But, as I will argue, self-government is about finding forms of governance that are culturally relevant so as to allow Aboriginal peoples to express themselves, on equal terms, within a revitalized Canadian state.

Flanagan suggests that the "new orthodoxy" contains eight propositions, and he addresses each of these in different chapters (Flanagan 2000: 6-7). He rejects the basic notion that Aboriginal people differ from other Canadians because they "were here first" and that this difference entitles them to special rights. Rather than acknowledging their historic and spiritual relationship to the land, he sees Aboriginal peoples as only the first of a series of immigrant populations. He states that Aboriginal advocates, including anthropologists, suggest that any distinction between civilized and uncivilized is racist and that Aboriginal cultures "were on the same level as those of the European colonists" — an argument that misrepresents anthropological ideas of cultural relativism and that becomes an excuse for the consequences of colonialism. In fact, much of Flanagan's book is a sustained rationalization for the conquest of Aboriginal peoples, an argument that rests on the claim that, because Aboriginal cultures and political systems were inferior or less developed than those of the European conquerors, Aboriginal people, by weight of history, have no claims to rights of self-determination.

Flanagan is at a loss to contest the idea, upheld by the courts and affirmed in government policy and in treaties, that Aboriginal rights exist by virtue of the fact that Aboriginal peoples inhabited Canada prior to the arrival of Europeans, that they lived in distinct communities, and that they had distinct cultures and political systems (see Flanagan 2000: 20-21). In other words, Flanagan attempts, through polemic, to strip Aboriginal people of their difference and to turn them into another type of immigrant. This is the myth that underpins the new assimilation arguments.[19] After all, if Aboriginal peoples are no different than other immigrants, it is possible to suggest "that the assertion of an inherent right of self-government is a form of racism" (Flanagan 2000: 25). But to differentiate rights on the basis of historical and Indigenous claims has nothing to do with race and everything to do with political (some would say diplomatic) relationships between original and settling societies.[20]

As the book's title indicates, Flanagan questions the very meaning of "First" Nations, arguing that Indian status in no way denotes unique political rights and that all forms of government must be subsumed under the Canadian state. However much Flanagan may dislike it, however, the reality is that Aboriginal cultures contained social, political, and legal processes that, though different from those found in European systems, are equivalent to those currently held by provinces and the federal government. Many of these powers have been recognized in treaties. For example, the right to "maintain peace and good order" has been effectively accepted as the right to have Aboriginal forces policing reserves, and Aboriginal rights advocates have argued that Indigenous systems of law should be sustained, which infuriates those on the right who argue for "one system" of law applicable to all Canadians.[21]

Like Smith (1996: 148, 271-73), Flanagan argues for a very limited form of self-government, is opposed to any redefinition of Aboriginal title in modern claims agreements (such as those in British Columbia), and is opposed to the concept of treaty renovation whereby the courts or the federal government attempt to recognize the spirit and intent of past treaties and interpret these in contemporary terms. Rather, he argues that treaties "mean what they say"; they must be interpreted literally, and any liberal interpretation is "both expensive and mischievous to the economies of all provinces in which treaties have been signed" (Flanagan 2000: 7, 151-54). Finally, Flanagan argues that economic development and self-sufficiency are impossible given the small size of reserves and that the only viable option for Aboriginal people is integration with mainstream Canada, for instance, by moving to cities where employment and investment opportunities exist.

But Flanagan never discusses urban Aboriginal people. The reason for this omission is revealed in his conclusion where he states that this portion of the Aboriginal population is "already on their way towards integration into Canadian society" (Flanagan 2000: 196). For Flanagan, like Jonathan Kay and Alan Cairns, the move to the city from the reserve signals an individual's choice of integration or assimilation (Kay 2001). He cannot recognize Aboriginal culture where it exists in the city, and he is only concerned that policies that encourage Aboriginal peoples to return to the reserve should be discouraged and that no land base should be created for Métis or other non-status populations.

Flanagan also implies that because Aboriginal peoples receive government subsidies and welfare they want a free ride. He goes so far as to state that Aboriginal peoples believe that "Being first in the Americas entitles [them] to receive from later arrivals the same standard of living that newcomers have obtained for themselves" (Flanagan 2000: 193). The intellectual shorthand for this argument is simple: assimilation equals economic integration. Thus, the only way in which Aboriginal people will break free from welfare dependency and escape poverty is to abandon the reserve and traditional hunting economies. As we will see, although the movement from reserve to urban environments for employment is an entrenched reality of Aboriginal life in Canada, Aboriginal peoples can envision an alternative economic future for reserve communities. At the same time, they wish to pursue cultural and economic practices that are sustainable over the long term. Flanagan's emphasis on individualism and free market competition makes it impossible for him to grasp how traditional, cooperative, and collective forms of economic activity can work to better the lives of Aboriginal peoples across the country for the benefit of all Canadians.

In comparison to Smith and Flanagan, the views of Alan C. Cairns seem reasonable and his intentions laudable. His book, *Citizens Plus: Aboriginal Peoples and the Canadian State* (2000),[22] is a widely cited and influential work. Cairns's arguments come closest to representing a small "c" conservative or small "l" liberal position on Aboriginal rights:

> A viable constitutional vision, I argue, must address two facts: Aboriginal peoples and other Canadians differ from each other; our differences are not total. There is much overlap — and we share a common space. Are our future constitutional arrangements going to foster some version of common belonging so that we feel responsible for each other, and will be eager to engage in some common enterprises, as well as accommodate our differences? (Cairns 2000: 5-6)

Cairns is concerned to improve the language of debate about self-government and to ask what place Aboriginal people have in the future of Canada. He believes in the recognition of Aboriginal rights as long as they do not impinge on the supposedly shared objectives of mainstream Canadians. The phrase Citizens Plus, which was suggested by the Hawthorn Report (and was subsequently adopted by the Indian activist Harold Cardinal) in the 1960s, still has significance and "could serve as the vehicle for a socio-political theory and as a simplifying label for public consumption" (Cairns 2000: 9, 52 passim).[23] Cairns is attached to this 1960s language for personal reasons — he was a senior staff member responsible for research in the area of constitutional policy and helped write the Hawthorn

Report. He recognizes this fact and tells the reader that he hopes that his commitment to the concept is not a result of his "naïve unwillingness to let go of his own past" and that his analysis is driven by "more than nostalgia" (Cairns 2000: 162 and 13). But Cairns's view has, in fact, since been surpassed by a more layered understanding of Aboriginal rights and citizenship.

Cairns rejects "basic assimilation policy" and questions how Aboriginal rights can be rationalized within the context of Canadian citizenship. He is careful to differentiate his position from that of Smith and Flanagan. He notes that 1950s assimilationist thinking was embraced by the left and then rejected, only to be adopted by the right under a slightly new guise. The former Reform Party platform "confirms the survival [of] ancient assimilation policy," the neo-conservative right thus continuing to claim assimilationist thinking as somehow progressive and to label contemporary left thinking as overly radical and unworkable. Cairns makes the important point that assimilation remains appealing to many Canadians because "its supporters have easy access to the symbolically potent rhetoric of equality" (Cairns 2000: 73).

But while Cairns obviously sees the new assimilation rhetoric as flawed, his argument promotes the idea of integration at many points. Unlike more conservative commentators, he presents a sophisticated understanding of culture and identity that draws on the contemporary anthropological literature and the writing of John Borrows, an Aboriginal lawyer. He recognizes, for example, that all cultures are hybrid and represent a complex mixture of characteristics that have emerged over time and through constant interchange with other societies (Cairns 2000: 104-05). But despite acknowledging contemporary anthropological thinking, he perpetuates the view of Aboriginal peoples as slowly having lost or abandoned their culture. Like Smith and Flanagan, he sees those people who have left the reserve as "integrated." For example, he views intermarriage, urbanization, and university education ("intermingling") both as signs of weakened culture that diminish the difference between Aboriginal and mainstream society and as examples of "modernizing Aboriginality" (Cairns 2000: 97, 73-74). Aboriginal scholars, in contrast, clearly demonstrate how intermarriage in either the past or the present does not imply the abandonment of one's cultural identity.[24] Likewise, university education and urban life in no way diminish Aboriginal peoples' identity; rather, they are apt to strengthen appeals to cultural values and traditions (see Chapter 6).

Cairns's views are widely shared. As recently as 2005, at the end of the First Nations-First Ministers Conference, *Globe and Mail* columnist Jeffrey Simpson hailed "citizens plus" as an alternative to assimilation or self-determination. Simpson states that the "plus" aspect of Aboriginal status "should be incorporated into the mainstream rather than placed outside it in various parallel ways, including dead-end reserves." The column is titled "Aboriginals are voting with their feet for a third way":

> Rather than assimilation or self-determination, the "citizen plus" model seeks to integrate aboriginals to a certain extent in mainstream society, without forcing them to become like the rest of us. In mainstream society, they learn modern skills. They work there. They hold on to their heritage. They negotiate, as do many citizens, between their specific identity and the broader, Canadian one. (Simpson 2005)

This paternalistic view gives the impression that Aboriginal people can only be successful if they leave the reserve — a place "where aboriginals can practice their tradition." And so we return to the essential stereotype: reserves equal out-moded culture and tradition; cities equal assimilation and integration.

Cairns sees self-determination and self-government as pertaining only to status Indians on reserves (Cairns 2000: 73-74, 112-13). Although opposing assimilation, he argues that Aboriginal discourse is too polarized and that there is a need for a middle ground — the conception of Aboriginal peoples as citizens plus. And here he suggests that "the most frequent image of self-chosen Aboriginal futures is of parallelism — Aboriginal communities and non-Aboriginal communities traveling side by side, coexisting but not getting in each other's way" (Cairns 2000: 6).[25] He attributes such parallelism to Aboriginal peoples and leadership (Cairns 2000: 95), although such a middle course would reverse the constitutional and policy gains they have achieved and would limit the form of self-government they hope to obtain. Thus, Cairns, like more conservative commentators, promotes an image of Aboriginal aspirations as somehow endangering fundamental Canadian values and, like the concept of a distinct Quebec society, as seeking to undermine a collective identity and national political agenda. The result is that a variety of Aboriginal claims come to look unreasonable and a very limited form of self-government more feasible.

Cairns's view of self-government is one that, like Flanagan's, is Eurocentric and unimaginative. Although he recognizes that Aboriginal governments may not be elected and might draw on traditional political values, he is clearly in favour of limiting Aboriginal jurisdiction and is troubled by any form of government that would increase the "civic distance" between Aboriginal and non-Aboriginal governments (2000: 140-41). The AFN recognizes that while some Aboriginal communities may opt for Eurocentric political forms and processes, such as municipal councils and bi-annual elections, others may prefer to develop political structures that are truer to their history and culture, such as those that reflect hereditary principles or specific roles for clans (see Chapter 11). But Cairns is reluctant to engage the idea of culturally appropriate political institutions because

48 Ending Denial

they may encourage parallelism and make it more difficult for Aboriginal peoples to engage in mainstream political goals (2000: 148-51).

Like Flanagan, Cairns disapproves of the use of the term nation for Aboriginal communities. He acknowledges that the term First Nation has relevance given the political status communities and tribes had during the early contact period and that today it is used to designate communities with common cultural, linguistic, and historical identities. But he is troubled by a discourse that makes "grandiose" jurisdictional claims for small communities. He reiterates that the Hawthorn Report "saw villages, not nations," but also that it wrote of the predominance of 'cultural flow' from European to Aboriginal societies and spoke of the 'Europeanization' of Indian communities as a major tendency in the social change that was occurring at the time. This is the assimilationist view that Cairns cannot shake, no matter how hard he tries (Cairns 2000: especially 94-95, 162-63).

Thus, using the phrase First Nations reinforces "competing, rather than complementary" identities. Cairns fears that First Nations claims might lead collectivities of reserves to have separate or different jurisdictions from those non-Native municipal communities that already exist. This ignores the fact that First Nations are different in jurisdiction, government relations, and culture from non-Native communities. It also ignores the fact that at the local and regional level First Nations are already interacting, rather than being integrated, with the local municipalities and regional economies that surround them. In most instances, First Nations exercise powers that are different from and sometimes greater than those currently associated with municipalities. For example, if we look at First Nations who have signed comprehensive claims, they have powers over land, resources, education, and health in addition to more municipal-like powers. This third order of government is different from municipal, provincial, or federal governments.

Cairns never rejects completely the possibility of self-government or the modern recognition of Aboriginal rights (and its defence by the courts). His analysis, at almost every turn, accepts the distinctiveness of status Indians and Aboriginal contributions to Canadian society. He recognizes the "interdependence and mutual borrowing" that has occurred between cultures, and he argues that this cultural and historical reality "does not challenge the desirability of self-government" but rather signifies the need for self-government so that Aboriginal peoples can sustain control over the type and pace of change influencing their communities (Cairns 2000: 205).

In his concluding remarks, Cairns suggests that he may suffer from a "failure of imagination" and that he may be "wedded to ideas of statehood and of political community that are anachronistic" (2000: 211). This is an honest and important admission by a writer who has made an important contribution to the scholarship on self-government. He gives us a cautious and conservative analysis of Aboriginal rights that, despite his best efforts, reveals a lack of understanding of how cultures change without being destroyed and how part, but only part, of Aboriginal identity is unquestionably linked to their status as Canadian citizens. Cairns's views are well in advance of those of Flanagan and Smith, and he, like many Canadians, is searching for better language and a deeper understanding of Aboriginal peoples that can point the way forward to solutions. He is not advocating a new or subtle form of assimilation, and he embraces the idea of diversity, of finding ways to "enhance the compatibility between Aboriginal nationhood and Canadian citizenship" (Cairns 2000: 211-13). On that sentiment, most Canadians can agree. We can further hope that in this search mainstream Canadians and their leaders educate themselves more fully on the nature of contemporary Aboriginal culture — and cultures.

NOTES

1 Aboriginal Elders or community members often preside over circle courts, which commonly hear only minor offences. The courts emphasize restitution and reconciliation between offenders and victims. See Proulx 2003 on alternative courts in the urban Toronto context; Borrows 2002 on the revitalization of Indigenous law; and Warry 1998, Ross 1992, and Ryan 1995 for analyses of Aboriginal justice and the emergence of circle courts.

2 The practice of Aboriginal medicine varies greatly across different provinces. Some centres, like Anishnawbe Health in Toronto have biomedical physicians as well as traditional healers who are available to clients (Skye 2006). In Ontario, Aboriginal Health Access Centres, funded through the province's Aboriginal Healing and Wellness Strategy, have traditional coordinators who arrange visits or consultations by traditional healers on an as-needed basis (see also Chapter 10).

3 The Nelson Canadian Dictionary (1999: 707) defines integrate as "to make whole by bringing all parts together; unify" and "to open to people of all races or ethnic groups without restriction" and integration as "the bringing together of people of different racial or ethnic groups into unrestricted and equal association, as in society or an organization; desegregation."

4 These raced-based arguments received new impetus in 2003 when Judge Kitchen of the British Columbia Provincial Court ruled that Aboriginal-specific fisheries should be eliminated because they violated the Charter of Rights and Freedoms equality provisions (see Chapter 11).

5 Smith's book was first self-published in 1995 by Crown Western and republished in 1996 by Stoddard. Melvin Smith was a public servant for 31 years and the "ranking official on constitutional reform" in four British Columbia governments. He died in 2000, but his book is still widely cited in conservative circles.

6 Smith's chapter on the White Paper is titled "A Vision Short-Lived."

7 Smith provides his emphasis to this phrase from a quote from a "government publication," which is listed (p. 16, note 17) as a "Submission to the Royal Commission on Aboriginal Peoples."

8 C-FAR stands for Citizens for Foreign Aid Reform; it is one of many right-wing websites. See
   <http://www.populist.org/cfar292.html>.

9 For example, Smith appeared before the Standing Committee on Aboriginal Affairs, where he
   presented his testimony (that is, his opinions) as the authoritative voice of an expert witness.

10 Rafe Mair, a cabinet minister in the Bill Bennett Social Credit government in British Columbia,
   talk show host, and long-time friend of Mr. Smith, wrote the Forward to the book. The two
   men worked closely in the late 1970s on British Columbia's constitutional proposals as part of
   federal-provincial discussions that preceded the repatriation of the Constitution. Mr. Mair notes
   that, after considerable work, these proposals went largely unread and were ignored by the federal government. Another friend, Gordon Gibson, is lauded by Smith in the book, as a "wise
   Canadian observer" (Smith 1996: 253). Elsewhere, Gibson's views are unreferenced and are
   passed off as factual evidence.

11 For Smith the critical turning point in Indian policy was the 1973 Supreme Court *Calder* decision,
   which acknowledged the existence of Aboriginal title to land. Smith argues that the government
   falsely interpreted the decision and gave it too much importance. Conservative writers commonly
   argue that the Supreme Court, as opposed to Parliament, has too much influence on government
   policy and action (see Chapter 9).

12 Canadian Human Rights Commission Annual Report 1996: 4; On-line at <http://www.chrc-ccdp.
   ca/publications/1996_ar/page4-en.asp>. In comparison, in the United States (excluding Alaska),
   where the Native population is proportionately smaller, 3 per cent of all lands are reserved for
   Aboriginal nations. The Commission notes that all the reserves in Canada would fit into half of
   the Navajo Nation Reserve in Arizona.

13 For example, Tom Flanagan (2001: 19) writes: "A sense of guilt over the colonial past should
   not prevent advocating the principles of individual freedom, legal equality, private property and
   open markets."

14 *First Nations? Second Thoughts* received the Donner Foundation's $25,000 book prize for works
   contributing to Canadian public policy. The Donner Foundation, well-known for its right-wing
   orientation and long-standing interest in Aboriginal issues, also financed Flanagan's research and
   the publication of the book. The Foundation's mandate "seeks to encourage individual responsibility and private initiative to help Canadians solve their social and economic problems." See
   <http://www.donnerfoundation.org/tocframe.html>.

15 Flanagan describes himself as a conservative or libertarian. His "core beliefs" include a privileging of the individual over collective rights, a valuing of representative forms of constitutional
   democracy, a commitment to free-market economies, and a belief that "the threads of progress
   are visible in the fabric of civilization" (2000: 8-9).

16 Early in his career, Flanagan wrote books and articles on Louis Riel and the North-West
   Rebellion before turning toward contemporary political analysis in writing on land claims and
   Aboriginal rights.

17 See also Scott 2004: 299-312. Scott's analysis is written for an academic audience and is at times
   quite esoteric. He is also less critical (or more generous) in his appraisal of Flanagan's analysis in
   First Nations? Second Thoughts.

18 This is a slippery slope argument often used by conservatives. There is no evidence that Aboriginal self-government would lead to demands by other ethnic groups that would require structural or constitutional changes.

19 These views are extremely common among mainstream Canadians; I have encountered them throughout the course of my life, both within and outside the university (Warry 1998: 33-34).

20 Aboriginal people find this comparison to other ethnic and immigrant groups offensive for it ignores the fact that they had established systems of government long before the first European settlers to North America arrived. But Flanagan spends an entire chapter trying to convince the reader that Aboriginal people are no different from later immigrants. He seems particularly perturbed by the use of the phrase "from time immemorial" which Aboriginal people often use to emphasize their historic and spiritual relationship to the land, for example, to describe how they were placed here by the Creator "from the beginning" (Flanagan 2000: 19).

21 See also Warry 1998: Chapter Five; Borrows 2002.

22 Cairns is a political scientist and former McLean Chair in Canadian Studies at the University of British Columbia.

23 H.B. Hawthorn was a leading sociologist; the Hawthorn Report, a major inquiry into Aboriginal affairs, was based on the contributions of a large number of social scientists. Cairns is careful to note that the subsequent White Paper ignored the recommendations of the Hawthorn report.

24 Skye (2006) draws on the work of Aboriginal scholars to demonstrate how intermarriage has always been an accepted part of Aboriginal-settler relations and how this in no way weakens self-identity claims.

25 This idea of parallelism is derived from the image of the two-row wampum, a common metaphor in Aboriginal discourse. See Chapter 13.

CHAPTER 3 Ending Denial: Acknowledging History and Colonialism

I n debates about Aboriginal peoples, history is often contested and white-washed. The neo-conservative right, in both Canada and Australia, relies for its arguments on historical revisionism or denial. They claim that Aboriginal poverty and ill health are the result of the failure of contemporary policies rather than the product of hundreds of years of colonialism and that any moral wrongs occurred as part of colonial history. On the other hand, Aboriginal advocates argue that clear government and public recognition for past wrongs, by apology and compensation, is necessary if reconciliation with Aboriginal peoples is to occur. As Robert Manne (2001) argues, only by acknowledging the state's active denial of its historical role can we come to grips with Aboriginal issues. Much like the alcoholic who refuses to acknowledge his or her behaviour, governments can be considered to be in denial when they fail to recognize the impact of their earlier policies and persist in actions that marginalize populations.

In its introductory volume, *Looking Forward, Looking Back*, RCAP (1996a) presents a Canadian history full of broken promises to Aboriginal peoples. During the period of early contact when "different but equal" cultures met, cooperation and mutual recognition between representatives of different political entities led to various agreements and treaties. We will see in the Conclusion to this book how this period of cooperation was symbolized in the Two Row Wampum as two nations pursuing parallel paths. This cooperative period gave way to "displacement and assimilation" as the settler society became entrenched in North America. As we saw in the last chapter, the government developed its doctrine of assimilation based on the assumptions that Aboriginal peoples were inferior to Europeans and incapable of governing themselves and that it was the state's responsibility to civilize them by imposing European values. This doctrine became the foundation for the Indian Act and other policies that were designed — through ignorance or ill intention — to attack Aboriginal institutions and to undermine their cultural values and identity. RCAP called for a renewed relationship between the government and Aboriginal peoples based on the principle of mutual recognition:

> the principle of mutual recognition ... calls on non-Aboriginal Canadians to recognize that Aboriginal people are the original inhabitants and caretakers of this land and have distinctive rights and responsibilities flowing from that status. It calls on

Aboriginal people to accept that non-Aboriginal people are also of this land now,
by birth and by adoption, with strong ties of love and loyalty. It requires both sides
to acknowledge and relate to one another as partners, respecting each other's laws
and institutions and co-operating for mutual benefit.[1]

As we have seen, neo-conservative commentators reject RCAP's portrayal
of Canadian history and any return to a more cooperative or nation-to-nation
model of Aboriginal relations. They uniformly condemn the commission for
laying a "guilt trip" on Canadians and blaming the current plight of Aboriginal
peoples on European actions. For instance, in *First Nations? Second Thoughts*,
Tom Flanagan borrows from now-antiquated archaeological theory to suggest
that civilization refers to societies that have reached a level of complexity which
is demonstrated by such characteristics as intensive agriculture, large permanent
settlements, specialization of roles and labour, intellectual and technological advances (metallurgy, writing systems, astronomy, etc.), and state political systems.
He then evaluates Aboriginal and European cultures on the basis of the presence
or absence of these characteristics. The difference between "simple" societies and
"complex" ones is important, Flanagan argues because "complexity is the hallmark of progress" in science, technology, and culture (Flanagan 2000: 31).

This view of culture contact bolsters the belief that conquerors have the
right to determine history and to dictate what rights the conquered will have.
For Flanagan, progress is marked by the "European tribes" who entered Canada
and established a new political order. It is only by way of British civilization that
Indian rights were recognized at all in the Royal Proclamation of 1763 (Flanagan
2000: 25). Flanagan notes that the concept of civilization has fallen out of favour in the social sciences, in part because of anthropological thinking about
the concept of cultural relativism.[2] Most anthropologists have abandoned terms
like "primitive," "simple," and "complex" to describe tribal cultures. There is, after
all, nothing simple about West Coast potlatches or Anishnabe ecological practices. It can take months and years of living in a culture for anthropologists to
fully appreciate the complexity of Indigenous beliefs and practices. Indeed, it is
analytically simplistic to rank cultures on some gross characterization of traits.
This does not mean that anthropologists or Aboriginal people fail to recognize
differences between cultures. Aboriginal peoples have never denied the value of
Western medicines or other technological tools, but claim that, on any analytical
scale, their ceremonies, cosmological systems, and political systems are no less
complex than European forms.

For Flanagan and other neo-conservatives like Smith and Kay the concept of
civilization is important because they believe that European cultural superiority
provides the rationale for the conquest of Indigenous peoples in the Americas,
Australia, and New Zealand. They cannot see that the attempt to destroy

Aboriginal cultures might be considered a sign of barbarism rather than civilization or that colonial actions came from societies that lacked the understanding
and moral integrity to search for ways of protecting Aboriginal cultures.

In the neo-conservative view, Canadian history, like history the world over,
is a natural process whereby hunters and gatherers are displaced by agricultural
peoples in a shift from "stateless" societies to organized society. Conquest was
inevitable, and says Flanagan, it is no more appropriate to talk of the morality of
colonial actions than it is to ask "whether it is right or wrong that childbirth is
painful, or that everyone eventually has to die" (Flanagan 2000: 39). Thus, conquest, both in the past and the present, is historically unavoidable, however re-
grettable. To assume the inevitability of history in this way is to be blind to the
lessons of the past and to abandon the insight that can lead to justice in our time
for the Indigenous peoples of the Amazon basin and elsewhere.

Flanagan's "moral defence" for colonialism and for the displacement of
Indigenous peoples comes from the Swiss jurist Emer de Vattel (1758), who argued that nations "live by plunder" and are destined by natural law to supplant
Indigenous peoples in order to cultivate land that is not being used for agriculture. Flanagan goes so far as to assert that, according to Vattel's criteria, the size
of reserves was "adequate" when they were first established. Furthermore, these
lands are today inadequate only because of the population growth on reserve
and because "various aspects of the legal regime adopted for Indians have inhib-
ited the migration from rural to urban locations that almost all other Canadians
have undergone" (Flanagan 2001: 42). In other words, farmers (Europeans) are
justified in taking land as long as they make the arts of civilization available to
the hunters who have been displaced. The exchange is simple — land for civilization. The method is equally clear — assimilation. For Flanagan there is nothing
racist in policies of assimilation or enfranchisement. He notes that the displacement of Aboriginal populations was a natural outcome of the spread of European
culture — helped by the spread of European diseases (Flanagan 2001: 39, 41-45).
The resulting drastic population declines among Aboriginal communities made
it easier for colonial settlers to follow practices aimed at destroying or undermining Aboriginal peoples and cultures.[3]

The denial of the destructiveness of colonialism is essential if Aboriginal peoples are to be blamed for their current problems. If Aboriginal poverty is not the
product of economic marginalization, then it must be the result of laziness or
welfare dependence. If there is nothing in our history to feel guilty about, then
we can ignore Aboriginal peoples' claims for compensation or contemporary redress. If the intentions of our ancestors and forefathers were good, then any harm
that was done can be rationalized, and we can start afresh. However, without
recognizing the damage done in the past, we cannot see how policies continue
to harm Aboriginal culture in the present. We should be able to recognize the

impacts of colonialism and use the lessons of history to recognize the poor intentions and paternalism in our own current thought and actions.

Debates about the intention behind colonial actions and the degree of harm
done to Aboriginal peoples are clearly illustrated in the bickering that surrounds
the use of the words genocide and cultural genocide in reference to the actions
of European settler societies. As a power word, genocide is rivaled only by its
sister term holocaust, connoting as it does the extermination of Jews and other
minorities in Nazi Germany. The word genocide (from the Latin *genus*, group
and *caedre*, to kill) was first used by Raphael Lemkin, a Polish-Jewish intellectual, to describe the Jewish holocaust (from the Hebrew ha-shoah). The word was
subsequently adopted by the United Nations (Evans and Thorpe 2001: 33) and
defined as the "systematic and planned extermination of an entire national, racial,
political or ethnic group."[4] Cultural genocide means the intentional destruction
of cultural practices, as opposed to peoples, through state policies; loosely, it also
means any harm caused to Indigenous peoples or other minorities. Authors such
as Ward Churchill have used the phrase "American Indian Holocaust" to suggest that the concept can be extended back in history and applied to the violence
that occurred against Indigenous peoples.[5] Not surprisingly, the use of both these
words to describe European actions against Aboriginal peoples is opposed by
neo-conservative commentators.

Systematic, state-sponsored violence experienced by Aboriginal peoples in
Canada was less than that which occurred in Australia at the hands of settlers
and paramilitary forces or in the United States by the military. The truth about
Aboriginal history and the extent of frontier violence has become another battle-
ground between the right and left, especially in Australia. In a three-part essay by
Keith Windshuttle (2000), a conservative Australian historian, published in the
right-wing journal *Quadrant*, the extent of historical revisionism is made clear.
Entitled *The Myths of Frontier Massacres in Australian History*, the essay examines four well-known massacres that occurred between 1834 and 1928. In each
case, Windshuttle claims that the number of killings has been exaggerated or that
the massacres were totally fabricated.[6] In an important rebuttal, Raymond Evans
and Bill Thorpe examine several critical flaws in what they term Windshuttle's
"random, chronologically challenged" approach.[7] Evans and Thorpe carefully
document the numerous examples of frontier violence that other more conservative historians avoid. They describe, for example, how the actions of Queensland
Native Mounted Police (circa 1860-1910), resulted in an "estimated, conservative count of 10,000 violent Aboriginal deaths in Queensland." They document
how these highly trained officers, under the guise of the euphemistically labeled
strategy of "dispersal," used hit-and-run tactics to track down and murder hundreds of individuals and to destroy Aboriginal camps and settlements (Evans and
Thorpe 2001: 26).

Perhaps as important, Evans and Thorpe argue that Windshuttle's "truth criteria" reflects a naïve approach to history, one that automatically biases the record against Aboriginal peoples. They note, for example, that Windshuttle claims that documentary evidence for White deaths is greater than for the killing of Aborigines. This is to be expected, because "white lives were considered more precious than aboriginal ones," which resulted in "a bias towards enumerating settler fatalities" in the historical record. Evans and Thorpe note further that precisely because the quantitative record is often unreliable, historians must be cautious and balanced in their interpretation and draw on both Aboriginal oral testimony as well as primary written sources. They conclude that Windshuttle's analysis is misguided, biased, and coloured by his desire to write an Australian history that shows White settlers as well-meaning and responding to Black violence as the frontier expanded:

> It is intensely discomforting to conceive of an Australian social order where the mass murder of a certain people, identifiable by their ethnicity, was a way of life, executed by a minority of perpetrators, tolerated by the settler majority, and winked at by a state which, in other settings, upheld the precepts of British culture, law and justice. This discomfort impels Windshuttle's analysis into denial, distortion and disremembering while contributing to its credibility. But the context of acceptable terror was the historical truth. (Evans and Thorpe 2001: 29)

Nonetheless, Evans and Thorpe remain uncomfortable about the implications of using the word genocide. They suggest instead, in an almost too carefully semantic argument, that the Australian situation requires a "revised redefinition" of genocide, for which they suggest the term Indigenocide (Evans and Thorpe 2001: 33). This term reflects the fact that killings took place on the basis of the perceived ethnicity or status of the victims as Indigenous peoples but also acknowledges that they were meant to remove Indigenous peoples as occupiers and owners of the land settlers so desperately wished to acquire. The logic of their argument suggests that Indigenocide would allow for discussion of the range of different situations and political conditions on the frontier (including different Aboriginal responses and resistance to settlement and encroachment) whereas genocide implies a concerted attempt at the elimination of an entire race or ethnic group.

In the end Evans and Thorpe say that it is inappropriate to speak of an "Australian Holocaust" and also caution against using the term genocide to describe postwar actions of forced assimilation and child removal because such a use risks "diminishing or conflating the Jewish experience, as well as being ahistorical." But they do suggest that it is completely accurate to characterize state actions against Aboriginal peoples during the frontier period as an example of "developmental genocide." These actions fit the contemporary definition approved by the United Nations *Convention on the Prevention and Punishment of the Crime of Genocide* (Evans and Thorpe 2001: 36).[8]

Canadians are fortunate that our frontier history does not contain this type of systemic violence against Aboriginal peoples. However, it is a myth to think of it as non-violent. We have the dubious distinction of bearing blame for one of two clear examples of the death of entirely discreet Indigenous cultures — the Beothuk of Newfoundland and the Indigenous peoples of Tasmania. Other Indigenous peoples, including tribes in the United States, were forced to migrate or disperse, but in these two island cultures an entire people and culture were eliminated through the effects of disease and purposeful violence by settlers.

Do Canadians know the history of the Beothuk or, for that matter, of the fur trade wars that resulted in significant death tolls and in the dispersal of Native tribes? Are we aware that the British may have been responsible for one of the earliest, if not the first, use of biological warfare, which occurred when plans were made to distribute blankets infested with small pox to Indians during the Pontiac Rebellion?[9] Do we know about such situations as the forced sterilization of Indian and Inuit women, which occurred until the 1970s and can be considered an act of genocide under the United Nations convention as "measures intended to prevent births within the group"?[10]

Such recent actions are labeled examples of cultural genocide by Aboriginal activists because they imply the continuance of state practice meant to destroy their peoples or cultures. In the United States, Canada, and Australia, Aboriginal scholars and students routinely employ the term to describe the many impacts of colonialism. Writing of Australian state violence against Aboriginal peoples, Manne prefers an expansive definition of the term genocide, one separate from our images of the holocaust.[11] He notes that one means by which genocide can be committed under the United Nations Convention is through the forced removal of children, if the intent is to destroy the racial group to which they belong (Manne 2001: 5). Such practices occurred not only in Australia but also in Canada where Aboriginal children were taken from their families and placed in residential schools or were "adopted out" of reserves to white parents in what came to be referred to as the "Sixties Scoop" by child welfare authorities (see Bennett *et al.* 2005).

In Australia these practices are generally referred to as the Stolen Generations policies, after a government report which so named them, a term which Manne has argued is a kind of "moral shorthand" for the abuses of government policy that encouraged removal of mixed-race Aboriginal children from their families. Prior to World War II, there was a "genocidal dimension in the thinking" of Australian administrators who were essentially attempting "biological absorption" of Aboriginal ("half-breed") children. Such attempts at "breeding out the colour" amounted to a type of eugenics movement and is an example of a deliberate genocidal campaign against Aboriginal peoples. With the end of the war and the association of eugenics with Nazism, this rationale for child removal policies was rejected.[12] However, Manne believes that the term genocide is inapplicable to postwar policies, which legitimated child removal as a part of the general ideology of assimilation, and justified it in the name of child protection (Manne 2001: 40, passim 34-41).

Inga Clendinnen, an Australian historian, strongly objects to the use of the term genocide being applied outside its contemporary context. For her, the word is forever linked to images of the holocaust and to the mass murder of innocent people by an organized authority. She believes "that to take the murder out of genocide is to render it vacuous, and I believe with Orwell that it is essential to keep such words mirror-bright because, given the nature of human affairs, we will surely continue to need them." Clendinnen is convinced that the use of the term genocide in the Stolen Generations report was not only misguided but a "moral, intellectual and (as it is turning out) political disaster." She notes that the response to the report on the part of those on the right is partially fueled by the use of this term and the "outrage at the use of that word 'genocide,' accompanied by the slamming shut of minds."[13] This position has been dismissed by Manne, Aboriginal advocates, and other left-leaning writers as an attempt to whitewash the seriousness of violence against Aboriginal peoples (Lucashenko *et al.* 2001: 16). Nonetheless, Clendinnen's cautionary comments are important; the debate about history and Aboriginal peoples requires language that is accurate and neither conciliatory nor polemical.

Clendinnen further cautions us to avoid "adversarial history" and the simplification of complex issues to score political points. She wants intellectuals to avoid "moralism, which discourages both subtlety in analysis, and patience and generosity in judgment" (in Brunton *et al.* 2001: 108). Judgements must rest on solid assessments of the information at hand and appreciation for the way in which individual opinions and state policy were coloured by the perceptions and attitudes of the time. Only when a generous and truthful reading of history is accomplished will we be able to remember our past; to be forgiven and to forgive ourselves; and, without forgetting, to use our history to move on to a shared future with Aboriginal peoples.

The use of the term cultural genocide is powerfully emotive, but does it reflect historical reality? Or is it merely a tool of left-leaning advocates and Aboriginal peoples to shut down debate about current policies that negatively impact their cultures? Writing in favour of assimilation in the *National Post*, Jonathan Kay echoes Clendinnen's words:

> Canada's 1969 White Paper, which supported the then mainstream policy of assimilation, is dismissed by critics as a relic of colonial thinking. Assimilation is

spoken of casually as "cultural genocide," a term whose very utterance pre-empts
debate and is often cited as the basis for many suits launched by those who attended
church- and government-operated residential schools. (Kay 2001)

Kay offers no examples of where the term cultural genocide is used to accuse
Canadians of intolerance or to shut down political debate. In fact, Aboriginal
academics use it cautiously and in strict reference to state policies, such as enfranchisement; the outlawing of Aboriginal ceremonies like the Potlatch and
Sundance; or, as Kay points out, support of residential schools or the child welfare
policies that led to the removal of Aboriginal children from reserves.

Aboriginal people sometimes do use the term cultural genocide in a casual way,
loosely associating all colonial practices with attempts to eliminate Aboriginal
peoples by way of assimilation and to end Aboriginal culture. That is, rather than
accurately describing attempts to eliminate specific cultural practices that were
thought incompatible with European (or Christian) values, the term is applied
to all the cultural changes Aboriginal peoples have experienced. In this way, the
phrase becomes a hindrance to any useful discourse. Kay's view is similar to that
of Clendinnen, who speaks of "minds slamming shut" when the term genocide is
broadly applied to situations where violence was not used or contemplated.

In both Australia and Canada major national inquiries into state historical
practices concerning Aboriginal peoples have come up with two very different
results.[14] When RCAP released its final report, which included over 400 recommendations, in November 1996, the government promptly shelved it, claiming
that the recommendations were too costly to implement. A year later it issued
a formal response in the form of the report *Gathering Strength*. Its "Statement
of Reconciliation" recognized in particular the harm caused by the residential
school system but stopped short of a formal apology to Aboriginal peoples for
historical wrongs:

> The Government of Canada today formally expresses to all Aboriginal people in
> Canada our profound regret for past actions of the federal government which have
> contributed to these difficult pages in the history of our relationship together....
> Sadly, our history with respect to the treatment of Aboriginal people is not some-
> thing in which we can take pride. Attitudes of racial and cultural superiority led to a
> suppression of Aboriginal culture and values. As a country, we are burdened by past
> actions that resulted in weakening the identity of Aboriginal peoples, suppressing
> their languages and cultures, and outlawing spiritual practices.... We must acknowl-
> edge that the result of these actions was the erosion of the political, economic and
> social systems of Aboriginal people and nations. (Canada 1997)[15]

The second section of the report stated government intentions to implement an array of measures dealing with employment, training, economic development, and land claims reform, among others. One of these was the Aboriginal Healing Foundation (AHF), which implemented a number of healing circles and community group processes for residential school survivors across the country. The report also spawned court actions against churches and the government and resulted in subsequent apologies by mainstream churches for their role in the residential school abuses.

Not all residential school experiences, of course, were bad. They can be credited with producing band managers, advocates, and political leaders with the skills necessary to effectively negotiate with, and oppose, government actions. But the abuses that did take place are well-documented. At least to date, courts have rejected claims for general damages—loss of language or damage to cultural well-being—but have upheld compensation in cases of actual physical or sexual abuse. There is no doubt that criminal acts—the physical and sexual abuse of individuals—occurred. At a collective level, the schools constituted a direct assault on Aboriginal culture and a conscious attempt to assimilate Aboriginal children. Aboriginal researchers have documented the intergenerational effects, which have contributed to addictions, loss of language and cultural esteem, and parenting problems. Residential school experiences have been identified as an important part of the culture and identity loss referred to by Aboriginal researchers as "historical trauma."[16]

Yet, as part of their denial of history, neo-conservative writers deny both individual and group claims for compensation for this type of historical injustice. For Flanagan, the money spent by the federal government in creating the AHF is wasted, and compensation for past wrongs only benefits "lawyers feasting on the fees" and threatens churches with bankruptcy. He cannot fathom the possibility that individuals who receive compensation might feel some sense of justice and that the closure that this symbolic restitution brings might actually contribute to healing. Rather, he believes only that compensation "encourages them [Aboriginal people] to see the problems in their own lives as the result of actions of others rather than as challenges for them to overcome by their own initiative" (Flanagan 2001: 13-14).

The reality, of course, is that the negative impacts of the residential school experience, particularly on families, are well-documented and have been for over 20 years.[17] Much—not all—of the work of the AHF has been profoundly important in helping communities to come to grips with the colonial causes for health and mental health problems. On Manitoulin Island, to take one small example, AHF monies helped to fund innovative approaches to community mental health and to develop community mentoring and training programs for parents and children still dealing with the effects of residential schools.

In November 2005, a decade after RCAP highlighted these issues, the Martin government announced a $2 billion compensation package for Aboriginal people who were forced to attend residential schools. The largest settlement in Canadian history, the agreement called for an initial payout for each person of $10,000, plus $3,000 per year of attendance at residential schools. Approximately 86,000 people are eligible for compensation. Significantly, the package also contained provision to continue funding of the AHF and of a truth and reconciliation process, a commemoration program, and other projects designed to promote healing in First Nations communities. While critics argued about the merits of this individualistic approach to compensation — mental health providers, for example, suggested that the money might be better spent on comprehensive counselling or other programs — it appeared that Canada, finally, had recognized the legacy of one of the most blatant colonial practices. Justice Minister Irwin Cotler called the decision to house Aboriginals in residential schools "the single most harmful, disgraceful and racist act in our history."[18]

RCAP had both Aboriginal and non-Aboriginal co-chairs and commissioners. Public consultations were held throughout First Nations rural and urban communities. And yet the mainstream Canadian public was never fully engaged and has largely remained uninvolved in subsequent efforts. Slowly, however, the language of reconciliation has entered the national vocabulary. In Alberta and Ontario, coalitions of Aboriginal and non-Aboriginal people are attempting to raise awareness for a National Day of Healing and Reconciliation to promote reconciliation between Aboriginal peoples and mainstream (particularly Christian) Canadians and to raise awareness of government policies that have affected Aboriginal peoples.[19] In British Columbia, the ministry responsible for land claims and Aboriginal affairs has been renamed the Ministry of Aboriginal Relations and Reconciliation Office. But, despite these provincial moves, the federal government remains responsible for reconciliation and building relationships with Aboriginal communities. It remains to be seen whether truth and reconciliation efforts will reach out to mainstream Canadians and whether some form of rapprochement with Aboriginal peoples can begin.

In Australia, the public response has been broader. Under former Prime Minister Paul Keating a unique national reconciliation strategy began in 1991 and lasted throughout the decade leading up to celebrations of the centenary of the Australian federation in 2001. A Council for Aboriginal Reconciliation was created, consisting of 25 prominent Australians drawn from all walks of life and co-chaired by an Aboriginal and non-Aboriginal person. The council implemented a series of events, celebrations, and public education campaigns "aimed at building bridges between Indigenous and other Australians." After the election of John Howard and a new Liberal (neo-conservative) party government in 1996, the council fell prey to political interference, most notably in the selection of its membership, which changed significantly.[20] In 2000 the Council presented to representatives of Australian governments the Australian Declaration Towards Reconciliation. The declaration is given more specific content or implemented through a plan called "'Roadmap for Reconciliation" that outlines four National Strategies. The Prime Minister then committed $5.5 million as seed funding for an independent foundation, Reconciliation Australia, to continue work towards Reconciliation in coordination with State/Territory and local Reconciliation groups.[21] Today, Reconciliation Australia, an independent not-for-profit organization supported in part by the government, continues to facilitate debate on the idea of a national treaty with Aboriginal peoples as well as other key Aboriginal issues.

For many Australians, the reconciliation process was an opportunity to express regret about the policies of the past, solidarity with the current generation of Aboriginal peoples, and hopes for the future. According to Jackie Huggins, the Aboriginal co-chair of Reconciliation Australia, beginning around 1997, a "spontaneous Peoples Movement for Reconciliation emerged and embedded itself in Australian society."[22] Over the course of many years, marches and other public celebrations attracted hundreds of thousands of supporters in major urban centres. The first walk across the Sydney Harbour Bridge in 2000 attracted roughly 350,000 people. Hundreds of thousands of Australians also signed "pledge books" to demonstrate support for the Declaration. "Sorry" became synonymous with a formal apology for past assimilationist policies and for the Stolen Generations actions in particular. Local "Sorry" groups formed throughout the country and took upon themselves the organization of events aimed at demonstrating solidarity with Aboriginal peoples and research into local Aboriginal history. National Sorry Days were later renamed National Days of Healing and Reconciliation to emphasize hope that animosities can be overcome.

A public call for an apology came after the tabling of the Stolen Generations report; this call was taken up and supported by the Council for Reconciliation. An apology was subsequently issued by all state and territory government, but the federal government would only issue a statement of regret. Melissa Nobles, an MIT political scientist, suggests that Prime Minister Howard has refused to issue an apology, because he reasons that "the policy of moving children can't be judged by the moral standards of today" and that to issue an apology "would endorse a view of Australian history as one of exploitation and racism."[23]

Jackie Huggins states:

The issue of an apology has also been fraught in other countries. In Australia, the common reasons given for not offering one is that today's Australians are not responsible for the deeds of the past. People claim that they have not committed any injustice, nor did their forbears (many of whom arrived in the country since the practice [of child removal] ceased) and therefore they have nothing to be sorry about. But, as we know, to heal and go forward there has to be a frank and honest acknowledgement of government policies that were wrong and harmful.

Huggins concludes that the "The word 'sorry' is still awaited.... As a historian, I can't contemplate the impact of that one word — with genuine intent — could have for the course of Australian history."[24] The issue, as she acknowledges, is intention and whether past or current actions are genuinely taken or taken for reasons of political expediency.

The question remains: why has public awareness of Aboriginal issues in Canada and Australia failed to translate into political action? In Australia, despite widespread public engagement with Aboriginal issues, the national government refuses to offer an apology, and Aboriginal policies continue to sustain the status quo. In Canada, the government recognizes past wrongdoings, and yet the public remains disinterested in the plight of Aboriginal peoples. In neither country, despite political rhetoric, are Aboriginal issues such as self-government, land claims, treaty renovation, or other critical issues high on the political agenda.

There is a huge chasm in public perception and belief that ranges on the one hand from those who whitewash history and deny the impact of colonialism on Aboriginal peoples to those who admit to past wrongdoings and move forward to begin the politics of reconciliation. The neo-conservative right in both Canada and Australia fears a truthful telling of the history of European-Aboriginal relationships as documented by academics and government inquiries. This fear is, perhaps, easily understood; to admit the history is to admit both to a record of racism in the past and to the possibility of continued racism and discrimination against Aboriginal peoples in the present. It is time to end this denial, to acknowledge the truth about our recent past, and to accept that the mistreatment of Aboriginal peoples should never be forgotten. Only then will an era of true reconciliation between Aboriginal and non-Aboriginal peoples begin.

NOTES

1 See RCAP 1996a, b at the Department of Indian Affairs website at <http://www.ainc-inac. gc.ca/ch/rcap/rpt/lk_e.html>.

2 As discussed in Chapter 2, at its most basic cultural relativism is the idea that all cultures are internally coherent and adapted to the environments in which they are situated. If all cultures must be understood on their own terms, it can be argued that none are inherently better or superior.

3 For a discussion of debates around virgin soil epidemics and their impact on Aboriginal populations, see Waldram et al. 2006.

4   Nelson Canadian Dictionary 1997. Under Article II of the United Nations convention, "genocide means any of the following acts committed with intent to destroy, in whole or in part, a national, ethnical, racial, or religious group, as such (a) Killing members of the group; (b) Causing serious bodily or mental harm to members of the group; (c) Deliberately inflicting on the group condi-tions of life calculated to bring about its physical destruction in whole or in part; (d) Imposing measures intended to prevent births within the group; (e) Forcibly transferring children of the group to another group." <http://www.preventgenocide.org/law/convention/text.htm#II>.

5   See Churchill 1994 and 1998. See also note 13, Chapter 6. Churchill is a controversial author who has gone so far as to suggest, for example, parallels between Nazi stereotypes and actions against Jews and contemporary images of Aboriginal peoples. His arguments concerning genocide, how-ever, are carefully argued in relation to the United Nations criteria.

6   He argues that this fabrication has taken place largely because of the over-zealous advocacy of Christian missionaries who were upset at the conditions faced by Aboriginal peoples on the fron-tier and later by ideologically driven (left-biased) historians who aimed to highlight impacts of the colonial project on the Aboriginal minority. A generous reading of Windshuttle's argument casts doubts on the numbers of deaths that occurred in these events. He also places the killings in the context of a contested frontier where individual (as opposed to mass or group) deaths of white settlers was not uncommon and, in so doing, calls into question, at least for these four events, the "truthfulness" of the historical record (Windshuttle 2000).

7   These historians point out, first, that Windshuttle is not an academically trained historian (he is a sociologist who before turning to Aboriginal history concentrated on media studies and journal-ism). While not dismissing the role of non-academic historians, they claim that either a lack of training (to be generous) or obvious bias caused Windshuttle to miss obvious, accessible, and crit-ical sources such as the British parliamentary papers, which document the numbers of Aboriginal and white homicides during the period he examines. In addition, Windshuttle fails to utilize a range of primary sources such as letters, witness depositions, and statements by both Aborigines and non-Aboriginals concerning the violent episodes he professes to carefully examine. However, their central criticism is that Windshuttle has been purposefully selective in examining specific massacres. If evidence prior to 1834 is examined, for example, an overwhelming case can be made for a long series of conflicts in which violence against Aboriginal peoples was an integral part of "opening up" the frontier for farming and settlement.

8   See <http://www.preventgenocide.org/law/convention/text.htm#II>.

9   See Steckley and Cummins 2001. Jeffrey Amherst, the Commander-in-Chief of the British forces, wrote to superiors in Britain with the suggestion that blankets infested with small pox be distrib-uted to Indians during the Pontiac Uprising. There is no written confirmation that this plan was implemented, though smallpox outbreaks did occur in the area around this time. These events are very much a part of Aboriginal oral tradition. I have heard, for example, of Aboriginal people who have been told by Elders to refuse blankets offered in hospitals even to this day.

10 A study by the United States Government Accounting Office during the 1970s found widespread sterilization by the Indian Health Services (IHS). In 1975 alone, some 25,000 Native American women were permanently sterilized — many after being coerced, misinformed, or threatened.

One former IHS nurse reported the use of tubal ligation on "uncooperative" or "alcoholic"
women into the 1990s. Canadian cases are less well documented but have been asserted by
Aboriginal women's organizations. See <http://members.aol.com/_ht_a/lillithsrealm/myhome
page/Sterilization/BrokenTreaties.htm>.

11 As noted in the Introduction to this book, Australian Aboriginal peoples face a very different
political climate than do those in Canada. They have, at least as yet, no constitutional recognition or protection of their rights; because there is no specific history of "treaty" relations, they do
not commonly possess land that is "reserved" for their sole use. The 1992 Australian High Court
decision in the Mabo case recognized Aboriginal title to land and resulted in the Native Title Act
1993. This act instituted a specific program of "land title" claims, which has allowed Aboriginal
peoples to lay claim to specific territories. Many anthropologists and historians are engaged in
this research.

12 These policies were documented in a government's inquiry, the Separation of Aboriginal Children
from their Families. The inquiry report came to be commonly known as the "Stolen Generations"
report.

13 Clendinnen, in Brunton *et al.* 2001: 106. See also Manne's response (in Brunton *et al.* 2001: 126).
Manne plays semantics with this quote by suggesting that the concept of genocide is "complex and
opaque" rather than "mirror bright," but, in so doing, I believe he misses the point that Clendinnen
is trying to make: that the state behaviours associated with the Stolen Generations are a different
order than killings associated with either the holocaust or the violence of the Australia frontier.

14 Some have attempted to place these national processes in the context of a wider movement of
historical review that has led, for example, to Germany's apology for the Holocaust, $80 billion
in reparations, and ongoing support for the Israeli government and to the South Africa Truth
and Reconciliation Commission process on apartheid. See E.J. Graff, "All Apologies" (2004) at
<http://www.radcliffe.edu/about/news/quarterly/200402/feature_01.php>.

15 Canada 1997. The statement continues:

     One aspect of our relationship with Aboriginal people over this period that requires par-
     ticular attention is the Residential School system. This system separated many children
     from their families and communities and prevented them from speaking their own lan-
     guages and from learning about their heritage and cultures. In the worst cases, it left lega-
     cies of personal pain and distress that continue to reverberate in Aboriginal communities
     to this day. Tragically, some children were the victims of physical and sexual abuse. The
     Government of Canada acknowledges the role it played in the development and adminis-
     tration of these schools. Particularly to those individuals who experienced the tragedy of
     sexual and physical abuse at residential schools, and who have carried this burden believ-
     ing that in some way they must be responsible, we wish to emphasize that what you expe-
     rienced was not your fault and should never have happened. To those of you who suffered
     this tragedy at residential schools, we are deeply sorry.

16 Duran and Duran (1995: 30, 43) first wrote of the impact of colonialism on mental health and of
intergenerational post-traumatic stress disorder. Maria Yellow Horse Braveheart and Lemyra M.

DeBruyn (1998) have pointed out a broader set of identity and mental health problems arising from unresolved grief and historical trauma.

17 See Aboriginal Healing Foundation 2005. This resource manual provides an excellent background to the causes, consequences, and healing approaches to residential school trauma.

18 As reported on the CBC website <http://www.cbc.ca/story/canada/national/2005/11/23/resi dential-package051123.html>.

19 See for example <http://www.ndhr.ca/default.php> and <http://www.reconciliationconference. com/vision/statement.html>.

20 The council also oversaw an extensive period of public consultations and, in two separate reports, made many recommendations to improve relations between White and Black Australians. These recommendations called for, among other things, legislation that would introduce formal treaties and political agreements to redress the absence of land and political treaties during the colonial period; and actions to protect the political, legal, cultural, and economic rights of Aboriginal individuals and groups.

21 The Australian Declaration Towards Reconciliation can be found at <http://www.austlii.edu.au/ au/journals/AILR/2001/7.html#Heading4>. The Reconciliation Australia is located at <http:// www.reconciliation.org.au/i-cms.isp>.

22 This synopsis of Australian events, and the quotations by Huggins, are taken from a speech, titled "Big Ideas and Small Steps — Australia's approaches to reconciliation and Indigenous self-govern-ment" that she gave at the First Nations Government Conference in Vancouver, March 2002. The speech is available at <http://www.turning-point.ca/index.php/article/view/101/1/28>.

23 As quoted by E.J. Graff, in "All Apologies" on-line at: <http://www.radcliffe.edu/about/news/ quarterly/200402/feature_01.php>.

24 See Note 22.

CHAPTER 4 The Media: Sustaining Stereotypes

In our rush to make sense of ever-increasing amounts of information, we often look for simple explanations. The media serves a useful purpose: they help us understand the surface reality of a complex world. Even where specific issues are given heavy print coverage, such as with health care reform, media analysis does little to improve our understanding of the issues. Jeffrey Simpson has lamented the average Canadian's ignorance of social policy by referring to polls such as one by Ipsos-Reid, sponsored by the *Globe and Mail*, that showed that even after extensive coverage of the Romanow Report on health care, over half the respondents (57 per cent) knew little or nothing about it (Simpson 2002). Simpson suggests that many Canadians get most of their information from television, which entertains rather than informs. Increasingly, many Canadians rely on websites for "news" that is more about celebrity and trivia that the events of the day.

How do the media influence, if at all, our perceptions of Aboriginal issues? On 26 October 2005, the CBC National News reported on the evacuation of the Kashechewan Reserve in Northern Ontario due to the failure of its water treatment system, which led to the contamination of drinking water. This was an important story that potentially could have been used to educate viewers about the poor water quality and other environmental health problems on hundreds of reserves. But the CBC chose to follow the evacuation story immediately with a feature on mismanagement by, and potential corruption in, the Natuashish Band Council. This community, formerly known as Davis Inlet, had been relocated, at an estimated cost of $350 million from their original home on the Labrador coast to a location that was more easily serviced. The story followed a previous CBC investigation that suggested there was over $3 million in missing funds. However, a subsequent investigation by the Department of Indian Affairs found no wrongdoing in the spending of the money Ottawa allocated for the community.[1] The October story focused on the alleged misuse of money stemming from the band's Voisey Bay income and the use of money by councillors for private airfares and family loans. It was based on an August 2005 letter from the band accountant that identified several questionable management practices.

Why would the CBC juxtapose these two stories? As I will suggest in Chapter 11, claims of mismanagement are overly exaggerated in neo-conservative critiques of First Nations governance. Linking these two stories by placing them back to back on the National News suggested that social and health problems are at least partly the result of mismanagement and corruption of First Nations governments. In short, such editorial decisions blame the victim and create the impression that Aboriginal peoples are responsible for their ill health, rather than decades of government inaction and centuries of colonialism. Is it a surprise, then, that many Canadians blame Aboriginal people for their problems?

Writing of the Kashechewan water quality crisis for the *Globe and Mail*, Richard Wagamese, an Aboriginal novelist and journalist, noted that the story had been placed third on evening newscasts behind lottery winners and a possible visit from Prince Charles and Camilla Parker Bowles. He noted that the Canadian media "still regard the lives of one of Canada's founding peoples as lacking in sufficient substance to matter to viewers"(Wagamese 2005).

On 30 October 2005, the Kashechewan crisis and other Aboriginal issues were addressed on CBC Radio's Cross Country Check-up, a national phone-in show. The host, Rex Murphy, a popular and respected CBC commentator, frankly admitted his inexperience and lack of knowledge about Aboriginal affairs. The CBC contacted National Chief Phil Fontaine, who tried to put the issue in historical perspective and to link environmental health issues to the need for improved federal-Aboriginal negotiations and strategies for change. Fontaine spoke eloquently about Aboriginal conditions, the failure of government policies, and AFN strategies to correct infrastructure deficits. Callers to the show, however, were unable to make these connections. One caller suggested that the water system had failed because poorly educated Natives were unable to maintain the system, and another not only spoke of his experience with Aboriginal people while referring to "reservations," a term inappropriately used in Canada, but also linked poverty and ill health to Aboriginal political corruption and mismanagement. Two weeks later, the *Globe and Mail* columnist Margaret Wente reduced the entire environmental crisis, and the boil water advisories on hundreds of reserves, to a story on how the incident could have been prevented if local workers had been better trained or the chief and council more decisive (Wente 2005). This view became a popular motif, repeated in letters to the editor which blamed Kashechewan residents and leaders for the problem.

Hundreds of Aboriginal communities live with boil water advisories as an everyday condition of life, while waiting years, and even decades, for sewage and water systems to be built. Skilled technicians to inspect and maintain the plants are desperately needed, and yet no comprehensive program to train and hire local residents exists. There are many other infrastructure problems; for instance, household mold resulting from poor building materials and inadequate ventilation compounds the existing housing shortage on reserves, a shortage which has been documented for decades. These problems remain unaddressed by successive Conservative and Liberal governments, who have been unable — or are unwilling — to initiate the comprehensive reforms recommended by RCAP.

It is naïve to assume that the purpose of the media is to educate the public about complex social issues. All too often what constitutes news is determined by crisis, drama, and fear, according to the Media Awareness Network, whose members have backgrounds in education, journalism, mass communications, and cultural policy.[2] The network notes that stories about cultural activities appear on some local television and radio stations, where they are usually given only passing mention. On the other hand, small newspapers often provide excellent coverage of local and regional Aboriginal issues. The *Manitoulin Expositor*, for example, has been recognized for its coverage of Aboriginal issues on Manitoulin Island.[3] A critical reading of its stories over several years shows that, although its coverage sometimes demonstrates a lack of understanding of Aboriginal culture, the paper does an excellent job of showing the complexity of community dynamics and attempts to include positive stories that focus on capacity building, the development of programs and services, and the revitalization of cultural ways. It also consciously attempts to include Aboriginal readers' letters in response to stories and so acts as a reasonable forum for debate. A 2004 survey of editorial positions, letters to the editor, and stories in 15 newspapers found that several Northern Ontario papers offered credible coverage of Aboriginal issues while the most negative and biased coverage was in large national papers.[4]

As early as 1992 following the Oka Crisis,[5] Fleras and Elliot noted that Aboriginal activism was subject to increasingly intense media publicity and that this coverage reflected the popular view of Aboriginal peoples "as a) a social problem b) having problems that cost the Canadian taxpayer and c) creating problems that threaten Canada's social fabric."[6] The Media Awareness Network notes that the treatment of Aboriginal peoples by major mainstream media is often focused on coverage "of political and constitutional issues, forest fires, poverty and substance or sexual abuse," adding that, for better or worse, the nature of reporting is that bad news gets all the attention: "Tragedies, conflicts and crises get reported; success stories rarely do." A number of causes for poor reporting include tight deadlines, lack of investigative time, and editors and other gatekeepers who are poorly versed in Aboriginal affairs. This is particularly problematic for Aboriginal peoples, because a crisis mentality means that the hard constructive work of building the capacity for a self-sustaining economy and government is lost amidst the "infobabble" (see Chapter 10). Rudy Platiel, who covered Aboriginal stories for the *Globe and Mail* for 27 years, notes, "there are an awful lot of good things happening that are not going to get reported in the mainstream press unless somebody pushes to get them there" (Media Awareness Network 2006). What is lacking in media coverage are, first, images and stories that would allow the Canadian public to truly grasp the capacity that is being built, and, second, an awareness of culture and history that would cast the shadow of blame away from Aboriginal peoples and toward the Canadian state and the public's ongoing indifference to Aboriginal poverty and ill health.

The Media Awareness Network uses a 2000 study by Henry and Tator (2002), leading experts on racism, to demonstrate journalistic bias in the reporting of the Jack Ramsay case. A former RCMP officer and Reform Party Member of Parliament, Ramsay was accused and convicted of the sexual assault in 1969 of a 13-year-old Aboriginal girl. Henry and Tator's research revealed that the media concentrated on "the girl's alcoholic and abusive parents, her impoverished childhood, and her own bouts with alcohol and drugs. By contrast, the review of Ramsay was more sympathetic. It focused on his career, his service to the community, and his supportive family." Such biased reporting is, in fact, all too common when Aboriginal people are the focus of media attention. Henry and Tator document different discourses that remain prevalent in neo-conservative thinking and mainstream media, including "discourses of denial," "equal opportunity," and "blaming the victim":

> The assumption is that because Canada is a society that upholds the ideals of a liberal democracy, it cannot possibly be racist. The denial of racism is so habitual in the media that to even make the allegation of bias and discrimination and raise the possibility of its influence on social outcomes becomes a serious social infraction, incurring the wrath and ridicule of many journalists and editors. (Media Awareness Network 2006)

The *National Post* is known for its anti-Aboriginal rights columns and pro-assimilation arguments. Its articles on Aboriginal affairs focus on government spending, the high cost of Aboriginal programs, the need for Aboriginal people to find jobs in the mainstream marketplace, and so on. Its coverage of the failed First Nations Governance Act, for example, relied on a *National Post*/Compas poll to suggest that two-thirds of Canadians say existing policy does not work and that the money Ottawa spends is doing little to improve Aboriginal conditions. The same article aired Flanagan's views that Ottawa could not deliver on the laudable goal of self-government and that funding reserve programs "creates perverse incentives for people where there is no future." Flanagan was then cited as suggesting that Ottawa cut funding for litigation and legal research by Aboriginal peoples (Chwialowska 2002).

The media often imply that Aboriginal affairs funding is wasted. Figures of $8 to $10 billion are often mentioned. A 2005 Canadian Taxpayers Federation report cites a figure of about $10 billion per year in federal and provincial expenditures on Aboriginal affairs. To put this into perspective, the federal government spends close to $4 billion providing subsidies to businesses and $11 billion on defence.[7] The press reports that money spent on Aboriginal affairs is poorly spent because it fails to change the horrendous living conditions experienced by Aboriginal peoples.

Are Aboriginal expenditures out of line? If we are prepared to neglect the differences in health and wealth between mainstream Canadians and Aboriginal peoples and the need for programs to reduce this gap, the answer is yes. Federal and provincial expenditures amount to roughly $7,693 per Aboriginal person. In comparison, the per capita expenditures on non-Aboriginal Canadians is roughly $5,496.[8]

The *National Post* is also where columnist Diane Francis is given a regular voice. Francis is well-known for her hard-line views. In a now infamous 1995 *Macleans* article titled "Time to Get Tough With Natives," she brought national attention to and supported the views of Melvin Smith (whose work we reviewed in Chapter 3). The article so outraged Aboriginal leaders that it was condemned by the AFN in a formal resolution, which stated "this type of thinking perpetuates misunderstandings, promotes intolerance and deepens the divisions between Native and non-Native societies."[9] Writing of Francis's views on Quebec, Gord Cruess states,

> Extreme positions spawn cycles of mistrust, non-dialogue, and hate. The Diane Francis's of the world manage to push people farther apart, because the rattling of their drums tends to drown out the more numerous, yet less histrionic, moderate voices. This shouldn't happen. We should use these sorts of propagandists not as instruments of division, but for our mutual benefit — they will always exist, and so we will always have a springboard from which we can launch more inclusive and truthful positions.[10]

These same observations might equally apply to other neo-conservative writing on Aboriginal affairs that appears in the *National Post*. It is there after all that Kay (2001) wrote directly of the need to assimilate Aboriginal peoples. The *National Post* editors ignored the Kashechewan story to run instead an editorial about "pipeline politics." It suggested that Ottawa "reassert itself" with the Deh Cho First Nation of the Northwest Territories who were continuing to be "obstructionist" in opposing the Mackenzie Valley oil pipeline.[11] That the editors of a national paper would consciously ignore such a major Aboriginal story like Kashechewan and instead choose to trumpet, once again, the stereotype that Aboriginal peoples are "in the way" of mainstream economic prosperity, speaks volumes about what they perceive to be the orientation of their readership.

A brief examination of the editorial positions, columns, and commentaries of what is, arguably, Canada's most important national paper, the *Globe and Mail* (the *Globe*), illustrates mainstream perspectives on Aboriginal affairs. On

Kashechewan, *Globe* stories alleged that drinking water had improved and that the residents need not have been evacuated; so, they focused on the costs of the evacuation. The *Globe* editors noted that the crisis was indicative of a much more widespread problem and that politicians used the event to "take potshots at their rivals." But, significantly, the editorial then used the events to talk of how Kashechewan residents were "stranded between two worlds" and "need a higher purpose, and a place to work at real jobs, somewhere within reach of those jobs, rather than on the remote Albany [River]" (Globe and Mail 2005; see also Erwin 2005). In short, the editors, rather than calling for progressive land claims policies or economic development opportunities, implied the need for residents to leave the reserve and integrate into the mainstream.

Globe editorials admit a genuine concern about the plight of Aboriginal peoples and the complexity of dismantling the Indian Act and progressing toward self-gov-ernment. However, they express a centrist position in opposing the First Nations Governance Act. The editors noted that the government demonstrated contin-ued paternalism in not engaging the AFN in the development of the legislation but clearly stated its favour for greater accountability and transparency for First Nations councils. Likewise, writing of Paul Martin's agenda, the editors suggested:

> No government can, or should, take away the Native rights guaranteed in the
> Constitution and upheld by the courts. But Mr. Martin should steer Native policy
> away from its obsession with exclusive Native rights and status toward a model that
> fosters integration through prosperity. (*Globe and Mail* 2003b)

This, unfortunately, seems the default position for the media. Of course, no one would object to shared prosperity for Aboriginal people, but while the plea for integration is constant, the implications of this strategy and its assimilationist assumptions are never argued. What, exactly, is an "obsession" with Aboriginal rights when they are protected in the Constitution? We can conclude that the *Globe*'s editorial positions remain essentially integrationist. Nowhere in them do we find an appeal for the protection of Indigenous cultures or an appreciation for non-Western values and institutions.

The *Globe* publishes neo-conservative columnists such as John Richards, an economist from Simon Fraser University's Public Policy Program and holder of the Roger Phillips Chair in social policy at the C.D. Howe Institute. Some of Richards's perspectives seem, at first glance, fruitful. For example, he argues for a greater role for provinces in addressing Aboriginal conditions and suggests that they have been too passive in allowing the federal government sole responsibil-ity for Aboriginal affairs. He advocates enhanced provincial funding for separate Aboriginal schools and cultural curricula for urban Aboriginals. At the same time, however, he assumes many neo-conservative positions, including those advanced by the Canadian Taxpayers Federation. He argues that RCAP exaggerated the possibility of on-reserve economic development and advocates providing treaty benefits to individuals and reducing the level of financial support for band governments. His perspective, like Cairns, is one that sees Aboriginal aspirations of self-government as a road to "separation" (Richards 2003, 2001). His ideas demonstrate a firm commitment to free market economics, the discourse of equality so favoured by the right, and an appalling ignorance of Aboriginal history, culture, and aspirations.

In 2001, five years after the release of RCAP, the *Globe* ran a 14-part "special investigation" by John Stackhouse, revealingly entitled "Canada's Apartheid."[12] Stackhouse's introduction to the series was a profile of Mathew Coon Come, then National Chief of the AFN, who had used an international forum on racism in Durban, South Africa, to note Canada's responsibility for the gross disparities faced by Aboriginal peoples. Although Coon Come asserted that Aboriginal peoples were being "pushed to the edge of economic, political and social extinction," he did not compare Canada's situation with that of apartheid. Instead, he drew attention to Canada's international reputation in opposing apartheid and its official position on self-determination. He also accused the government of "serious double standards...concerning Indigenous rights at home and in the United Nations' system." Coon Come was in fact quoting from recent findings of the United Nations Human Rights Committee and the Canadian federal government's own commission.[13]

Coon Come's remarks became the focus of many neo-conservative commentaries and some outright racist rants, particularly on the Internet.[14] Stackhouse seized the apartheid label—a powerful metaphor—to suggest that Aboriginal peoples have been separated from mainstream society and that this separation must end. Such anti-parallelism discourse, as previously discussed, is used to support arguments that reserves be abolished, that incentives to move Aboriginal people off reserve be encouraged, and that integration and assimilation are the solutions to Aboriginal conditions. This theme is subtly played out in Stackhouse's series. At times he equates separation with "two solitudes" and Canada's inability to come to grips with Aboriginal issues. More often, he uses it to suggest the failure of the reserve system and the futility of strategies of self-determination. He suggests, for example, that Aboriginal people are becoming disinterested in self-determination and that they realize "their communities can exist as islands no longer."

Stackhouse's series is, at times, both insightful and hopeful. In different articles he details how Aboriginal people have teamed with businesses and industries to promote economic development, the biculturalism of urban Aboriginal peoples, and the desire of Aboriginal peoples to fully participate in the "two worlds" of Canada and their own communities. He, like most Canadians, wants a country in which economic development and greater participation in the marketplace are possible for Aboriginal people. But as in many media representations, much of Stackhouse's investigation is built on the personal stories of individuals. He never seriously engages larger issues of colonialism or post-colonialism. As a result, when Stackhouse concentrates on well-known social pathologies on and off reserve, including addictions and family violence, we are left with images of hopelessness and are never asked to examine mainstream political indifference and responsibility.

Throughout the series, Stackhouse also falls prey to a blaming mentality. In the end, he turns to the need for increased accountability for First Nations governments and suggests that too many Aboriginal leaders have "retrograde attitudes" that keep their people in a second-class status. Thus he calls the revitalization of Aboriginal ways a naïve "going back" to the past. Although he rejects the word assimilation, he finally turns to integration and even the potential abandonment of reserves as the solution to Aboriginal problems. In his conclusion, he notes that a new generation of Aboriginal people no longer talk of assimilation but speak of integration and of "dismantling the hidden apartheid." This article, titled "First Step: End the Segregation," suggests that "only a radical change in thinking, and ending the reserves as we know them, will make a real difference." While he admits the potential of re-creating reserves with improved resource-bases exists, Stackhouse sees Aboriginal leadership as incapable of good government. In fact, his perspective remains remarkably devoid of any recognition of the inherent rights of Aboriginal citizens or of the complex work on self-government that has been accomplished. Rather than speaking of the need to recognize or renovate treaty rights, to expand reserves, or place other natural resources under comprehensive claims, Stackhouse instead focuses on the "rampant corruption and nepotism" of leaders — charges that we will see are not only misplaced and stereotypical but that are themselves evidence of a double standard.

More often than not, mature readers know the orientation of the writer before they pick up a column and are thus able to provide their own counterspin to opinion pieces. The power of political commentary is that it comes preformulated and often tailored to our built-in biases and political orientations. It is meant to spark debate and to present simple summations of complex issues. In the process, unfortunately, it over-simplifies and falls back too easily onto common stereotypes and common sense solutions.

One difference between media stories and issues-driven academic research is that the media generalizes from individual cases in order to make the news personal and to connect to readers on an emotional level. As a result, exceptions to the rule not only apply, but are sought after, because they demonstrate the failings of systems and bureaucracies that must respond not to individual cases but to all cases. Academic arguments, more often than not, are concerned with structural solutions to social problems. Individuals are used to illustrate and to put a human face on problems, but researchers are taught not to generalize from individual cases — to do so is to elevate the anecdotal to the level of statistical truth.

The treatment of child and family issues by the media clearly demonstrates the Eurocentric attitudes of most commentators. Margaret Wente, the well-known columnist for the *Globe*, writes on a variety of issues, often tackling stories that reflect neo-conservative views on contemporary feminism and family values. In "Race politics and Emma's fate," she examined the issue of Native adoption.[15] It was a heart-wrenching tale of someone caught in what, at first glance, appears to be inane bureaucratic red tape. Emma (a pseudonym), three-and-a-half years old, had been placed in foster care by the state and raised by White foster parents. Emma's mother, a Native, and her father, who is White, are drug addicts. Shortly after Emma was born, her parents moved to Hamilton, Ontario — Wente says "they decamped for Ontario." By choosing a word that implies sudden or secretive movement or a nomadic existence, she casts aspersions on the parents' motivations for moving. In Ontario the state intervened and placed Emma in foster care. It is clear from Wente's story that Emma received much love and excellent care from her White foster parents. There is evidence also that Emma, who is a fetal alcohol syndrome child, responded exceptionally well to her foster parents and that, in Wente's words, they "are sensitive to her native heritage and eager to make sure she grows up exposed to it" (Wente 2003a).

But Emma's mother's First Nation, the Squamish, stepped in and asserted their right to determine who would care for the child. And it is this fact that Wente finds objectionable, even though, under provincial legislation, the First Nation has the right to determine the best interests of the child. In the end, the Hamilton Children's Aid Society sided with the Squamish band's plan to place the child in care with a non-Native foster parent who lived in British Columbia near the reserve and who had connections to the First Nation.

Interestingly, Wente makes much of the foster mother's fear of potential psychological risk in having to relocate Emma geographically but downplays the potential value of placing Emma near her home reserve. Wente also emphasizes Emma's mixed race and the fact that in appearance the child looks "more Irish than native." This is a misrepresentation of Aboriginal identity and equates intermarriage with loss of culture. The matter of appearance, for example, means little except to those who continue to equate cultural identity with the colour of skin.

Wente's reason for writing about this case is to single out "race-based childcare policy." What she leaves unstated is that Aboriginal child welfare policy is broadly supported by both Native and non-Native child welfare experts, as well as provincial and federal governments. She concludes with the foster mother's words: "Everything else should play second fiddle to the best interests of the child. But because she's native, everyone assumes she has no rights." For Wente, "as long as race politics comes before child welfare, we'll continue to have a double standard in this country—one for children somebody decides are native, and one for everybody else." In another article, Wente suggests that these cases of Native children being removed from non-Native foster families can be compared to the residential schools experience and that "in the name of redressing the past, we are repeating it."[16]

This suggestion is fallacious in its conclusion that non-Native authorities, rather than First Nations, should be able to control Aboriginal child welfare. The creation of Aboriginal Child and Family Services and government recognition that First Nations have a right to define and control their membership are two ways that the wrongs of the past have been redressed by recent policy and legislation. First Nations now demand the right to say where their children are placed and will no longer see their children taken away by the state and adopted into White families unless they deem it in the best interest of the child. Their right to repatriate children to foster care parents that meet their community's standards can in no way be compared to the state's forced removal of thousands of Aboriginal children from reserves with the express purpose of eradicating any vestige of cultural identity in favour of a European worldview. To suggest that Aboriginal people and Aboriginal child welfare agencies are not aware of the significance of cultural identity in the context of adoption, or that they do not have the best interests of the child foremost in mind, is paternalistic in the extreme. It is no doubt true that individual social workers and child welfare agencies are less than perfect, but to question the right of Aboriginal agencies to make these decisions, when these rights are legislated, is the worst form of post-colonial thinking.

In one respect at least Wente is right. In this case two individuals who came to love a child were prevented from adopting that child because of ethnocultural policies designed to recognize Aboriginal peoples' right to self-determination.[17] Wente correctly notes that, right across the country, First Nations are "asserting their right to decide what becomes of native (or part native) children in need of protection." Although she doesn't like this, she has to accept it. Aboriginal peoples' control over child welfare is a modern corrective to the colonial practice of Native child adoption by state authorities, which in Australia and Canada led to a generation of children being "stolen" from reserves as their families stood by helpless to argue their fate. Wente's columns also ignore how First Nations are becoming interested in developing custom adoption systems.[18]

Wente is also wrong when she states that "Other child protection services are afraid to fight back." Non-native agencies are in fact respecting the legislated authority of Aboriginal child welfare agencies. She is wrong for the same reason when she suggests that "federal and provincial governments look the other way." Both governments, for sound historical, social welfare, and legislative reasons, acknowledge First Nations rights to determine their membership and to develop child welfare agencies that can provide culturally appropriate foster care. Child and family issues are particularly interesting in light of neo-conservative "family values" arguments. Consider the following statement by Flanagan:

> Aggregate statistics show some improvement in the average income and material well-being of aboriginal people in Canada, but this improvement is mainly concentrated among the elite. At the same time as members of the aboriginal elite are doing very well for themselves, aboriginal poverty and associated pathologies remain acute and perhaps even growing. Welfare dependency is higher than ever as is illegitimacy. About half of aboriginal children are born to single mothers and grow up without a father, their chances of ending up on welfare or in prison are frighteningly high. (Flanagan 2001: 18)

Ignore the ironic assertion that an Aboriginal elite benefits from economic development.[19] There is some truth in this passage. There is a higher than average percentage of single parent families and, specifically, single mother families in the Aboriginal population — about 23 per cent, roughly double the mainstream figure.[20] However, about 25 per cent of single mothers report that the child's father is involved directly in their care. It is true that Aboriginal children have higher than average risks in life — they are more likely to end up on welfare or in prison. What is *not* true, and indeed what is misleading to suggest, is a connection between these two facts. If there is a correlation here, it is because Aboriginal children are at greater risk of a range of problems because they are poor and experience marginalization and racism. We have no evidence to suggest that Aboriginal children are at greater risk because they are often raised in single parent families. This is simply the traditional family values perspective so dear to the neo-conservative right.[21]

Formal, legal, and Christian marriages in Aboriginal communities have always been less common than in mainstream society. However, the numbers of "illegitimate" (that is, illegitimate according to Eurocentric thinking) children cannot be taken as evidence that they lack care. Such privileging of mainstream ideas about the "proper" family led to the Sixties Scoop discussed in Chapter 3.

Anyone who has even a small glimpse into Aboriginal values understands their deep cultural concern for children and child protection (Maar *et al.* 2005). Aboriginal people value children highly, and Aboriginal women often have children at a young age, often in their teens. The reasons for teen pregnancy are complex, but many youth suggest that Aboriginal communities and culture are more accepting of adolescent pregnancies and that families are supportive in such cases.[22] Young Aboriginal couples face enormous emotional and social pressures, not least of which is to obtain a job and education, which often requires one or both spouses to leave the reserve. But Aboriginal extended families offer a safety net for children; Aboriginal children are loved, and raised, by a network of kin, including single mothers, relatives of both parents, and grandparents. When we take into account this environment, we can argue that Aboriginal children are as well-protected as any children.

When elections loom, both federally and provincially, Aboriginal affairs are given particularly short shrift by the media. Campaign rhetoric is all about the big three domestic concerns: the economy, health care, and education. Rarely are Aboriginal questions even posed during leadership debates. During the 2004 election, when Tom Flanagan served as a key strategist to Stephen Harper, Aboriginal issues gained momentary notice when his views were revealed and condemned by the AFN. But Harper quickly affirmed a commitment to Aboriginal rights and distanced himself from Flanagan's controversial positions. As always, Aboriginal conditions disappeared from the electorate's radar. On election day, 44 per cent of voters mentioned health care as first of 15 critical issues; Aboriginal issues failed to make the list.[23] They are low on the media's priority list because they are low on Canadians' agenda. A 2004 survey by the Centre for Research and Information found that, among 11 possible priority areas that people were asked to rank in importance, quality of life for Aboriginal peoples was ranked second last (Seidle 2005: 11).[24] Nearly half (49 per cent) believed that the situation of Aboriginal Canadians is about the same or better than that of other Canadians; only 44 per cent believed it is worse.

If there is any hope for improving the cultural awareness of mainstream media, it lies, not at all ironically, in the fact that there is a growing Aboriginal media that is beginning to present an alternative and culturally informed reading of major events. Aboriginal peoples have long used regional print media and radio to reach their communities. As Buddle-Crowe (2001) has demonstrated, they have always seen mainstream media as both a powerful threat to their cultures and a potential tool for the promotion of Indigeneity. Native-owned and operated broadcasting developed only in the mid-1970s when the CBC began beaming southern Canadian and American television via satellite into Northern communities. Aboriginal leaders saw southern programming as a threat to their language and cultural traditions and began to demand a voice in the production of their own programs.

Currently, 13 Aboriginal communications societies are funded under the federal government's Northern Native Broadcast Program to serve status and non-status Indians, Inuit, and Métis, primarily in rural and remote communities.[25] Aboriginal media now include several hundred local radio stations, 11 regional radio networks, the beginnings of a national Aboriginal radio network, six television production outlets, a pan-Northern Aboriginal television network called Television Northern Canada, and numerous newspapers.[26] The Media

Awareness Network notes that, until recently there has been a dearth of experienced Aboriginal journalists. Aboriginal people make up over 3 per cent of the Canadian population, but in a 1994 study by the Diversity Committee of the Canadian Newspaper Association, of the 41 mainstream papers surveyed, only four of 2,620 employees were Aboriginal. Today there are about 200 Aboriginal reporters employed in various media. However, many more need to be trained to fill positions in this rapidly increasing industry. Journalism and broadcast training is one more area of capacity building that needs to be supported by federal and provincial education strategies. A small number of Aboriginal students attend general communications and journalism programs at universities and colleges, but most are trained on the job. The Aboriginal journalism program at the University of Western Ontario has closed, but a communication arts program at the University of Regina has been successful, as have Aboriginal Media programs offered by the First Nations Training Institute at Tyendinaga Mohawk Territory and Humber College. These programs, as with other Aboriginal educational initiatives, are increasingly rooted in Aboriginal learning styles and Indigenous knowledge. Aboriginal people are also engaged in the production of mainstream television and Internet communication.

A quick survey of Aboriginal newspapers, such as the National Aboriginal newspaper *Windspeaker* and Ontario's *Birchbark*, quickly offers a cultural corrective to mainstream coverage of most Aboriginal stories.[27] Unfortunately, these papers generally fail to reach a mainstream readership. An increasing, although still modest, number of non-Aboriginal peoples are being exposed to Aboriginal representations and news stories through the Aboriginal Peoples Television Network (APTN). Nielsen ratings place its regular viewership at roughly 58,000 to 68,000 people. This has been accomplished despite flat-lined budgets and poor channel placement.[28] And while the APTN falls back on mainstream movies or television series for some of its programming, it has been successful in producing and developing many Aboriginal-specific shows. Anyone who has watched APTN talk shows or news reports will recognize that, once again, Native and non-Native media are inherently different. While there is coverage of the dark side of Aboriginal life — from poverty to concerns with inner-city prostitution and drug abuse — there is more positive reporting and coverage of innovations in many fields. Aboriginal issues — from health concerns to questions of sexuality and identity — are discussed in ways that give honour to the diversity of cultures and the complexity of daily living on and off reserve.

Thus, there is the faint promise that as Aboriginal media grows and as more Aboriginal writers and reporters enter the mainstream media, editors and media owners will be forced to take notice — or at least take issue — with culturally informed interpretations of Aboriginal issues and events. Aboriginal media could be the mechanism for educating mainstream media in the complexity of Aboriginal cultural ways. We can even hope that, in the decades to come, a real dialogue in the media about the nature of self-government will begin and that there will be many positive stories about the development and capacity building that are occurring across the nation. The question that remains, of course, is whether mainstream Canadians are prepared to listen to these Aboriginal voices or whether they will once again tune out and turn their backs on Aboriginal peoples.

NOTES

1 The issue of the Natuashish band finances had been followed closely by CBC since as early as 2000, when an Auditor General report questioned the expenditures associated with the Natuashish relocation. The story is on-line at <http://www.stjohns.cbc.ca/regional/servlet/View? filename=natuashish-051026>.

2 This discussion draws heavily on the perspective of the Media Awareness Network, a non-profit organization concerned with media literacy programs. See <http://www.media-awareness.ca/ english/issues/stereotyping/Aboriginal_people/Aboriginal_education.cfm>.

3 The paper has covered many contentious issues, including the awarding of communications contracts to Aboriginal-owned companies and criminal cases involving Aboriginal people accused of medical negligence and murder where cultural arguments were used as part of the defendant's defence.

4 See "Expositor coverage of First Nations issues lauded," *The Manitoulin Expositor* 1 September 2004: 5. The survey was conducted by Communitas Canada, a non-profit educational institute. The *Toronto Star* also faired poorly, though mainly because of the low number of stories (five) it covered in the three-month period monitored by the survey.

5 In the summer of 1990, a confrontation between the Quebec provincial police and Mohawk Warriors at Oka gained national and international attention. The Mohawks created a barricade to protest the expansion of a golf course onto Native lands and burial grounds. One police officer was killed during the confrontation, and the Canadian military intervened. Over a period of 78 days, mainstream press coverage evoked images of fierce Native warriors and focused on the threat of present and future violence from Aboriginal people. As in the more recent confrontation at Six Nations/Caledonia, the confrontation aggravated relations between the Aboriginal and non-Aboriginal local residents. The federal government subsequently bought the disputed land and made it available to the Mohawks.

6 Fleras and Elliot 1992: 9, 92-98. The Media Awareness Network also notes the biased reporting of the 1990 Oka Crisis. Gail Guthrie Valaskakis suggests that media images drew on "exaggerated monolithic representations of Aboriginal activists." The Aboriginal filmmaker, Alanis Obomsawin provides an alternative view in documentaries that include the history of the Kanasetake reserve, the violence of federal army and provincial police, and the lawlessness of non-Native protestors who hurled rocks at innocent Aboriginal men and women.

7 Increases announced by the Martin government for Aboriginal affairs in the Kelowna agreement, which was subsequently abandoned by the Harper government, were equivalent to increases in defence spending, which was projected at $12.8 billion over five years (see Chapter 11).

8 These are my own admittedly rough calculations, based on the best and most current population figures and recent budget expenditures. Aboriginal figures were reached by dividing the $10 billion figure by an Aboriginal population of 1.3 million. Canadian figures divided the federal budget of $175 billion (less $10 billion) by a non-Aboriginal population of 31,020,000. The amount of federal-provincial expenditures per person varies between provinces between $5,000 and $6,000 per person, as does per capita expenditures, according to the size of annual expenditures.

9 19 July 1995, Resolution No.19/95. The resolution drew on Francis's remarks but was actually aimed at the Department of Indian Affairs.

10 Gord Cruess 2005, "History's What You Make It Re: Speak White: A Little History," *Quid Novi*. Available at <http://www.law.mcgill.ca/quid/archive/2003/03111803.html>.

11 *National Post*, 29 October 2005: "Pipeline politics," A22, A23. The editors did, however, print a letter from Rachel Bartels of Toronto that decried the poor water quality on reserve and implied an inherent racism in Canada by suggesting that Canadians cared less about First Nations people than about those in the Third World.

12 The series began on 5 November 2001 and ran weekly in the *Globe*'s Focus Section through 19 December 2001. Quotations below come from this source.

13 A copy of Coon Come's comments on Canadian policy, racism, and human rights can be found at <http://www.sabcnews.com/wcar/chiefcomesept1.html>.

14 Racist blogs, comments, and rants against Aboriginal people are easy to find and quickly demonstrate the hostility and illogic of racist thinking. For one example, go to <http://jamesbredin.tripod.com/numberfour/id35.html>.

15 Wente 2003a; see also Wente 2004. Quotes from Wente below come from these sources. For an Aboriginal media commentary on this case, see Dan David's commentary for *Windspeaker* at <http://www.ammsa.com/windspeaker/windguest2003.html#anchor5192633>.

16 Wente followed up this story with another similar case in "What Lisa wants" (Wente 2003b). That case involved another foster child in British Columbia, aged 14, who although under legal age expressed an interest not to return to her reserve. The essential issues in that case remain the same, but are complicated by the problem of whether children not of legal age can speak on their own behalf and be heard by state authorities.

17 These cases are, unfortunately, not uncommon in pitting Aboriginal communities, who want their children returned, against children who are now living, often in good care, away from First Nations. In another similar case involving the Sto:lo nation, an informal agreement (which does not set a legal precedent) was reached between the First Nation and the foster parents which led to the children being allowed to stay with their non-Native foster parents. See Crawford 2003.

18 See Maar *et al.* 2005 on adoption and Aboriginal child development. Custom adoption entails encouraging First Nations' members to act as foster parents, identifying members of the extended family or clan as adoptive parents, and bringing traditional values and teaching into the adoption process.

19 This remark is ironic in that conservatives often assert that in mainstream society the wealthiest members are critical to driving economic success for the middle class. The improvements in material well-being that have occurred in Aboriginal society might just as easily be taken as a sign of significant improvement to Aboriginal economies.

20 According to 1996 Census data. See DIAND <http://www.ainc-inac.gc.ca/pr/ra/smt/exsm_e. html>. An Ontario Federation of Indian Friendship Centre Report (OFIFC) study of urban Aboriginals places the figure higher, at 27 per cent. The mainstream rate is about 12 per cent (see OFIFC 2002).

21 Flanagan chooses to ignore the fact that the percentage of couples living together outside of marriage has been increasing for the past two decades and that there has been a corresponding increase in the number of children born "out of wedlock" to common law or same sex parents in mainstream society.

22 OFIFC 2002 explores youth sexual health and pregnancy, including social norms and other factors contributing to teen pregnancy.

23 CBC/Environics poll of five electorates is available at <http://www.mapleleafweb.com/election/ quick/federal.html>.

24 The last ranked item was spending money on Canada's largest cities. The environment and health care were the top ranked priorities.

25 For a history of Aboriginal broadcasting and federal financial support of Aboriginal media, see the Northern Native Broadcast Access Program website at <http://www.pch.gc.ca/ progs/pa-app/progs/paanr-nnbap/broadcast/2_e.cfm>.

26 See note 25.

27 Aboriginal on-line newspapers are easily accessed at the Aboriginal Multi-media Society's website <http://www.ammsa.com>.

28 The Nielsen numbers also cannot truly reflect viewership given the bias toward measuring urban rather than rural and remote homes. See Barnsley 2002.

PART II

UNDERSTANDING
ABORIGINAL ISSUES

CHAPTER 5 Putting Culture into the Debates

The concept of culture is central to anthropology and the social sciences. Anthropologists examine how cultures change, cultural boundaries are created, and cultural identity is protected. But they have not always been able to convey to the public just how significant the concept of culture is for human behaviour. And confusion about the nature of culture is a key problem in the debates about Aboriginal peoples.

In early formulations, cultures were thought of as the sum total of beliefs, behaviours, customs, and rituals expressed, often in the form of institutions, by humans as members of a society. This allowed anthropologists to characterize and classify different customs and to differentiate distinct cultures through time, for example, by comparing hunting and gathering cultures with agricultural ones or by distinguishing between state and stateless societies. Early anthropology assumed an evolutionary perspective, hunting and gathering cultures were seen as lower than agricultural societies. Thus, European society came to be equated with civilization and European values viewed as superior to those found in other parts of the world. Indeed, it can be argued that as late as the 1970s, anthropological and other social science analysis of Indigenous peoples still contained implicit evolutionary assumptions that privileged Western systems of thought, values, and institutions and so continued to foster the value of acculturation models and assimilationist thinking.

This view has since been discarded. Evolutionary comparisons and references to European society as the "only" form of civilization ended as cultural relativism — the idea that all cultures are equal but different — became the hallmark. Anthropological research has demonstrated that different cultures have their own internal logic, beauty, and complexity. Each is understandable in its own terms, so behaviours that at first seem bizarre or immoral to Westerners (polygamy, first cousin-marriage, initiation rites, and so forth) are made understandable, if not rational, given that they serve specific social, economic, or political functions. Of course, different values and principles, as well as the morality of cultural practices, can be argued and questioned. Some cultures are less technologically advanced (another word that conveys an implicit evolutionary perspective), but all cultures can be shown to be internally sophisticated.

In the past anthropology often argued that traditional ways were lost or that cultures were endangered by contact with colonial powers. They described the ethnographic present, picturing contemporary societies as if they existed in the same way prior to contact with Europeans, even when the impact of colonialism had already caused great changes to their institutions. For example, anthropologists working in Papua New Guinea as late as the 1980s were still describing cultures as if they were pre-contact stone-age societies, even though that country was an emerging and modern nation. Such stereotypes of traditional culture continue to exist in such popular media as *National Geographic*, which emphasizes exotic and traditional views of Indigenous peoples. Thus, the idea of culture as static continues to be prominent in mainstream and neo-conservative thought: traditional cultures become opposed to modern society, and Indigenous values are considered to be antiquated or inappropriate in contemporary life. However, as used by Aboriginal peoples and in contemporary anthropology, the term traditional culture (or medicine, or values) conveys ever-changing and adaptive qualities.

With the end of European rule in Third World nations and increasing globalization, most anthropologists have turned their attention to interactions between cultures, multicultural societies, and culture change. Examining the colonial process, they understand not only how smaller, more vulnerable cultures often resist taking on the values and ideas of dominant cultures[1] and how some cultural traits continue while others are abandoned, but also how cultural identity and beliefs are products of cultural interaction; for example, being Hindu in India is different than being Hindu in Canada. Culture has been redefined as a system of ideas, values, and metaphors that are consciously and unconsciously used or enacted by people in their everyday lives. It is not a rigid set of behaviours and traits but a fluid and adaptive system of meaning. It is this malleable understanding of culture that many Canadians do not comprehend.

Ronald Niezen succinctly defines this new definition of culture:

> As many anthropologists have recently pointed out, cultures are often impermanent, complex, "creolized," hybrid and contested. Culture is a verb, not a noun, a process, not a thing in itself. (Niezen 2003: 6)[2]

Cultures are hybridized in many ways. Since at least the 1970s researchers have referred to religious belief as syncretic. Syncreticism arises most obviously in cultural encounters where traditions are "fused either deliberately or more usually unconsciously and over a period of time — into a novel emergent form whose meanings and symbolic expressions are in some respects different from either of the original traditions" (Gualtieri 1984: 1).

For instance, Aboriginal cultures adapted and changed prior to contact through the interaction of different Indigenous societies. Many Aboriginal beliefs and institutions now viewed as historical or traditional are, in fact, the product of early contact. For example, the Code of Handsome Lake, viewed as one of the foundations of Iroquoian Longhouse religions, arose during a period of intense colonization in the 1800s when Iroquoian cultures were experiencing rapid culture change (Wallace 1972). Kathleen Buddle-Crowe (2001) has shown how the Aboriginal use of media, including the APTN, is the most recent of countless adaptations that have occurred during the past 300 years. The adoption by Indigenous peoples of syllabic writing, literacy, newspaper production, and, more recently, Internet technology has been a strategy used to sustain culture and to reject and confront colonial policies and practices. Aboriginal peoples' use of media, then, should not in any way be misinterpreted as a sign of assimilation into mainstream culture.

To understand the difference between a view of culture as static or as fluid is to take the first step in understanding Aboriginal peoples. Otherwise, Aboriginal culture can be seen as something belonging only to the past and cultural change taken as proof that Aboriginal peoples have assimilated or chosen to adopt European ways, as we have seen neo-conservative critics argue in previous chapters. This distinction, the difference between *adaptation* and *adoption*, is fundamental to debates about Aboriginal peoples.

Aboriginal people do not want to go back to the past, nor do they have to — they have never left their culture. Traditions change, but culture endures. However, many mainstream Canadians believe that Aboriginal culture has changed so much that it is impossible to distinguish it from mainstream culture or lifestyles. This belief in turn gives rise to the idea that Aboriginal people have already assimilated and that they should be treated the same as other Canadians. Yet, Aboriginal culture is alive in the city and on the reserve, it is evident in ceremonies and in the practice of everyday behaviours.[3]

Why would neo-conservative writers like Flanagan and Kay expect Aboriginal peoples to cling to prior technologies or practices when they become outmoded? European culture is itself an amalgam of many earlier cultures and traditions, yet many commentators routinely take the adoption of Christianity or the acquisition of literacy and education as a sign that Aboriginal peoples have become civilized or, in other words, that they have adopted European cultural ways (Flanagan 2000: 45). As I have stated elsewhere (Warry 1998: 33-35), we no longer use children to work in factories or transport ourselves by horse and buggy. Why do we expect Aboriginal culture to be static when ours is not? Much commentary on Aboriginal peoples fails to make this obvious distinction and in the process denies both the uniqueness and diversity of Aboriginal culture.

This static view of culture is necessary for neo-conservatives to argue that Aboriginal people have abandoned their culture in order to take up "superior" European cultural practices that are better equipped to the needs of contemporary society (see, for example, Flanagan 2000: 31-37). It seems they cannot grasp the fact that Aboriginal culture has been sustained despite policies that aimed, over centuries, to promote assimilation into the mainstream. They see the loss of specific traditions as loss of *all* culture: because Aboriginal Christians attend church, they have abandoned their traditional spiritual beliefs; because they no longer subsist by hunting and trapping, their traditional economies are defunct or obsolete. The truth is completely different. Aboriginal Christianity is a complex hybrid of Aboriginal and European beliefs and practices. Hunting is still a vital aspect of Northern economies and decreases community reliance on economic subsidies and social assistance.

Neo-conservatives often assume that culture is an integrated block of traits and institutions and that, if critical aspects of a culture change, then the culture is lost, damaged, and, over time, on the verge of extinction. In this view, surface appearance is evidence of assimilation and integration. But culture, like race or ethnicity, is not skin deep, and the surface attributes of a culture can change while its underlying values, identity, and logic persist.

Such an understanding should be self-evident. Our Western traditions remain based on fundamental values, even though they have changed tremendously in their practice. Over the past century, Christmas has become highly commercialized, but few Christians would debate the importance of its celebration or the significance of the key values its story conveys. The wording of our national anthem has changed, as has its performance by rap artists and rock stars, but its singing remains an essential part of Canadian identity. The art of letter writing has all but disappeared, but new email languages and web-design software are emerging, replacing the thank-you note and invitations of the past. At times, traditions change so much that they become almost unrecognizable or their meaning becomes lost. Few young people can articulate the reason a wedding ring is placed on the ring finger or explain why the bride's and groom's family sit on separate sides of a church; both reflect ancient symbolic behaviour whose meaning is clouded by the passage of time.[4] Is the emailing of a wedding announcement a less authentic expression of changing social status than the public announcement of banns in a church? Both announce individual intentions to a broader community of family, friends, and work-mates.

These are examples of what anthropologists call the "reinvention of tradition."[5] Tradition is constantly changing, its value questioned, and its practice reformed and in some cases abandoned. A Canadian Christmas is different from that in Europe or the United States, but it is no less authentic for having borrowed from other historical traditions. When cultures collide and meet — especially when

Indigenous cultures have been under assault by a dominant culture for hundreds of years — it is sometimes difficult to see that the minority values persist and remain vibrant. But although many Aboriginal communities have been severely colonized in the sense that specific traditions have been abandoned, their cultural values have persisted. Our own hubris — our belief that our culture is superior — often blinds us to the continuing presence of these Indigenous ways and to their resistance to assimilation. This resistance takes place in the form of outright protest and demonstration as well as in "everyday acts" (Scott 1985). We know, for example, that in residential schools, students risked corporal punishment by speaking their language in secret and that Aboriginal spiritual practices, dances, and ceremonies continued to be held even when outlawed by the Indian Act. Aboriginal resistance continues today in fights over fishing rights and land claims, demonstrations against the First Nations Governance Act or other paternalistic legislation, legal actions over residential school abuse, Indigenous teaching and education, and the daily actions of Aboriginal people who quietly practice Aboriginal medicine and spirituality.

It is easy to fall back on stereotypes rather than try to understand the complexity of contemporary Aboriginal culture. We must appreciate how specific cultural practices combine, change, and renew to comprehend that "Native and Christian" are synonymous, not dichotomous (see Treat 1996). Here, actual experience is helpful. If you attend an Aboriginal church service — be it Catholic or Protestant — you will be instantly struck by how different the iconography, sermons, and rituals are, how Christianity is transformed in the Native context. The artwork of Norvel Morrisseau is ripe with Christian images that have been transformed and interpreted through his Ojibway worldview. Morriseau's Christ appears as a shaman, his body flowing with power. Similarly, the work of artist Carl Beam blends Eastern, Western, and colonial images to produce powerful statements about Indigenous identity and colonialism. He reveals a contemporary and vibrant Aboriginal identity that moves us beyond stereotypes of the past while still being linked to history.[6]

Indigenous cultures and economies are alive and well, and Indigenous peoples have adapted (not adopted) technology to their own values and practices. Some First Nations, like the Cree of Quebec, have instituted income security programs that have "enhanced the viability of hunting as a way of life" and as a result "participation in hunting has intensified" (Feit 2004b: 117). For many people, hunting, trapping, and fishing are recreational or seasonal labour (see Berkes et al. 1994). But hunting and trapping on many Northern reserves still provide significant amounts of food to the community, and recreational activities remain an important way of connecting to, and gaining spiritual sustenance from, the land. And where Aboriginal people participate as entrepreneurs in the mainstream market, their values permeate their activities: they are collaborative and cooperative rather than competitive in the dog-eat-dog style of the mainstream marketplace.

We are accustomed to cultural difference and, at least in superficial ways, embrace it. We like variation in the food we eat. Twenty years ago you might find Canadian-Italian or Canadian-Chinese restaurants, in which hot and spicy dishes were made more bland and thus palatable to mainstream tastes — yet another example of cultural blending. Today, many of us actively seek out Mexican, Middle Eastern, Szechwan, Japanese, Vietnamese, Thai, and a host of other cuisines. Fusion cooking blends European cooking styles with influences from the South, East, and West. Yet, this appreciation of other food styles is seldom seen as a threat to Canadian tastes, or that a hunger for Pad Thai interferes with the ability to appreciate Yorkshire pudding. Most of us would argue that this taste diversity improves our culinary culture and that the diversity of ethnic groups in general is a positive trend in our society and one that is to be encouraged. We agree that this diversity enhances, rather than undermines, our sense of Canadian identity, and we say that we belong to a Canadian culture that embraces diversity as a fundamental value.

In a similar way, not only have Aboriginal peoples embraced many values of the dominant society, but many of our mainstream values have been subtly altered by centuries of interaction with Aboriginal cultures. Again, evidence of this process abounds, especially when we think of how we have adopted Indigenous technology, such as snow shoes and canoes, to adapt to our environment. Native iconography — for example, the Inuit's stone marker, the Inukshuk — exists in virtually every tourism shop and promotional video, including those used to capture Olympic games and international trade. So, although many of us deny the significance of Aboriginal cultures and marginalize Aboriginal peoples in our political discourse, they have had an impact on our national identity. Many of our basic values — including our desire for collective solutions, our concern for equality and egalitarianism, our reticence, and our awareness of environmental ethics — owe much to our centuries' long engagement with Aboriginal peoples (Saul 2002).

To appreciate that deeply held values are shaped by cross-cultural interaction allows us to embrace, rather than fear, multiculturalism and to release ourselves from ethnocentrism — the presumption that our values and behaviours are intrinsically superior to those of other societies or religions. Clifford Geertz has written about how difficult it is for us to truly escape ethnocentrism, how rewarding this exercise can be, and how important an appreciation of diversity is for contemporary social and political practice (Geertz 2000: 42-67, 68-88). Escaping ethnocentrism is difficult in part because it can also lead to feelings of dissonance. Once we assume any sort of relativistic stance and acknowledge the possibility that our values are culturally constructed, we begin to question the validity of our own beliefs. If another culture's belief in God (or ghosts, or spirits, or flying saucers) is seen to be arbitrary, or non-rational, then what does this tell us about our own belief in God or the devil, saints, or angels? If we officially recognize homosexual marriage, how can we condemn the practice of polygamy?[7] And on and on. For some, learning, accepting, or tolerating different beliefs or behaviours is dangerous. People who are inherently conservative may fear that their own cultural beliefs will be abandoned or be seen as arbitrary should other cultural beliefs become accepted. Many do not want to take the risk of uprooting their worldview or considering the possibility that there is not a single right or appropriate way of behaving.

Clearly, other values and beliefs test our own. Some beliefs can be assessed by science; for example, claims about the healing power of herbs or alternative medicines can be validated.[8] Others rest on faith and cannot be proven. Recognizing other cultural beliefs as valid may make it hard to argue the superiority of some behaviours or ideologies over others. This perhaps accounts for the fear of Indigenous peoples (and other ethnic groups) and the belief systems they espouse — not just their different spiritual beliefs, but their different ways of organizing economic activity and of thinking about law, as well as their different political processes and forms. Many mainstream Canadians think that tolerating these alternative ways of being will threaten or make less valid their own beliefs.

However, we have learned that different values or rituals can be reconciled with our own beliefs through familiarization. As with learning a new language, new knowledge supplements and complements our mother culture, and we move toward biculturalism. Geertz suggests that by escaping ethnocentrism and appreciating difference, we are able to expand our imagination and augment our self-understanding. Thus, being able to question the arbitrariness of our beliefs is a fundamental step in the process of consciousness-raising that Tim Wilbur argues will allow human society to reach its full potential (see the Conclusion).

Many neo-conservatives cling to ethnocentrism in the belief that the status quo and Western values are inherently superior. Representative democracy, respect for individual rights, and encouragement of competition in open markets are seen as essential to human progress, while cultural relativism is considered to be dangerous because not all cultural values can be equal. But, as previously discussed, cultural relativism, which demands that we understand cultural values in their own terms, does not require us to be blind to the injustice of specific cultural beliefs. Here again, neo-conservatives use a simple, uninformed view of culture to suggest that the search for cultural tolerance will undermine our concerns for human rights.

According to anthropologist Sally Engle Merry (2003), an expert on the anthropology of law, "the idea [of] cultural relativism is often seen as anathema to human rights activists," because they work with an out-of date notion of culture.

For those who see culture as a "coherent, static and unchanging set of values," culture is a problem. Cruel and inhumane behaviours — for example, female genital mutilation (or female circumcision) or "honour killings" sanctioned by tribal elders as punishment for having an affair — are immoral by any standard and need to be reformed. But only those who assume a model of culture as static would suggest that these practices be protected in the name of culture or tradition. As Merry notes, this antiquated view of culture "is increasingly understood as a barrier to the realization of human rights by activists and as a tool for legitimating noncompliance with human rights by neo-conservatives." This is as true of a Muslim cleric's defence of female circumcision as of a fundamentalist Christian's rationalization of the death penalty as "eye for an eye" justice.

As Merry notes, anthropologists have come to understand culture as being historically produced, porous to outside influences, and incorporating "competing repertoires of meaning and action" (Merry 2003). This allows each and every belief and practice to be openly debated and, as necessary, rejected without rejecting the entire culture. We do not dismiss American culture because of its continued use of the death penalty, a practice condemned by Amnesty International and banned from virtually all Western democracies. Nor should we condemn Islamic regimes because of their adherence to shari'a law. Instead, we must encourage appreciation for diversity and respect for traditions while confronting and debating, at every turn, actions that are unethical or immoral. A modern view of culture opens us to respect for cultural diversity and is in no way antithetical to the search for human rights.

This sophisticated view of culture is necessary if Canada is to become a model for other countries in the areas of multiculturalism and Indigenous rights. Alan Cairns is one of the few commentators who has made an effort to understand the culture argument. He notes that some Aboriginal scholars also appeal to outdated views of culture as bounded and discreet, rather than permeable, because it allows them to make arguments that emphasize autonomy and the incommensurability of beliefs. He suggests, for example, that Mary Ellen Turpel has asserted that Aboriginal and Western conceptions of law are incompatible and that she draws on Ruth Benedict (an anthropologist who was influential in the pre- and post-World War II era) to suggest that Aboriginal "cultures are oriented as wholes in different directions. They are travelling along different paths in pursuit of different ends, and these ends and these means in one society cannot be judged in terms of those by another society because essentially they are incommensurable" (cited in Cairns 2000: 179). Cairns correctly asserts that this idea would receive little support from contemporary anthropologists. It is a version of the kind of strong relativism argument that has given way to the more contemporary belief that cultures are interrelated. Because of this interrelationship (in the form of globalization, multiculturalism, and so forth), it is reasonable to challenge specific cultural processes and behaviours and to assert basic human rights and responsibilities within the context of an ethnocultural society. Those like Turpel who call for separate institutions ignore the fact that Aboriginal and mainstream institutions will always need to be interfaced and that it is through this discourse on how Aboriginal politics and law interconnect to mainstream political and legal institutions that incommensurable practices and values are accommodated or transformed.

Cairns, unlike other neo-conservative commentators, acknowledges that culture is open to renovation rather than destruction. He draws on the late anthropologist Sally Weaver who explained:

> Old paradigm thinking sees culture in some quantum sense in which "traditional" or "real" Indian culture diminishes under the forces of acculturation to the point it disappears. Thus the Cree cannot eat pizza and remain "real Cree" ... New Paradigm thinking does not reify "traditional" culture as a state First Nations seek to freeze in some form. Under the new paradigm, First Nations cultures continue to be reconstructed into the distant future, as all cultures are, and some 500 years from now there will be First Nations chiefs and Cree culture in existence in Canada. (Weaver 1990: 12)

Cairns acknowledges the usefulness of the phrase "the invention of tradition" (Hobsbawm and Ranger 1983), which captures how cultural groups reinvent and recover the past while participating in the modern world (Cairns 2000: 104).

Cairns also draws on the work of John Borrows, who stresses that Aboriginal peoples have always adapted to Western ways. Borrows argues, for example, that the adoption of Christianity, farming techniques, and education provided the means for Aboriginal peoples to sustain their claims to self-governance (Borrows 1992; as cited in Cairns 2000: 105). This perspective on the continued maintenance of Aboriginal culture in the face of forces of colonialism is common in anthropological writings today, which stress that Aboriginal cultural identity is not abandoned when particular cultural practices are lost or the ways of other cultures adapted. Thus, Cairns is one of the few mainstream writers who recognizes that this view of culture, and cultural identity, opens the door to many possibilities, including a view of Canadian identity and citizenship shared between Native and non-Native peoples (Cairns 2000: 107).

But in Cairns we also have proof of Geertz's assertion of how hard it is to sustain diversity thinking. At times Cairns appears to be skeptical of this new paradigm and speaks of it as almost a temporary intellectual perspective that has been accepted in part because of the success of the Aboriginal rights movement. On the contrary, current views of culture have been developed in countless research studies dealing with ethnicity, culture change, and identity around

the world. So, despite his deepened understanding of culture, Cairns cannot escape his ethnocentrism. Late in his analysis, it becomes clear that he sees certain
behaviours — for example, intermarriage and the migration to cities — as important signs of a merger between cultures, of "modernizing Aboriginality." By this
he means the "ongoing, selective, eclectic incorporation of values, behaviours,
and identities with their updated Aboriginal counterparts." He labels this, after
the anthropologist Anthony Giddens, as "de-traditionalization" brought about
by globalization (Cairns 2000: 107). Rather than seeing cultural change as pre-
senting Aboriginal peoples with multiple paths to engage actively in Canadian
citizenship and as ways to sustain their culture, Cairns perceives change as a sign
of the inevitable loss of culture and as the reason Aboriginal autonomy cannot
reasonably be sustained in the modern world. Like Flanagan, he sees the obvious
evidence of any form of cultural blending or hybridity as a sign of assimilation.

Thus, Cairns believes that the overall weight and direction of Aboriginal cultural change has been toward modern Euro-Canadian ways; that is, he believes
that Aboriginal cultures have become more like Euro-Canadian culture. As a
result, it is difficult for him, as it is for many Canadians, to see the continuing
integrity of Aboriginal culture as sufficient reason for claims to autonomous
social and political relations. In contrast, Borrows sees Aboriginal culture and
peoples as "traditional, modern, and post modern" (Borrows 1997; as cited in
Cairns 2000: 206). This is a view that Canadians should work hard to understand, because it most accurately sums up the complexity of Aboriginal lives.
For Borrows, for example, intermarriage, urban migration, educational pursuits,
and participation in mainstream Canadian institutions are obvious facts of life
but not signs of assimilation.

The difference between Borrows and Cairns is subtle and significant. Cairns's
more mainstream outlook reflects a reasonably sensitive analysis of contemporary Aboriginal identity, one with which many mainstream Canadians would
agree. But Borrows points us both to acceptance and tolerance of Aboriginal cultural identity and to reconciliation. By accepting Aboriginal culture as vibrant
and alive, we can encourage the re-invention of systems of law, governance, and
health that will allow Aboriginal peoples to find culturally appropriate solutions
to the challenges they face.

Part of the ongoing debates about Aboriginal peoples in Canada and abroad
revolves around the use and misuse of the concept of culture itself. In this sense
there is a culture war in this country. It exists between neo-conservative commentators and politicians and Aboriginal advocates. But while the political war
is ongoing, the intellectual war has long been decided. A view of Indigenous cultures as discreet blocks that disappear with prolonged exposure to dominant cultures no longer exists in social science. Where it appears in political commentary,
as we have seen, it signals ignorance and a failure to keep pace with a contempo-

rary understanding of how culture and identity are at work in the world. There is no intellectual or philosophical position, no view of culture, that can support the idea of assimilation in a modern multicultural world.

NOTES

1 The now classic work in this area is Scott 1985.

2 This is, of course, an analogical metaphor—you will be hard pressed to actually use culture as a verb in a sentence. The metaphor is meant to suggest that the qualities of culture are fluid and dynamic rather than fixed or static.

3 See Waldram 1997 for an account of spiritual healing in a prison environment. There is a direct relationship between forms of healing that occur in these institutional settings and the broader processes of individual and community healing in urban and reserve settings. See also Warry 1998.

4 The wedding ring itself is probably derived from the ancient symbol of the *ouroborus*, the snake swallowing its own tail, and is a symbol of eternity; the blood of the veins of the ring finger were thought by ancient Greeks to flow directly to the heart. The seating of families represents a time when women were more formally exchanged between clans or groups of extended families.

5 This term, used by Keesing and Tonkinson (1982), and the "invention of tradition," used by Hobsbawm and Ranger (1983; see also Cairns 2000: 104) convey attempts to revive traditional practices as well as the purposeful and sometimes political manipulation and idealization of past customs and events.

6 Carl Beam, whose image "Fast Forward" is reproduced on the cover, tragically died during the summer of 2005, from complications of diabetes, shortly after being recognized with the Governor General's Award. His work lives on and can be viewed at <http://www.neonravenartgallery.com/carl/carl.html>.

7 This, of course, was one of the many slippery slope arguments advanced by conservatives in the gay marriage debates.

8 To a certain extent. Whether specific values or practices should be put to Western scientific tests is a question for debate. For example, in many Indigenous cultures there is a spiritual component or endowment to herbal remedies, so that the chemical compounds represent only part of the "curing" capacity of the plant.

CHAPTER 6 Being Aboriginal: Identity

When we think of ourselves, we conjure up tiny parcels of the culture — or cultures — that influence our ways of thinking, feeling, and behaving. The types of food we enjoy, the music we listen to, the key values (privacy, respect, justice) we hold dearly — all are part of our internalized culture. Thus, individual identity can be seen as personalized culture.

We can speak of individual, group, and cultural identities, which are intertwined with one another. We each have a nested layer of such identities that helps orient us to others in the world. A person is a mother, daughter, spouse, teacher, tennis player, and Canadian all at the same time. Schools, neighbourhoods, workplaces, cities, and our nation act as reference groups. A person's cultural and national identity may also be multi-faceted. We can be Aboriginal, Chinese, Canadian, or have multiple-ethnicities — like Italian-Canadian — that are important to us. Our cultural identity is also influenced by the languages we speak, whether we are monolingual, bilingual, or multilingual. Thus, language and culture are intimately connected, but not synonymous. Those Aboriginal people who no longer speak their language sustain their Aboriginal identity in the same way that third-generation Italians who do not speak their language still think of themselves as Italians first and Canadians second. It is just as possible, and happens regularly in Aboriginal contexts, for parents who were forbidden from speaking their language in residential schools to encourage their children to learn it.

Canadians have a particularly ambivalent national identity, one played out, at least in part, in relationship to the United States. Our national inferiority complex *vis-à-vis* our neighbour to the south is itself a characteristic of our cultural identity. Pages of ink have been spent on what, if anything, makes us unique or how our identity is defined in this opposition. The success of the Molson "I am Canadian" campaign and the collective sigh of relief that followed the Canadian win of the Olympic Gold Medal in men's hockey over the American team in 2002 is proof enough that a Canadian national identity does exist even in the face of the forces of globalization. The differences between what might be called the Canadian national and cultural identity are many, but the two forms are ultimately overlapping. For present purposes, we will assume that the former has more to do with politics and with our feelings of independence, sovereignty, and control. The latter is about the fundamental values, behaviours, and ideals that distinguish us

from others. We see, then, that identity (and culture itself) is formed through the
interaction of individuals, groups, and cultures. I cannot be a father unless I have
a son. I cannot identify as Canadian unless I have the United States, or another
nation, to compare and contrast Canadian characteristics against.

To take one metaphor, culture can be thought of as light: it is comprised of
dual qualities, particle and wave. Cultures are fluid (wave-like) and malleable and
so change through time and flow into other cultures. Yet they also have solid
(particle-like) attributes, which allow them to bump up against, resist, or contrast themselves to other cultures. Interactions between different cultural processes lead to border behaviours that are essential in the formation of personal
and cultural identity. Identity, too, is fluid; it changes and matures with time. As
Niezen points out (2003: 6), while social science has come to recognize culture
as impermanent and constantly changing, the process of overlap and contesta-
tion between cultures actually draws identities more firmly as individuals choose
between various beliefs, meanings, and metaphors to suggest what culture they
belong to and the ways they can differentiate themselves from Others. Thus, the
process of identity formation is highly contentious, invoking not only personal
meaning but often political meanings, images, and symbols that Others use to
describe us.[1]

Several studies have shown how our images of Aboriginal peoples have varied
throughout history and at least partially reflect the dominant political agendas of
the time. For example, during the early contact phase of Canadian history, when
Aboriginal knowledge and assistance were necessary to open up the country,
Aboriginal peoples were portrayed sympathetically as noble savages and adaptive
wilderness survivalists (Coates 1999: 25). Early stereotypes of "Godless" pagans
allowed for aggressive missionary policies and conversion. Much later, when First
Nations communities were in the way of expansion, they were portrayed as violent enemies and, later still, as child-like peoples who were in need of the protection of the state.

Coates suggests that, although this process of image-making and identity formation continues today, it has been transformed by Aboriginal peoples themselves as they have assumed greater political control and have begun to participate in the production of media images about their culture and communities:

> The creation and definition of identity is a process that is both internal and external.
> It is internal to the extent that the community defines itself and seeks to determine
> how it is viewed in the broader world. The values, images and experiences presented
> to the broader public spring from the communities themselves. At the same time,
> even the internal definition emerges through the references to the dominant society
> and to the non-Aboriginal world. Internal and external images are intertwined and

interactive, each one developing with explicit and implicit reference to the other.
(Coates 1999: 28)

Enduring stereotypes of Aboriginal peoples as natural environmentalists or as
traditionalists who subscribe to Indigenous spiritual values or participate in ceremonies are both common. Yet these representations are simply that — stereotypes. Coates suggests that we see Aboriginal people in these ways because we
believe that spiritualism and environmentalism are qualities that are lacking in
mainstream Canada (Coates 1999: 26).[2] As we have seen in earlier chapters, stereotypes of Aboriginal poverty, welfare dependency, and assimilation by leaving
the reserve are used by neo-conservatives to advance specific political agendas.

Canadian cultural identity is comprised of an amalgam of many cultures and is
concerned with the search for shared values, like tolerance, which make Canada
a multicultural country. John Ralston Saul (2002) argues that this amalgam is
characterized by four distinct layers in two waves. The first wave is comprised
of newcomers, the English and French settlers who interacted and reacted to an
existing Aboriginal culture and created Canadian culture. The second is the dynamic influx of non-European immigrants who are reshaping Canadian culture
today. An important part of the solution to Aboriginal issues is national recognition that Canada is built on the foundation of interaction with Aboriginal cultures. This requires Canadians to remember how Aboriginal peoples have helped
shape Canadian history and how central Aboriginal images and values are to
Canadian identity.

Aboriginal cultural identity is the product of a complex history of culture contact, history, cultural change, and resistance. Berry identifies it for RCAP "as an
internal (symbolic) state (made up of cognitive, affective and motivational com-
ponents) and external (behavioural) expression of being an Aboriginal person
(individual emphasis), and a member of an Aboriginal community (social emphasis)" (Berry 1999: 6, 8-10). His analysis makes it clear how Aboriginal identity
is influenced by the myriad of factors associated with colonialism, including residential school experiences, media representations, racism, and discrimination.

The nature of Canadian Aboriginal identity, past, present and future, was the
focus of a 1998 Association of Canadian Studies conference.[3] The papers presented there ranged over a wide map of Aboriginal identity politics from the role
of government in the creation of arbitrary categories of Aboriginality, to the false
images of Indians as portrayed by mainstream media, to the reappropriation of
this media and the use of film, video, and text as the basis for the construction of
contemporary Aboriginal identity at the individual and collective level.[4]

We can learn three interrelated lessons from these studies. First, cultural identity and personal and community health are closely connected.[5] Second, most if
not all of the problems associated with Aboriginal identity politics are directly

attributable to the legacy of misguided government policy. Third, we must distinguish between an Aboriginal person's political status and cultural identity.

1. CLOSE CONNECTION BETWEEN CULTURAL IDENTITY AND PERSONAL AND COMMUNITY HEALTH. When our collective identity is in play, our personal worldview is engaged. Actions at a state, regional, national, or international level impact on the emotional well-being of individuals. Culture imbues personality with specific traits and has important psychological benefits. When the relationship between culture and identity is disturbed or is called into question, the result can be personal disorientation that can have serious emotional and psychological consequences for individuals, families, and communities. Family learning environments and parenting skills, as well as formal religious and state educational systems, play important roles in informing children about core cultural values and creating a healthy sense of personal and community identity. Thus, the state, through educational and other institutions, comes to shape cultural identity in important ways.

Control over issues of personal and cultural identity — essentially the right to say who you are — is one of the most critical aspects of self-determination. Our sense of self and feelings of personal worth are linked to how we think about and experience our culture. When I recently spoke about Aboriginal history and health in Ontario Cancer Care Centres, I often remarked that "Aboriginal peoples carry history on their backs" to suggest that past colonial practices directly impact on current health and illness. At one site, an audience member remarked that *all* people feel the impact of their cultural history — and this is certainly true. The phrase "je me souviens" ("I remember"), for example, captures this reality for the Québécois. But no culture has been more savagely attacked with discriminatory practices, stereotypes, and policies of assimilation for a sustained period of time than Aboriginal cultures worldwide. The burden of this colonial history is deeply felt in Aboriginal people's identity in Canada today.

When children see negative images of their culture in school texts, when as adults they experience racism or discrimination or when their culture is denigrated or marginalized, they can feel unworthy, embarrassed, humiliated, or enraged. Aboriginal identity has historically been defined by the state, as we saw above. The residential school system was a direct assault on this identity; indeed, educational practices were strategically honed to strip away Aboriginal identity and replace it with a European one. As a result, many — not all — who attended residential schools lost a sense of themselves as Indians. Issues of cultural identity can also arise for children adopted out of their culture or for children and grandchildren of parents who lost their status. Coates notes that questions of Aboriginal identity are crucial at both the level of the individual and society. For individuals, personal identity crises can be a cause of interpersonal conflicts, risk-taking behaviour, and mental health problems, including suicide (Coates 1999: 23-41).[6]

A great deal of research has demonstrated that a strong sense of personal cultural identity is critical to good health. Jeff Reading, an Aboriginal epidemiologist and Scientific Director of the Institute of Aboriginal Peoples' Health, has documented the long-term and intergenerational health impacts of the residential school syndrome (Reading 1999: 29-54). More recently, under the rubric of historical trauma, Aboriginal researchers have attempted to explain many contemporary problems — suicide, family violence, alcoholism — as the result of the identity confusion caused by colonial policies, which included forced relocation of communities, attempts at educational assimilation, and the removal of children from reserves (Braveheart and DeBruyn 1998). Elsewhere, I have argued that the recovery or establishment of a strong sense of cultural identity by individuals and communities is an essential part of community health and integral to self-determination efforts because it instills those feelings of self-worth and control that are essential to capacity building (Warry 1998). It is this link between culture and ill health that also provides a critical rationale for the need for culturally appropriate health services (see Chapter 10).

2. LEGACY OF MISGUIDED GOVERNMENT POLICY. As well as distinguishing between settlers and Aboriginal peoples, colonialism also created political divisions, which continue to this day, between status and non-status Indians, on and off reserve Indians, and Indian and Métis, giving each access to different resources and different rights. The net effect of the federal government's policies has been to divide and conquer Aboriginal peoples both through relocation and marginalization and through the politics of enfranchisement. Thus, in certain cases, even when individuals know themselves to be Aboriginal, they can be denied their status and rights by the state. Defining different types of Aboriginal people has led to political divisions and fights about the resources available to different communities. These artificial identity divisions also influence how Aboriginal communities interact and how individuals think of themselves.

Coates describes the division between status and non-status Indians as a "classic example of government intrusion into the cultural and social affairs of First Nations and the inappropriateness of legislative definitions of Indigenous identity" (Coates 1999: 23-41). The creation of status and non-status Indians, Inuit, and Métis is the historical by-product of colonial policies, including enfranchisement policies by which Indians had to relinquish their status in order to obtain certain rights that were available to other Canadians (see Chapter 2). Over time, there came to be a growing population of non-status Indians and Métis who had a different set of rights than status Indians still recognized under the Indian Act. Some redress has been made: Bill C-31, passed in the mid-1980s, allowed many Indian women who lost their status when they married a non-Indian man, and their children, to reclaim their Indian status.

Questions arising from these historical divisions of Aboriginal people continue to plague the administration of Indian Affairs and greatly impact on the lives
of individuals. Limited resources, including money for housing and essential services, have forced some bands to reject non-Native spouses as potential members
and, in extreme cases, to force the eviction of non-members, even if this meant
breaking up couples or families.[7] Because of the arcane relationship between
Aboriginal peoples and the Crown, the collective rights of First Nations override
the rights of individuals, even though they are protected from discrimination under the Charter of Rights and Freedoms. In rare cases, bands have discriminated
against members but remain immune from human rights legislation as long as
their actions occur pursuant to the Indian Act (Dickson-Gilmore 1999: 22). Such
cases draw the wrath of a great many people because they give precedence of
collective rights over the individual. However, such discrimination is driven by
these inadequate, if not oppressive, government policies that have forced bands to
prioritize services when they would prefer to provide them to all.

Cultural protection and cultural sovereignty, self-determination and self-government, are linked. The quest for self-determination is to overcome these artificial divisions and obtain the right to say who is — and who is not — an Aboriginal
person. And when this right is asserted, and injustice occurs in individual cases,
the media is quick to suggest that reverse discrimination or racism is occurring.
Thus, for example, First Nations that legally assert their rights to raise children,
sometimes taking those children from White foster parents, have been accused of
not having the best interests of the child at heart (see Chapter 4). White spouses of
Aboriginal people have been forced to move from reserves in order to make space
for Aboriginal-only families, a situation exacerbated by housing shortages on reserve and the federal government's insistence that First Nations pass membership
codes, which, in many cases, disadvantage status Indians involved in intercultural
marriages. These situations, however painful, unfortunate, or even unjust to individuals, are the inevitable by-product of a process of cultural recovery whereby
First Nations are attempting to undo decades of colonial and postcolonial policies
that stripped individuals and communities of their right to control and proclaim
their cultural identity.

At the other extreme is the issue of the rights that accompany Aboriginal status. A Supreme Court of Ontario decision gave Métis as well as status Indians the
right to hunt on Crown land. Yet, the court was unwilling to provide a method for
defining who was, or was not, Métis (Coates 1999: 29). As rights once reserved
for status Indians are expanded to include non-status and Métis, the possibility
of "status fraud" arises: there may be individuals who wish to claim Métis status
in order to obtain special exemptions to hunt and fish, to claim medical or other
services, and even to request tax exemptions reserved for Aboriginal peoples.
But is this a realistic concern? In several provinces, a simple declaration that a

person is Métis is sufficient for recognition as an Aboriginal person. Once identified, a person has some potential advantages over other citizens. The Ontario
Métis Aboriginal Association website notes that members have special rights to
harvesting (hunting, fishing, trapping, gathering), employment and education
programs (employment equity; Aboriginal-specific bursaries and scholarships),
and procurement of specialized government services contracts.[8] There may be
cases where people have rediscovered or reclaimed their Aboriginal status for
personal gain, but instances of such identity fraud seem rare. It is highly unlikely
that a non-Aboriginal person would want to claim to be a member of a marginalized minority. An essential quality of cultural identity is that it is self-ascribed.
Individuals identify with a particular cultural or ethnic group because it has
meaning for them.[9] The issue of who is, or who is not, an Aboriginal person must
be resolved by accepting the principle of self-identification, not the arbitrary divisions that government policy has created. As Coates remarks,

> On the broadest national scale, an Aboriginal person is one who identifies as an
> Indigenous person. For decades, there have been strong political and legal reasons
> for suppressing such identification and many individuals did so. The resurgence
> of Indigenous pride, cultural assertiveness, and political rights over the past thirty
> years has brought many individuals back into the Aboriginal fold — although less
> often back onto the reserve. (Coates 1999: 33)

Enhanced cultural awareness has lead to the self-identification of Métis and
of Aboriginal people who live off reserve, and this in turn has lead to calls for
improved culturally specific services for urban Aboriginals and for the exten-
sion of rights normally associated with status Indians to non-status individuals.
In the past, some Aboriginal people living in cities may have "passed" as non-
Natives — they denied their Aboriginal heritage in order to improve their chances
of being hired for work or to escape prejudice or discrimination. Today, however,
non-status Aboriginal peoples are asserting their rights and seeking to develop
culturally appropriate institutions that can better represent their urban communities (see Chapter 7).

3. POLITICAL STATUS AND CULTURAL IDENTITY. Neo-conservatives draw our attention to
the many Aboriginal people who, they assert, live mainstream lives and who can
be considered to be assimilated or integrated. There may be many Aboriginals
who appear no different from mainstream Canadians on the surface and some
who, for whatever reasons, renounce their heritage. For others, their Aboriginal
heritage is a meaningful but not dominant part of their character and personality.
There are those who embrace their culture and for whom it is, at least in a political sense, a defining characteristic of their lives. In short, we should expect a wide

range of individual approaches to identity within the Aboriginal population. If there is one primary characteristic of contemporary Aboriginal identity, however, it is the appreciation for diversity, the divergent paths that lead to degrees of cultural awareness.

First and foremost, Aboriginal people are members of a particular culture — Ojibway, Cree, or Dene, for example. Their cultural identity is also shaped by the reserve on which they were born, the reserves of their parents and extended kin, and their tribal area and history. Of course, many Aboriginal people have, over time, either through choice or through government policy, lost touch or have moved away from their home reserve. Secondly, Aboriginal peoples are members of a larger or pan-Indian culture; some see themselves as part of a group of Indigenous nations or cultures worldwide. Third, they may then identify as Canadian. The extent to which a person privileges their Aboriginal identity over their Canadian identity varies greatly, but by and large Aboriginal people have a significant personal cultural investment as Canadians, even where they may recognize links to Indigenous nations in the United States and elsewhere.

Social scientists have used the term hybridity to capture individual ways of being and thinking in two or more cultures. Because humans are capable of moving easily between different frames of reference, the choice between cultures is not black and white, but one involving shades of grey or a pastiche of colour. People act out their hybridity when they are aware of the juxtaposition of different roles and value systems. Edward Bruner, for example, notes that anthropologists carry an ethnographic and a personal self — they fit in and adapt to the cultural worlds they study while remaining outsiders who cling to their culture of birth.[10] But everyone experiences hybridity to some degree in their personal and professional lives: we leave work and the values and rules that accompany it and (as best we can) return to values associated with home, family, and friends. Occasionally, we comment on how we have to put on airs when in professional settings or take off professional cloaks when at home. Tourists experience temporary hybridity as they attempt to accept local cultural ways and leave behind the foods and flavours of their home. Indeed, the mark of a good tourist is the ability to learn and adjust, as opposed to the stereotype of the "ugly American" tourist who carries cultural standards and expectations into a foreign setting.

But for many people, such as children of mixed marriages, immigrants, and Aboriginal peoples, hybridity becomes a central way of being. I sometimes speak of Aboriginal peoples as being fluently bicultural: they are capable of understanding their own cultural ways as well as the rules of mainstream society. The specific hybrid ways they see themselves are many and varied. There are non-status Aboriginal people who have lost touch (often through several generations) with their reserves, who believe that Aboriginal people should integrate into mainstream society, and yet who think of themselves as Aboriginal. There are status and non-status Aboriginal people who live in the city and practice their culture every day. And there are many Aboriginal people, both new-status and non-status, who wish to re-establish ties to the reserve but who cannot move back because of a shortage of housing or other resources.

The nature of a persistent Aboriginal identity is misunderstood by neo-conservative commentators, who see it as rigid, rather than fluid. This view essentializes Aboriginal peoples, denies difference, and sees culture as only a superficial aspect of identity. It suggests that individual and cultural identity can be separated. Writing in Australia, Johns states:

> The best prospects for aboriginal self-determination lie in individual acts of self-determination, reconciled to the modern world. The contradictions of collective, internal self-determination, retaining elements of pre-modern culture are inimical to reasonable aboriginal outcomes. The orthodoxy assumes aboriginal salvation lies in identity and collective solutions. It places identity before all other considerations. The main reason for the 'culture' argument is that the other grounds for separateness; race, colour and an economic system are disappearing. (Johns 2001b: 41)

Johns, working with the static view of culture, is unable to see that Aboriginal culture is not in the process of disappearing. His argument posits cultural identity as a superficial aspect of politics, something that Aboriginal people grab onto as their culture disappears. He thinks that it is all right for Aboriginal people to be proud of their culture or assert an Aboriginal identity as long as they do not do so politically in the public realm. So Aboriginal culture, in clinging to past values, fails to provide the means for ensuring "reasonable" outcomes, as measured by participation in mainstream society. Johns suggests that it is appropriate for Aboriginal people to seek individual self-determination and to express their identity through private association. It is wrong, he argues, to provide public support for culture or to encourage separate rules or institutions for specific cultural groups. This should occur only where "the consent of the entire body politic" exists (Johns 2001b: 42). In these arguments Johns assumes that anything that is contrary to mainstream identity should somehow be hidden away or that diversity should not find its way into public policy. This is akin to arguments about gay and lesbian identity. It is fine to be gay in private but wrong to take sexual politics into the realm of public discourse. However, when discrimination is entrenched in public policy, we are no longer dealing with issues of sexual preference but with issues of human rights.

Johns's argument is illogical because it rests on the idea that self-identity and collective identity are somehow discreet and separable. Nothing is further from the truth. Identity, as demonstrated in countless studies during the past 30 years, is intimately connected to larger social institutions and political processes. If Johns is capable of separating his private identity from his work in public institutions, it is, perhaps, because his identity is connected to the mainstream Australian-European organizations that provide him with comfort and privilege.

Borrows, in contrast, calls for "new narratives of Aboriginal political participation" and soundly rejects assimilation, which implies "loss of political control, culture and difference." He believes that Aboriginal peoples' participation in Canadian politics can "change contemporary notions of Canadian citizenship." It is possible to see Aboriginal citizenship as distinct from Canadian citizenship while sharing many of the same attributes and aspirations, such as our mutual appreciation of and respect for the landscape and environment (Borrows 2000: 332, 326).[11]

So, culture and identity are integrated concepts and cannot be opposed. Cultural identity is not singular and solid; it is multi-faceted and nested. Culture does not, therefore, drive people apart and lead to different solitudes.[12] For this reason, we have nothing to fear from Aboriginal self-government except the fear produced when identity politics are played. A person with a traditional Aboriginal spiritual orientation does not automatically become a radical advocate for self-government any more than a Native Canadian working for IBM denies his Aboriginality or votes for a conservative party. Individuals assume their identities by consciously selecting from a wide repertoire of cultural symbols and ideas. They interpret their cultures consciously or unconsciously (this distinction being an indicator of how reflective and reflexive a cultural member is). Cultural identity and political orientation are related in a complex manner, but they are not synonymous, any more than language and culture are synonymous.

The American Indian College Fund runs a series of print advertisements with the caption "Have you ever seen a real Indian?" They picture a variety of young men and women in street and work clothes, training to be physicians, veterinarians, lawyers, and other professionals.[13] At first glance, the photographs fail to reveal any outward sign of Indian identity, and the models could easily pass for any American teenager. They remind us that culture lies not in surface characteristics but in the hearts and minds of individuals who carry with them their culture and use it, each day and hour, to make choices in their lives. This is the understanding of cultural identity that should be built into our public policy and into our advocacy for Aboriginal rights. We must learn to "see the Indian" where, at first glance, none appears. We will then be in a position to respect the rights and responsibilities that accompany Aboriginal status. What is at issue here is Aboriginal peoples' right to protect their culture and their right to self-identify and to pursue their rights to self-determination. The search for self-determination is inseparable from self and cultural identity and is an individual and collective project.

NOTES

1 The reference to "Other" here draws on the work of Edward Said (1979) who demonstrated how Western or mainstream conceptions of "Other" cultural groups were the product of colonialism. Said's work showed how Western stereotypes of Arabic and Islamic peoples were formed; how they misrepresented Middle Eastern cultures; and how they demonized entire nations, allowing the West to more easily pursue and rationalize its colonial and contemporary policies. Said's work has been highly influential in the social sciences and humanities. Today, analysts routinely speak of representations or constructions of the "Other" to describe how specific cultures, subcultures, or minorities are symbolically created in social and political discourse.

2 Coates also notes that this view is so dominant that it comes to shape current scholarship, so that, for example, we have a much better picture of reserve communities and of Indians who continue to engage in hunting and trapping or other "traditional" social and economic practices, than we do of individuals who choose to live in cities or who have essentially mainstream religious beliefs or materialist attitudes.

3 Papers presented in that conference have been edited by Michael Behiels (1999).

4 For the use of media by Aboriginal people, see Restoule 1999; Buddle-Crowe (2001) traces the history and development of Aboriginal media in Canada.

5 See also Berry 1999 on the health and mental health consequences of identity conflict.

6 See also Waldram 2004 for a review of mental health in colonial and postcolonial perspective.

7 See Dickson-Gilmore (1999: 44-62) for a careful examination of the Jacobs case in Kahnawake. This study clearly demonstrates that human rights activists would be able to intervene in individual cases and to ensure families obtain compensation or assistance when they are the subject of discriminatory actions by bands were it not for the Indian Affairs Department's failure to live up to its statutory responsibilities.

8 See <http://www.omaa.org/page_11_Join_or_renew_membership.htm>. See also the Métis Nation of Ontario <http://www.metisnation.org/programs/MNOTI/home.html>.

9 In a recent and controversial case, the American Indian Activist Ward Churchill had his Aboriginal status questioned. Churchill received national attention for an essay he wrote following the 9/11 terrorist attacks in New York City and Washington, DC. The subsequent media coverage led to an examination of his academic qualifications, allegations that he had violated scholarly and journalistic standards in his writing, and claims that he had mischaracterized or lied about his Aboriginal status. Churchill has always asserted that the right to self-identification is paramount given the American government's history of identity politics. This controversy can be followed through Wikipedia accounts and numerous websites. See for example <http://en.wikipedia.org/wiki/Ward_Churchill>, <http://www.frontpagemag.com/Articles/ReadArticle.asp?ID=16917>, and <http://www.realchangenews.org/archive3/2005_03_23/current/interview.html>.

10 See Bruner 1993, cited in Narayan 1993. Narayan, for example, has written on the role of Native anthropologists and the difficulty of writing for a Western academic audience about familiar Native experiences.

11 Borrows (2000) argues that Aboriginal peoples' relation to the land is critical. He speaks of "land-ed citizenship" in the original sense and of Aboriginal "citizens *with* this land." He argues that better understanding of Aboriginal values would influence how Canadians view the land and land use policies.

12 Cairns's appeal to the notion of solitudes conjures up Canada's historic problems with Quebec sovereignty and suggests that Aboriginal political claims are as troublesome or problematic to a Canadian national identity or political agenda (Cairns 2000).

13 The advertisements remind us that many Indian graduates return to the reservation and that economists project that every dollar of a graduate's income will turn over two-and-a-half times so that an investment in Aboriginal education is an investment in the larger economy.

CHAPTER 7 Culture in the City

Perhaps the greatest myth about Aboriginal people is that when they move to the city, they abandon their culture. Propagated by the neo-conservative right, it is a myth assumed to be true by many mainstream Canadians. There are several assumptions behind it: that Aboriginal culture is tied to the reserve; that relations to the land — hunting, trapping, environmental concerns — are synonymous with Aboriginal culture; and that leaving the reserve is a conscious choice to adopt mainstream lifestyles and values. In each of these assumptions, there is some truth; for example, relations to the land remain an important part of Aboriginal culture. However, the survival and revival of urban Aboriginal culture demonstrates the failure of government assimilation policies. Urban Aboriginal peoples, and the choices they make, are central to cultural revitalization. Indeed, the Aboriginal cultural revitalization movement was born in the city and not on reserve.

Social scientists are partially to blame for perpetuating the myth of urban assimilation; until recently there have been few good studies and no true ethnographies of the normal daily lives of Aboriginal people who live in cities. Research on urban communities continues to be viewed as less important, and the majority of researchers remain focused on the reserve or remote locations.[1] There are also significant methodological challenges to researching urban populations. The Aboriginal community is often dispersed throughout the city and does not live in discreet neighbourhoods[2]—there is no equivalent to a "Chinatown," for example. Surveys are therefore difficult to implement. Organizations like Aboriginal friendship centres or health centres, which service inner city or street populations, sometimes serve as the focal point for research, but using their clients to accumulate data tends to perpetuate images of Aboriginal people as the urban poor. Those middle-class or wealthy Aboriginal people (including those who work for government and agencies that service the marginalized) are seldom the subjects of research and are therefore poorly understood. Although they are represented as assimilated, what little research exists suggests that issues of culture and Aboriginal identity remain important to them; this area requires further study.

The significance of culture in the city has been documented for well over 40 years in such works as Hugh Brody's study of "Indians on Skid Row in Edmonton" (1971), written for the Department of Indian Affairs; Edgar Dosman's *Indians:*

The Urban Dilemma (1972), set in Saskatoon; Mark Naglar's Toronto-based report, *Indians in the City* (1973); and David H. Stymeist's research in a northwestern Ontario town, *Ethnics and Indians* (1975). Not surprisingly, these early
studies contain many outmoded ideas and a conception of culture that has been
subsequently discarded. Nonetheless, a careful reading demonstrates that, even
in the 1960s when the research was done, the urban Aboriginal population was
diverse, reasons for migration to the city were complex, and urban migrants had
an interest in sustaining Aboriginal values in the face of mainstream or White
urban ways. For instance, Stymeist demonstrated how Aboriginal people were
distinguished and set aside from other ethnic groups and how "virulent" was the
discrimination and prejudice they faced. Naglar interviewed 150 Indians from all
walks of life. In a chapter on "Cultural Influences," he speaks of the historical in-
justices that produced Indian resistance and distrust of Whites, suggests that the
"degree of Indianness" affects adjustment to urban life, and that "cultural overlapping" leads to an identity that incorporates both mainstream and Aboriginal
values into an individual's living pattern (Naglar 1973: 25). Brody's and Dosman's
studies concern the urban poor on skid row and the early Aboriginal organizations that serviced them. Both document the continuing persistence of Aboriginal
values and behaviours in the urban context. Dosman's study, in particular, provides evidence for the beginnings of Pan-Indianism and interest in the revival
of shared Indian ideology in the face of policies of assimilation. Dosman notes
that the urban affluent ("native aristocracy") and welfare dependent populations
share a common sense of Indianness. Indeed, he states that affluent Aboriginals
"share a common consciousness of Indianness," a rejection of Christianity, and
an interest in Aboriginal spirituality and culture (Dosman 1972: especially 42, 55,
and 179-80, passim).

Dosman's call for new policies and forms of organization can be considered
an early plea for distinct and culturally appropriate urban institutions by the
Aboriginal urban elite who refuse assimilation. That urban Aboriginal people
retain an interest in traditional culture and spirituality and are often more ori-
entated to Indigenous spirituality and knowledge than those living on reserve
was later confirmed in Don McCaskill's multi-city survey of attitudes among
Aboriginal urban migrants (McCaskill 1981). Although these findings have been
rejected by many neo-conservative and mainstream commentators, they show
that Aboriginal urbanization, rather than defining the success of assimilation,
has provided the conditions and means for the rebirth of Aboriginal culture and
identity. How this occurred is most clearly understood through the example of
the Indian friendship centre movement.

The concept of the friendship centre originated in the mid-1950s when a no-
ticeable number of Aboriginal people were moving to the larger urban areas of
Canada, primarily to seek an improved quality of life, jobs, and/or higher educa-

tion. According to the 1951 census, for example, there were only 85 Aboriginal persons in Toronto; by 1961, this number had grown to 1,196, a number which was undoubtedly low as census data do not accurately capture highly migrant Aboriginal populations (Naglar 1973: 8). Aboriginal and non-Aboriginal community leaders began to advocate for the establishment of specialized agencies that could provide assistance to people moving to cities from reserves.[3] These agencies would provide referrals and offer counselling on matters of employment, housing, education, and health, in liaison with other community organizations. In 1951, the first friendship centre, the North American Indian Club, was created in Toronto. This was followed by the creation of the Coqualeetza Fellowship Club in Vancouver in 1952 and the Indian and Métis Friendship Centre in Winnipeg in 1959. By 1968 there were 26 friendship centres across Canada, which were linked through provincial and territorial organizations. Throughout their early history, friendship centres were largely voluntary organizations. They were literally places of friendship where Native and non-Native volunteers could meet. They relied on small government grants, fundraising events, and private donations to provide job counselling and other services to urban migrants and the poor.

In 1972 the government of Canada formally recognized the National Association of Friendship Centres and implemented the Migrating Native Peoples' Program (MNPP) to assist Aboriginal migrants in adapting to urban life and, given the thinking of the time, to encourage the adoption of mainstream ways. By 1983, the government was providing core funding through the Secretary of State to 80 centres across the country. In 1988, permanent funding was secured with the formation of the Aboriginal Friendship Centres Program (AFCP). Currently, the National Association of Friendship Centres represents the concerns of 99 core-funded and 15 non-core-funded friendship centres, as well as seven Provincial Territorial Associations (PTAs), across Canada.

Unlike the United States, where the government sponsored resettlement programs to encourage Indians to move to cities, Canada did not have any formal assimilation policies aimed at encouraging Natives to leave the reserve. Nonetheless, given the assimilationist thinking at the time, it is fair to say that early government support for friendship centres and the MNPP were designed with the intent of encouraging urban migrants to assimilate to mainstream life. What happened, however, was just the opposite. As Dosman notes, even by the 1960s there was an emerging Aboriginal elite, many of whom were affiliated with these centres and took an active part in leadership or management of Aboriginal services. They were interested in ensuring the revival and survival of Aboriginal cultural practices in the city.

Early friendship centres were often located in inner city areas in order to service hard-to-reach street people, who often fell prey to addictions, in part because they had lost a sense of their Aboriginal identity. Some of the first programs developed were addiction programs (AA programs are still regularly found in friendship centres) and street patrols that provided outreach to the indigent and homeless, both Native and non-Native. The centres became important leaders in urban social services and often advocated for the development of additional services where they were lacking. Today they commonly offer an array of health and social services, including visiting physician programs, day care, employment counselling, court worker programs for Native people in conflict with the law, and Native inmate liaison programs, which send volunteers to visit individuals and Native inmate groups[4] in prisons and correctional institutions. In some cases, they also provide lunches for members, arts and crafts programs, and home care programs for Elders and seniors.

Friendship centres are at the forefront in creating and maintaining culture in the city, for instance, by bringing Elders and traditional persons into the city to provide cultural and spiritual counselling. The National Association of Friendship Centres has as its mandate:

> To improve the quality of life for Aboriginal peoples in an urban environment by supporting self-determined activities which encourage equal access to, and participation in, Canadian Society; and which respect and strengthen the increasing emphasis on Aboriginal cultural distinctiveness.

Provincial and federal friendship centre associations also conduct research on Aboriginal people living in cities and advocate for policy changes and for the development of culturally appropriate services.

Since the 1960s, the Aboriginal population in Canada has become more and more urban, and today roughly half of Canada's Aboriginal population live in cities.[5] According to census figures, the urban Aboriginal population grew by 62 per cent, compared to 11 per cent for other urban Canadians, during the decade 1981 to 1991. Population growth in urban areas is fuelled by natural increases (birth rate) as well as net migration from rural areas.[6] Because Aboriginal people do not commonly participate in the national census, these estimates of urban populations are unreliable. Census figures place the Toronto population at 20,000, although Aboriginal agency estimates range from 70,000 to 80,000 (Proulx 2003).[7] According to census figures, Winnipeg has the largest urban Aboriginal population: census data places it at 55,755, or 8 per cent of the city. But this figure does not accurately capture the homeless, so that Aboriginal agencies claim that the total population is closer to 70,000 and project that this will grow to more than 100,000 by the year 2020. Aboriginal communities vary greatly as a percentage of the total urban population and are more visible in cities in the North and West. In Thunder Bay, Aboriginal people constitute about one-third of the population, while in Toronto, despite similar total numbers, they make up less than 5 per cent of the metropolitan population.[8]

Today, in addition to friendship centres, many other Aboriginal organizations service clients in large metropolitan areas. These include legal and alternative justice services, halfway houses, Aboriginal community health clinics or health access centres, addictions treatment centres, urban cultural survival schools and Aboriginal language programs, and Aboriginal child and family service agencies, among others. All these offer culturally sensitive and appropriate services to clients.

One service offered by friendship centres deserves special note. Native inmate liaison programs have long been offered to assist Aboriginal inmates in jails and prisons and with their transition back to society. Aboriginal people are greatly overrepresented in the Canadian correctional system as the result of crimes committed while intoxicated, the inability to pay fines for offences leading to default, and, over time, cumulative records of offences that lead to longer and longer jail terms. Significantly, prisons are also an important site for cultural revitalization (see, for example, Waldram 1997). It is in prison that many Aboriginal persons have their first exposure to Aboriginal culture and spirituality. Inmates may attend Native Sons or Native Brotherhood meetings. Inmate liaison workers assist these groups, recruit volunteers and Elders, and help organize a variety of ceremonies, including sweat (purification) lodges or pipe ceremonies. The revitalization of Aboriginal culture has been aided by the work of ex-inmates, many of whom leave prison with a renewed sense of their Aboriginal identity and who begin their rehabilitation by participating in the friendship centre movement or other urban social services.

Our understanding of the urban Aboriginal community, then, begins with the fact that there are numerous services that place Indigenous practices and values at the heart of service delivery. Unfortunately, mainstream perceptions of urban Aboriginal peoples tend to be dominated by images of the clients of these organizations—the homeless and urban poor. As Brian Maracle, an award-winning journalist and author of *Crazywater*, says,

> The perceptions of Native people that most Canadians have are defined and limited largely by the second-hand images they see in the media and by the first-hand encounters they have on the street. Given these limited and superficial sources of information, it's not surprising that the stereotype of "the drunken Indian" looms so large in the warped perception that many Canadians have of native people. Although this stereotype is not fully shared by all Canadians, it is nevertheless deeply rooted in the Canadian psyche. (Cited in Dennie 2001: 14)

Part of the problem, as Roger Obonsawin, of the Aboriginal Council of Toronto has noted, is that "Aboriginal people who find steady employment and social acceptance in the city blend into the increasingly multicultural urban scene, while those who encounter difficulties are highly visible and reinforce the stereotype of urban Aboriginal people as poor, marginal, and problem-ridden."[9] However, as we have seen, there are many middle-class Aboriginal people for whom their culture and spirituality remain important. A 2003 survey by Statistics Canada and the Alberta government found that the Aboriginal off-reserve population had a higher labour force participation rate — 75.5 per cent — than the overall Alberta rate of 74.2 per cent. The employment rate for off-reserve Aboriginal people in Alberta is 66.9 per cent, while the unemployment rate is 9.5 per cent.[10]

The reasons Aboriginal people move to the city have always been varied and are classically categorized by "push" or "pull" factors (McCaskill 1981). For example, people are pushed from the reserve because of unemployment and pulled to the city by improved employment opportunities. Many who move to the city sustain a regular relationship with their reserve, returning on weekends or holidays to spend time with family. In heavily urbanized parts of the country such as Southern Ontario, many Aboriginal people commute from the reserve and work full time in urban locations. For status Indians, urban migration is cyclical and changes through the life course. They may leave the reserve for higher education or work in cities and temporarily return to the reserve for periods of varying length during their life; if in good health, they may retire to the reserve. Although long-term care and other medical services are increasingly available on or near reserves, many elderly or disabled Aboriginal persons live in cities to have access to specialized medical services.[11]

There are also more personal reasons for moving to cities. Aboriginal people who have experienced conflict with the law or imprisonment may choose to seek the anonymity of the city, rather than return to the reserve if they have been socially isolated or ostracized for their behaviour. And there remains the urban poor, the street population who have, for a variety of reasons, come to the inner city after leaving the reserve or who have, like a host of other Canadians, simply ended up on the street after losing their jobs, experiencing mental illness, and/or developing an addiction. Gays and lesbians (called "two-spirited people" in Aboriginal culture) sometimes find reserves to be less tolerant of their lifestyle and seek out gay communities in large cities. An important segment of the Aboriginal community are middle- and upper-class professionals, entrepreneurs, artists, leaders of service or political organizations, civil servants, lawyers, consultants, and so on. Aboriginal artists — musicians, playwrights, novelists and poets, painters — seek the creative communities and audiences that are available in cities. The urban Aboriginal community is therefore made up of many economic and social layers and interwoven social, economic, and political networks. The majority of Aboriginal political organizations are based in cities and are led by talented and well-educated professionals who are advocates, policy-makers, and managers. Those who are professionally trained as lawyers, physicians, or academics migrate to the higher paying jobs that are unavailable in rural areas.

Urban populations are divided into those status Indians who sustain some relationship to their home reserves and permanent city-dwellers who include non-status Indians who have lost any connection to a specific home reserve. This is an important distinction for two reasons. First, for at least some Aboriginal people, the urban and reserve communities are linked in a fluid and dynamic political relationship. For example, status Indians living in cities believe they should continue to have a right to vote for First Nations (band council) elections, a right that was upheld in the Supreme Court's *Corbiere* decision.[12] Second is the need to build capacity in rural and remote areas. Increasingly, Aboriginal youth leave the reserve for higher education but want to return to rural environments (either at home or in other Aboriginal communities) in order to improve the health and economic well-being of First Nations. Sustaining a participatory political relationship while off reserve enhances the likelihood that well-educated professionals will return.

The nature of community in the urban context has recently been addressed by Craig Proulx, who studied with the Community Council Project (CCP), an Aboriginal-run justice/diversion program operated by Aboriginal Legal Services of Toronto. This project mediated cases involving Aboriginal offenders, which were referred by the Crown attorney and heard by a panel of Aboriginal volunteers, community leaders, and Elders, who assisted both offenders and victims in reaching agreements about culturally appropriate ways of solving disputes and reconciling grievances. Proulx argues that Aboriginal service and political organizations are both the locus and nexus of the Aboriginal urban community. He notes that many of the board members and other volunteers of these agencies are leaders in the larger community and very much committed to the goal of Aboriginal self-determination. It is these individuals who define the nature of culturally appropriate institutions; seek to sustain relationships between reserves and urban organizations; and locate cultural knowledge-keepers, Elders and spiritual leaders, to participate in the guidance and delivery of programs. Proulx demonstrates that it is through conceptualization and the delivery of services that Aboriginal people bring to life their culture and values (Proulx 2003). Thus, the creation of culturally appropriate services is an exercise in cultural revitalization and self-determination.

One of the challenges facing urban peoples is how to practice culture within the context of Pan-Indianism or Aboriginal cultural diversity. In cities such as Toronto, Montreal, or Vancouver, the Aboriginal community is comprised of many different cultures, from Blackfoot and Dene to Inuit and Cree. Jairus Skye, an Aboriginal researcher who studied Indigenous healing at Anishnawbe Health in Toronto, has shown how Indigenous healers work within the context of a culturally diverse urban community and, in so doing, sustain Indigenous values and address illness and identity issues among their patients and clients. Aboriginal healers maintain their own authentic Indigenous health and healing practices (Cree, Dene, or Haudenosaunee, for example) and yet work with patients from other Aboriginal cultures as well as non-Native clients. These healers also cooperate closely with non-Aboriginal physicians, consulting them on diagnoses, explaining herbal medications, and referring patients to other mainstream caregivers.

The questions of how culture is sustained in the city and the nature of urban Aboriginal communities are important and related. Many mainstream Canadians fail to understand the nature of culturally appropriate institutions and perceive Aboriginal service agencies as just another (expensive) way of providing health and social services. Why, they ask, can't Aboriginal people use the same services as other Canadians? The answer is that White services have failed to provide the same levels of care and service to Aboriginal clients as they do to mainstream Canadians and that culturally appropriate services have been proven to be both effective and cost effective in doing so.

The neo-conservative argument is clear: Indians in the city are somehow less Aboriginal and more mainstream in their identity. If they have not been assimilated, they are on their way — and this is a good thing because it means that they are more fully Canadian. It is true that some Aboriginal people, whether married to other Aboriginal people or to non-Natives, maintain steady employment and have little or no contact with Aboriginal organizations; others consciously choose not to practice their culture. But there is no evidence to suggest that all urban Aboriginal peoples have relinquished their cultural beliefs or that the city somehow forces them to abandon their culture. Quite the contrary, their culture is alive and well as they seek to enhance the development of Aboriginal-specific services and to move toward a form of Aboriginal self-government. If the move to the city contributes to a loss of culture, as the neo-conservatives maintain, there is no Aboriginal-specific population to govern and there is no future for self-determination or self-government in any urban setting. Whatever political powers Aboriginal people might be entitled to are linked to the reserve and are weakened in the city (see Cairns 2000: 184).

This is a drastic oversimplification of the RCAP position, which made it clear that while culture survives in the city, urban Aboriginal peoples are caught in a jurisdictional quagmire and need culturally appropriate services and institutions that can serve to facilitate rather than impede self-determination. RCAP consulted widely with urban Métis, non-status Indians, and Aboriginal people and took submissions from urban organizations, including associations of friendship centres. It conducted a National Roundtable on Urban Aboriginal Issues and reported its recommendations in Volume 4 of its report in a section on "Urban

Perspectives." RCAP (1996d) acknowledged that urban populations are culturally diverse, so that, for example, Cree, Ojibwa, and other values are often in play.
And it also acknowledged the lack of the sense of community that is tied to a land
base and environment as naturally occurs in rural, reserve, and remote settings.
However, RCAP was primarily interested in recognizing that, with 50 per cent of
the Aboriginal population in cities, Aboriginal culture needs to be supported and
enhanced in urban areas. This could be accomplished in many ways, including,
for example, recognition of communities of interest, changes to existing forms
of governance, and financial supports for Aboriginal programs. RCAP's most innovative suggestion was that governments set aside land in urban areas to be
dedicated to Aboriginal culture and spiritual needs.

RCAP was reluctant to take on the issue of government in the city for many
reasons, not least of which is that, until jurisdictions for First Nations are clarified
and implemented, urban self-government will be difficult to tackle. Currently,
there is no federal or provincial policy that would advance the authority of urban
Aboriginal institutions. Because the problems of urban Aboriginal people begin
with the definition of who is and who is not an Aboriginal person (see Chapter
6),[13] there is little clarity about whether federal or provincial governments should
fund services or who would regulate Aboriginal governance structures.[14] As
Cameron notes, the federal government has exclusive power to propose and pass
legislation regarding Aboriginal people. For historical reasons, once people are
off reserve they are treated as normal members of a province, and it is often the
provincial and/or municipal government that provides funding for direct services to them. The federal government can have legislative and often funding control
for specific initiatives, but it does not have the accompanying responsibility for
service planning and delivery. This jurisdictional conflict creates challenges for
Aboriginal people. New urban services can take years to fund and implement as
various levels of government negotiate responsibility for funding, control, and
reporting of programs.

RCAP identified three main problems arising from this jurisdictional conflict.
First, urban Aboriginal people receive a lower level of service than their counterparts on reserve. Second, compared to all Canadian citizens, they have a difficult
time accessing any services because service providers often do not know who is
entitled and because provincial governments will not fully accept responsibility
for providing services to them. Finally, even where urban Aboriginal people are
eligible, there remains in many smaller cities a lack of culturally appropriate services, particularly a lack of services delivered in Aboriginal languages.

Because the federal government refuses to fund (at least with any consistency)
services or organizations for urban Aboriginal peoples, at least some advocates
have claimed that it has encouraged them to move to the city in order to reduce
its financial responsibilities for Aboriginal programs on reserve (RCAP 1996a:

543). There is no way to document this claim, but it is clear that, as a result of jurisdictional confusion, there is considerable disparity in how different provinces respond to the needs of urban Aboriginals and to what extent they are prepared to fund Aboriginal-specific services. Ontario funds the Aboriginal Healing and Wellness Strategy (AHWS), which provides a variety of Aboriginal-specific and culturally appropriate services, including healing lodges for victims of family violence. AHWS also funds Aboriginal health access centres in cities and on reserves, as well as a variety of community-based health promotions and illness prevention services.

Following RCAP, as part of the Aboriginal Action Plan, between 1998 and 2002, the federal government developed an Urban Aboriginal Strategy (UAS) designed to improve policy development and program coordination at the federal level and with other levels of government. Ottawa began to discuss how it could support efforts on the ground that were aimed at serving urban Aboriginal people. While many challenges remain, the UAS has achieved successes in small but important ways. For example, it contributed significantly to a greater awareness by governments and others about the circumstances facing urban Aboriginal people, and this led to increased collaboration among provincial and federal governments. In 2002, the government reaffirmed its commitment to the UAS in its Speech from the Throne, stating that "In a number of cities, poverty is disproportionately concentrated among Aboriginal people. The government will work with interested provinces to expand on existing pilot programs to meet the needs of Aboriginal people living in cities."[15] The 2003 Budget allocated $25 million over three years to support the UAS. Most of this money was used to fund pilot projects in eight urban centres: Vancouver, Calgary, Edmonton, Saskatoon, Regina, Winnipeg, Toronto, and Thunder Bay. All are cities with an Aboriginal population of more than 15,000 according to the 2001 census, representing at least 5 per cent of the total population. The pilot projects are meant to test new ideas on how to better respond, through partnership, to the local needs of urban Aboriginal people.

Although many mainstream Canadians find the notion of urban self-government improbable or unfathomable, there already are political experiments that could eventually lead to truly self-determining and autonomous Aboriginal urban political institutions. One such experiment is evolving in the Greater Toronto Area where the Aboriginal Council of Toronto (ACT) aims to build a self-sufficient, united, and influential Aboriginal community and to develop forms of political representation for the urban population. ACT was founded by a community meeting of about 100 Aboriginal people held (appropriately) at the Native Canadian (Friendship) Centre in 2001. Sixteen people were appointed with a mandate to develop options and recommend processes for the establishment of a council which would politically represent the Aboriginal people of Toronto. In 2003, Roger Obonsawin, an Aboriginal consultant, was elected as ACT's first chair.

ACT is composed of representatives from the treaty areas reflected in the Toronto Aboriginal community as well as other Métis, Inuit, and non-status Indians. It has been recognized by Toronto Mayor David Miller and effectively serves as the political voice for the urban Aboriginal community. Although still in its infancy, it is exploring possible governance and administrative structures, including the possibility of serving as an administrative and law-making body.

In short, urban Aboriginal leaders have moved beyond RCAP and are actively working toward a vision of urban self-government. Although this is difficult for most mainstream Canadians to understand, Aboriginal people can see a day when an urban administrative body, elected by popular vote, will oversee programs and services and carry out other responsibilities for community affairs. Such a vision is realistic given that, at least in large urban centres, networks of culturally appropriate services are entrenched and accepted by mainstream social and health agencies. Canadians will begin to understand this vision and the possibilities of urban self-government only when they come to appreciate that Aboriginal cultures and communities are alive and well in the city. The move from the reserve does not mean that culture, and cultural identity, is left behind. Urban Aboriginal people wish to carve out an urban space that allows their children and families to obtain appropriate housing, education, health care, and social services. They want agencies that are based on Aboriginal values, ways of caring, and ways of learning. In order to obtain such culturally appropriate services, they are building urban alliances and political organizations, reaching out to non-Native urban leaders and volunteers as they did in the 1960s when friendship centres were first created. The difference now is that this urban population is large and that claims to urban Aboriginal self-determination are proportionately powerful. Aboriginal peoples in the city are creating a political voice that can no longer be ignored, even when the blinkers of assimilationist thinking remain in place.

NOTES

1 This is also true of my own work. During the late 1980s, I was involved in several projects involving friendship centres and child welfare agencies that focused more directly on urban life. Since the early 1990s, however, I have worked predominantly on reserve. However several of my students—Judy Clark, Jennifer Ranford, Kathleen Buddle-Crowe, Craig Proulx, and Jairus Skye—have worked with urban organizations and peoples. My analysis in this chapter is derived in part from my own knowledge of urban Aboriginal agencies as well as this student research.

2 There are exceptions to this statement; Winnipeg, for instance, has sections of high or predominant Aboriginal populations.

3 This brief history is taken in part from the website of the National Association of Friendship Centres <http://www.nafc-Aboriginal.com/aboutus-history.html> where the quotations below can be found.

4 These groups are known by a variety of names across the country, but in federal institutions they are commonly called Native Brotherhoods and Sisterhoods. In Ontario correctional centres, the groups are known as Native Sons and Daughters.

5 Readers interested in trying to understand contemporary urban Aboriginal issues might begin with the following website: The Aboriginal Portal <http://www.Aboriginalcanada.gc.ca/acp/site. nsf/en/index.html>, has listings of urban and rural locations across the country. Each has urban directories for Aboriginal and government organizations and agencies. There are also independent sites, such as the urban Aboriginal organizational directory for the Greater Toronto Area <http://www.cfis.ca/GTA_directory.htm#Organizations> and the Native Canadian Centre <http://www.ncct.on.ca/>. Similar sites are available for all major cities.

6 This does not necessarily mean that reserve populations are shrinking. The 2001 census showed a slight increase in reserve populations as the result of natural growth as well as migration to reserves from surrounding rural areas.

7 The difference between these figures is partially accounted for by census survey techniques, the fact that many Aboriginal people do not participate in the census, the fact that people living in the city may be considered part of reserve census figures, and the difficulties associated with self-identification of Aboriginal status in the census itself.

8 For census and other data on urban peoples see the Urban Aboriginal Atlas on line at <http://www. gismap.usask.ca/website/Web_atlas/AOUAP/>. Morris, Cooke, and Clatworthy (2004) review some of the problems with population figures and the policy implications for urban peoples.

9 As cited in a speech by Charley Coffee, Executive Vice President, Government and Community Affairs, Royal Bank of Canada Financial Group (2002), "Urban Aboriginals and 'Promising Practices': Our Call to Action," available at <http://www.rbc.com/newsroom/20020919coffey. html>.

10 See "The 'Other' Aboriginal: Reconsidering the Urban Aboriginal Image" available at <http:// www.opinion-canada.ca/en/articles/article_43.html>.

11 Little is known of Aboriginal people living with disabilities; however, the lack of sidewalks, ramps, and other amenities makes reserves hostile physical environments for those with disabilities.

12 See the government backgrounder on this decision at <http://www.ainc-inac.gc.ca/nr/prs/s-d20 00/00168bk_e.html>.

13 For a full discussion of the legal and constitutional standing of status, non-status, and Métis in relation to federal and provincial jurisdictions see RCAP 1996a, d.

14 I have been aided in this brief review by Angela Cameron's (n.d.) "Canadian Urban Aboriginal Peoples: Focus on Law and Policy," available at <http://www.sfu.ca/~fisls/Canadian_Urban_ Aboriginal_Peoples2.doc#_Toc10602854>.

15 Speech from the Throne to open the Second Session of the 37th Parliament of Canada <http:// www.pco-bcp.gc.ca/default.asp?Language=E&Page=sftddt&doc=sftddt2002_e.htm>.

CHAPTER 8 Courts and Claims: Aboriginal Resource Rights

Land claims and rights to animal, forest, and mineral resources are central to the future economic development of many, if not all, First Nations and Métis communities. For neo-conservatives this is a critical issue because they believe Aboriginal rights, as collective rights — especially rights concerning resource industries, particularly both inland and ocean fisheries — are at odds with mainstream interests and antithetical to a small "l" liberal ideology that emphasizes the protection of individual rights. They see rights-based arguments for control of resources (salmon, lobster, or fur-bearing animals) as arguments for race-based rights and therefore a threat to non-Aboriginal sport and commercial hunters, trappers, and fishers. Further, they fear that the gradual expansion of treaty and land rights that would give Aboriginal peoples access to sub-surface minerals or to forests would limit mainstream corporate use of these resources. As significant as these issues are in and of themselves, they also highlight neo-conservative attitudes to the role of courts — specifically, the Supreme Court — in interpreting the special rights of minorities and collectivities.

Let us begin by recalling that existing Aboriginal rights are protected in the Constitution under Sections 25.1 and 35.1 of the Charter of Rights and Freedoms (the Charter).[1] The Charter guarantees that other Canadian rights and freedoms "shall not be construed as to abrogate or derogate" from any Aboriginal, treaty, or other rights or freedoms that pertain to Aboriginal peoples, including any rights or freedoms that were recognized by the Royal Proclamation of 7 October 1763, and any rights and freedoms that now exist or may be so acquired. Section 35 further affirms existing Aboriginal and treaty rights; defines Aboriginal peoples to include Indian, Inuit, and Métis; and clearly states that treaty rights include those that exist by way of land claims agreements and rights that may be acquired in future. Finally, the Charter states that Aboriginal rights are guaranteed equally to all male and female persons.

The constitutional recognition of Aboriginal rights is tied to treaties signed between the Crown and individual First Nations in either the historic or contemporary periods.[2] While neo-conservatives are forced, given current realities, to acknowledge existing treaty rights, they are not happy about it. Flanagan, for example, begins his well-researched and parsed argument concerning treaties by arguing that a treaty is, in theory, a written international agreement between states.[3]

He notes that the Supreme Court holds Indian treaties to be unique because they have not been created according to the rules of international law and that, prior to 1982, courts ruled that they could be changed by the federal government. Since that time, however, treaties have been regarded as essential documents that can be interpreted as one source of Aboriginal rights. Flanagan bemoans the fact that recent Supreme Court decisions have regarded Indian treaties as if they were based on a nation-to-nation status — an interpretation RCAP and Aboriginal rights advocates argue is needed if Aboriginal self-determination is to be realized (Flanagan 2000: 134-35).

Canada's constitutional entrenchment of Aboriginal rights is considered an important model by Indigenous peoples internationally. Flanagan has gone so far as to warn his Australian colleagues to "avoid putting vague statements of principle in the constitution" because constitutional recognition of Aboriginal rights "limits the legal flexibility for experimentation" (Flanagan 2001: 19). Just what type of experimentation Flanagan is referring to here is unclear — presumably he means policies that would assist in the forced integration of Indigenous peoples — but he clearly prefers not to mention Aboriginal peoples (or minorities) in national constitutions. It is just as easy to argue that, without such constitutional entrenchment, Aboriginal rights would never be recognized in practice and that any experiment with collective approaches to law, health, and economy would not occur.

The Charter is also clear that Aboriginal rights are subject to change; that is, additional rights may be acquired in future as new treaties are made or old treaties reinterpreted. This distinction reinforces the fact that the Charter is a living document. Currently, comprehensive claims have been signed by those bands that never had treaties in the past, such as those in British Columbia and the Northwest Territories. The claims, which often take decades to negotiate and sign (and which cost many millions of dollars in the process), are comprehensive in the sense that they include agreements on issues such as health, social services, education, governance, and rights to land and resources. In this way they can be considered modern treaties. For example, the James Bay and Northern Quebec Agreement (JBNQA), signed in the 1970s, includes provisions for Aboriginal access to hunting territories and defines different categories of land over which the Cree have varying degrees of access to resources. Later claims, including the Nisga'a Final Agreement in British Columbia and the Nunavut Agreement, follow this essential pattern and go so far as to designate highly specific rights to resources — for example, to soapstone or quarry deposits necessary in the production of Aboriginal arts, repatriation rights for cultural artifacts, fishing rights (including allowable catches) in specific waters, and so forth. These modern treaties also provide plans for the transition away from Indian Act legislation and designate political control over various jurisdictions. Thus, they come close to roughing out the nature of Aboriginal self-government.[4]

The fact remains, however, that many Indian bands throughout the country do not have this type of agreement and are bound by historic treaties. Treaties signed between 1850 and 1921 laid out various actions the Crown would take and the responsibilities the Crown would assume in return for land ceded by specific Indian bands; they also designated particular parcels of land for the sole use of these bands.[5] The historic and contemporary understandings of these treaties are highly contested. While neo-conservatives state that treaties should be narrowly or literally interpreted, most social scientists and Aboriginal peoples argue that the written portion of the treaty must be understood in its broader historical and intercultural context. Venne, for example, has demonstrated that Aboriginal oral tradition and an appreciation of Aboriginal authority to negotiate treaties are essential to a complete understanding of treaty relationships (Venne 1997a, 1997b, 2001). Any reading of the social science literature, however, makes it clear that treaties are not simply transactions about ceding land but rather are complex statements about the political relationship between Aboriginal groups and the Crown.

That said, the amount of land given to Aboriginal peoples varied significantly across the country and over time, as did the particular conditions of individual treaties.[6] After the treaties were signed, the federal government assumed various responsibilities for the protection of these lands — again, the precise nature of federal responsibility can be debated in specific cases. It is clear, however, that in many cases the government failed remarkably in its responsibility to protect reserve lands. For example, errors were often made in the boundaries of the territory originally designated for reserves, and land was also subsequently ceded or sold by the government for any number of reasons. Where the Crown failed to uphold its responsibility, treaties can be reopened under the government's specific claims policies. Where a claim is considered reasonable enough to be heard, bands are provided with funds by the government to do land claims research. If they can prove the federal government has acted improperly, they can be given new land or financial compensation for land lost. It is not uncommon, for example, for bands to receive millions of dollars in these cases, money that can be used for economic development or, in some cases, to purchase additional land.

Nonetheless, even where modern treaties have been negotiated, federal and provincial governments continue to be negligent in their responsibility to ensure that the agreements are policed. Harvey Feit documents how governments have failed in their obligations under the JBNQA and how Cree have engaged in a series of court battles in order to ensure tighter regulation of forestry activities and to obtain a stronger voice in forestry management on Cree territories (Feit 2004a).

Flanagan, Smith, and many mainstream Canadians believe the federal government should be under no obligation to reopen treaties, revisit land claims, or take a liberal interpretation of treaty rights. They believe that, with conquest, the Crown has obtained the right to override any territorial claims and to unilaterally determine reserve boundaries and property rights (Flanagan 2000: 121-22). This view runs contrary to modern legal decisions and to an evolving notion of Aboriginal rights.

RCAP (1996b) argues that treaty rights are a "minimal, partial compensation for the loss of lands and resources since the advent of European colonisation." It views treaties as social, moral, and political compacts between Aboriginal peoples and the Canadian state. But the nature of Aboriginal rights or federal obligation derived from treaties is complex, and to date the federal government has resisted any broad interpretation of them. Indeed, it has commonly enacted policy and legislation only after decisions on Aboriginal rights by the Supreme Court.

Before turning to the issue of resource rights, let us look at one well-known example of treaty interpretation. Treaty Six (1876), signed with the Plains and Wood Cree in the Calgary area,[7] contained this clause, which has become known as the medicine chest clause:

> In the event hereafter of the Indians comprised within this treaty being overtaken by pestilence, or by any general famine, the Queen ... will grant to the Indians assistance necessary and sufficient to relieve [them] from the calamity that shall have befallen them.
>
> And ... That a medicine chest shall be kept at the house of each Indian Agent for the use and benefit of the Indians at the direction of such agent. (Waldram et al. 2006: 174-75)

The medicine chest clause was subsequently interpreted by the Supreme Court to mean that the government must provide all medical supplies free of charge (*Dreaver versus King* 1935). It is for this reason that the federal government, rather than the provinces, assumed responsibility for health care for status Indians[8] before development of universal or socialized medical plans for all Canadians. The precise nature of this treaty clause has never been tested in court, and the federal government continues to deliver medical care to Aboriginal people as a matter of policy, rather than as a treaty right. It pays for the delivery of health services to status Indians, though it has tried to curtail expenditures at every turn. Aboriginal people continue to have poorer access to health services, poorer quality services, and poorer health than Canadians; as a result, it can be argued that an expansive interpretation of the medicine chest clause has not occurred (Waldram, Herring, and Young 2006; Jacklin and Warry 2004a; Warry 1998).

The nature of specific rights is, therefore, contested and has changed over time. Ultimately, it is the responsibility of the federal government to settle claims, taking into consideration the needs of specific First Nations, local history, and regional interests. And it is the responsibility of the courts to determine the contemporary nature of Aboriginal rights on a case-by-case basis. They are concerned with a general notion of Aboriginal rights, so that a decision made with respect to a status Indian in Ontario applies also to status Indians throughout the country and potentially can be extended to non-status and Métis peoples, even though they, or their ancestors, were never signatories to treaties.[9]

Even though Aboriginal rights are recognized in the Constitution, many mainstream Canadians believe they should be restricted. This is most evident in the area of hunting and fishing. Neo-conservatives argue that Aboriginal rights give Aboriginal peoples a natural and unfair advantage over mainstream Canadians as if, despite their obvious poverty and economic disadvantage, they are somehow privileged because they have access to special programs and a land base that other Canadians do not have.

Why should Aboriginal peoples have special rights? One argument holds that the pre- and early-contact use of land and resources was based on needs and practices that no longer exist, so they should not serve as the basis for contemporary claims. Some social scientists argue that property was collectively or communally held prior to European contact and that no real sense of ownership existed. Others claim that there were distinct concepts of individual and communal property and that a sense of private property rights did exist. Certainly, in many Indigenous cultures personal belongings, clothes, tools, and weapons belonged to specific owners. But other items, particularly ceremonial objects, canoes, and even lodges (housing), were better regarded as communal property. In some areas, there were distinct hunting territories, and men assumed the role of guardians, inviting friends or family members to hunt on their territories. Among agriculturalists, as in Iroquoia, land was owned by matrilineal clans (extended families), and entire villages were moved after periods of sustained planting and harvesting so that the land could be left fallow to rejuvenate. Animals, as well as land, needed to be cared for, so that territories were also left to recover from periods of sustained hunting. There was, then, a difference between individual rights to land and broader collective rights to territories or to certain resources — for example, to fish and game — which were often shared collectively by members of a tribe.

Should traditional property rights be interpreted to include the right to sub-surface resources? Some mainstream Canadians say no, because the use of diamonds, oil, or natural gas was unknown to Indigenous peoples. Aboriginal advocates counter that their ancestors did utilize sub-surface minerals and quarried stone for tools and other uses so that the contemporary assertion of sub-surface rights can be seen as a continuance of such traditional practices. In 1993, Inuit signed the Nunavut Land Claims Agreement, the largest such claim in Canadian history: 18,000 Inuit received rights to land and renewable resources, gaining control of about 318,000 square kilometers of surface land rights and another

38,000 square kilometers of sub-surface rights for oil, gas, and minerals. As well, they received a $1.1 billion payment. The 2004 Labrador Inuit land claims recognized the Inuit's exclusive right to carving stone, ownership of 3,950 square kilometers of quarry materials, and a 25 per cent ownership interest in sub-surface resources. We can expect future land claims to press further the Aboriginal right to sub-surface resources.

The nature of resource use has become the focus of Supreme Court interpretation in several cases. Aboriginal rights to hunt and fish on Crown land for personal use have been recognized. The 1990 *Sparrow* decision was the first time the Supreme Court interpreted Aboriginal rights within the context of Section 35 of the Constitution. Ronald Sparrow, a member of the Musqueam band in British Columbia, was charged with fishing with a net longer than that permitted by his subsistence fishing licence and so in contravention to the Fisheries Act. Sparrow did not dispute the facts. Instead, he argued that he was exercising an existing Aboriginal fishing right, that is, a constitutional right protected under Section 35(1). The trial judge and county court held that an Aboriginal right could not be claimed unless that right had been ratified by a treaty or other official document and so convicted him. This ruling was overturned by the British Columbia Court of Appeal whose decision was upheld by the Supreme Court. Further, the Supreme Court used this case as an opportunity to comment on the nature of Aboriginal rights, stating that "existing Aboriginal rights" must be interpreted flexibly in order to allow them to evolve over time. It categorically rejected the idea that Aboriginal rights were "frozen" according to prior treaty language or terms. It also emphasized that Section 35 must be given a generously liberal interpretation in light of its objectives.

Following this case, and with the Supreme Court's directive that Aboriginal groups should be consulted when their fishing rights might be affected, the federal government launched its Aboriginal Fisheries Strategy (AFS) in 1992. The AFS subsequently came under fire and became the focus of additional litigation. The *Sparrow* decision recognized Aboriginal rights to fish for food for personal, social, and ceremonial purposes. This has led to the assertion that Aboriginal peoples have commercial rights to resources because game and fish were traded between tribes as well as between settlers and Indians. While admitting that Aboriginal peoples have the right to hunt and fish for personal use, the neo-conservative argument insists that *Sparrow* has been blatantly misread and poorly interpreted by the government and that there should be no treaty-based right to commercial fishing (see Smith 1996: Chapter 6). It goes on to state that any rights claim to the commercial use of resources is ludicrous because it cannot be traced to pre-contact resource use; that is, commerce is itself a European, not Indigenous, practice.

Some mainstream Canadians fear the potential reinterpretation of treaties. Flanagan, for example, argues that the Supreme Court should continue to hold to the 1988 *Horse* decision, which stated that treaties should be viewed as a form of contract and interpreted as written documents. However, in both treaty negotiations and court testimony, the oral history of Aboriginal peoples and the historic and contemporary cultural context of treaties have been taken into account, so that treaties have come to be more liberally interpreted. The Supreme Court in the 1997 *Delgamuukw* decision stated that oral tradition was not subject to the same standards of assessment for evidence as written testimony but that it should be taken on equal footing to historical documents. Flanagan draws on a paper given by Alexander von Gernet at a Fraser Institute conference following this decision to denigrate the value of Aboriginal oral tradition and to assert the superiority of European historical methods (Flanagan 2000: 157-62; von Gernet 1996, 2000).[10] In contrast, Borrows has offered a compelling analysis of the significance of Aboriginal oral history as an alternative and corrective to European history. In fact, he goes so far as to suggest that Aboriginal legal values can be used to develop new systems of law to better serve not only Aboriginal peoples but also newcomers (Canadians) (Borrows 2001, 2002).

The *Horse* ruling was effectively overturned in the *Marshall* decision, which was exactly the type of liberal interpretation stemming from *Sparrow* that many feared. In 1993, Donald Marshall Junior (who had formerly been falsely imprisoned for murder) was arrested and prosecuted on three charges under the Fisheries Act for selling eels without a commercial licence, fishing without a licence, and fishing during the closed season with illegal nets. Marshall admitted to having caught 463 pounds of eels in a Nova Scotia harbour and to have sold them for $787.10. He believed he was exempt from complying with the fishery regulations because of a 1760-61 treaty right to catch and sell fish. However, he was found guilty by both a provincial lower court and the Nova Scotia Court of Appeal, which denied his treaty right. A 1999 Supreme Court ruling acquitted him on all charges on the grounds that he had a treaty right to secure a "moderate livelihood" by fishing and gathering natural resources. However, it also held that this right was a regulated one, which did not allow him to freely pursue unlimited economic gain. That is, the court decided that the treaty allowed Marshall to have some commercial gain from his harvesting (out of season) of a resource. This decision opens the way for further rights, which need to be tested through other treaties, to commercial harvesting of fish and forest resources.

The *Marshall* decision changed Fisheries and Oceans Canada policies and practices to allow the entrance of Aboriginal fishers into a lucrative economic market. To begin with, the department made a commitment to increase access to the commercial fishery for the 34 Mi'kmaq and Maliseet First Nations affected by the decision, and since 2001, Canada has reached multi-year fisheries agreements with many of them. Although these actions have not been without conflict and protest from non-Aboriginal commercial fishers, the impact on First Nations communities has been exceptionally positive, with an increase in access to commercial fishing and the beginnings of collaboration between the Aboriginal and non-Aboriginal fishing communities. Thus, a treaty right, upheld and interpreted by the Supreme Court, has laid the foundation for federal policies that provide culturally meaningful employment not just for individual fishers but for collective First Nations fishing enterprises. This lays the groundwork for other enterprises, such as the development of fish-processing plants and other related industries.

Mainstream opposition to these decisions occurs because they establish a natural or historic right of access to resources for Aboriginal peoples as members of a collective group and so privilege Aboriginal claims over those of non-Native sport or commercial hunters and fishers (see Koenig 2005: 4, 17). In the extreme view, special rights or policies for Aboriginal peoples are labeled as race-based (Smith 1996: 214, 199-226). For instance, in the aftermath of *Sparrow* and *Marshall*, the federal government looked for innovative ways to ensure equal Aboriginal participation and expansion in the fisheries, especially in British Columbia. However, this meant that Aboriginal fishers could fish at times when non-Aboriginal fishers could not. In 2003, Judge Kitchen of the British Columbia Provincial Court ruled that such Aboriginal fisheries should be disallowed under the Charter of Rights and Freedoms (Mickleburgh 2003: A1; Simpson 2003: A13). In his decision, which resonated with the arguments put forward by Melvin Smith (see Chapter 2), he argued that to have Native-specific fisheries amounted to "racial discrimination" against non-Native fishers and compared the practice to government-sponsored or legislated examples of discrimination such as the Japanese-Canadian internments in the 1940s.[11] Kitchen's decision was greeted with enthusiasm by neo-conservative commentators and has since infiltrated numerous references to Aboriginal issues in arguments concerning the "privilege" they hold because of treaty rights and/or specialized programs.

Kitchen's decision, as Simpson notes, "utterly rejected the premises of the Aboriginal Fisheries Strategy because it expressly favored one group (Aboriginals) over another (non-Aboriginal commercial license holders)." He suggests that "the courts have been, to some extent, all over the map on the issue of Aboriginals' right to fish." In fact, lower provincial courts have often been confused, but the Supreme Court has been consistent in its interpretation. As Simpson notes, the Court has been "a pillar of equality jurisprudence throughout the age of the Charter" (Simpson 2003: A13). In 2006 the Kitchen decision, which was appealed by the federal government, was reversed in a 5-0 decision by the British Columbia Supreme Court which ruled that the method of allocation used in the Aboriginal Fisheries Strategy was not, in fact, raced-based, and that it was in keeping with Aboriginal peoples' constitutionally entrenched rights.[12]

Can "special" treatment be broadly interpreted as "unequal" treatment for entire groups in society? Does a preference for hiring women or visible minorities disadvantage particular men in specific job competitions? Almost certainly yes. But does this form of affirmative action disadvantage all men? It does not, in part because relative merit and qualifications must still be considered and in part because most men are already privileged in most occupations by social attitudes and organizational inclination. However, this comparison, like all comparisons to other minority or human rights, is only partially valid. We must not forget that Aboriginal rights are distinct precisely because they are derived from treaty relations and that they are entrenched in the Constitution.

Certainly, we need to find better ways to ensure collaboration between Native and non-Native fishers. As Simpson notes, the harsh reality is that fish stocks are a limited resource, and both communities want access to them. The federal government is looking for ways to level the playing field; in some parts of the country, it has purchased or bought out commercial licences from non-Natives and has awarded them to Natives (Simpson 2003). We must also recognize, as Koenig has argued, that many non-Native fishers have long family and historical community interests in the fisheries (Koenig 2005). Aboriginal peoples have historically contributed to a mixed or integrated fishing economy, and only since World War II have they lost their competitive advantage — in part because of prior federal policies that are only now being corrected and in part because of changes in the industry, including the cost of technology which made their fishing activities uncompetitive. A stable fisheries policy must engage a range of Native and non-Native interests to commercial, recreational, and ceremonial uses of resources and encourage co-management agreements. In the process, there will need to be recognition of "different but equal" access to fish stocks, which may not fully please special interest groups.

The reinterpretation of treaties over time, both within the context of specific rights to resources and in the reclaiming of land or financial compensation for land, leads some Canadians to comment that Aboriginal people should consider themselves lucky to have special rights to huge tracts of land or that land claims take away land that should be for all Canadians. These views ignore Aboriginal peoples' historic claims and their special cultural and spiritual relationship to the land. Equally misguided is the idea that land claims take land and resources away from mainstream resource companies who fuel a major portion of Canadian economic growth. As a result of the prevalence of these notions, the federal government has proceeded cautiously, taking into account each new Supreme Court interpretation of Aboriginal rights and attempting to integrate this new understanding into modern land claims negotiations. Each new agreement builds upon previous ones and attempts to be a "state of the art" treaty that encapsulates current judicial thinking on Aboriginal rights.

For those First Nations who signed numbered treaties in the historic period, it is only by reopening and renovating treaties that they can hope to gain access to resources that will allow them the opportunity to develop sustainable economies and so end their reliance on welfare and other government subsidies. It is for this reason that the nature of treaties must be open to reinterpretation. The net effect of modern treaty negotiations is to leave different bands with different access to resources, land, and financial capital. As a result, Aboriginal organizations are constantly attempting to level the playing field and reopen treaties. New statements of claim for Alberta Treaties 6 and 7, in order to include natural resources, have been filed (Flanagan 2000: 156), leading to the question of whether Aboriginal treaty rights can or should be extinguished; in other words, in return for the settlement of claims, must Aboriginal peoples abandon (extinguish) their claims to future undefined Aboriginal rights. The concept of extinguishment has been pursued by the federal government for more than three decades and has been resisted, at every turn, by Aboriginal leadership. Some mainstream Canadians argue that Canadians and business interests need closure to the land claims and that claims should not be revisited. Proponents of the "new orthodoxy" such as Michael Asch and Norman Zlotkin, assert that there is nothing in the surrendering of Aboriginal title through historic treaties that implies extinguishment and that Aboriginal peoples only ever intended to share access to lands with newcomers. Flanagan sees this assertion, that treaties imply access to a shared resource, as the "mantra of treaty revisionism" (Flanagan 2000: 153).

Cairns expresses a more moderate view when he notes that RCAP argued "compellingly" that "given their spiritual connection to the land, extinguishment produces a loss of identity" and that, significantly, the "certainty and clarity" around claims that Ottawa demands on behalf of citizens can be accomplished without extinguishment. Because the common view of the claims process is that it is adversarial among separate parties with arguments between "nations" about distinct claims and autonomous power (Cairns 2000: 188-200, especially 193), Asch and Zlotkin argue that what is required is the abandonment of the extinguishment policy, so that a negotiating process of "mutual accommodation" can be entered into whereby Aboriginal communities and the federal government act in a "mutually legitimating partnership among equals" (Asch and Zlotkin 1997: 218, 228). In other words, the conventional wisdom emerging among Aboriginal advocates of the current claims process is that the policy of extinguishment hinders the development of a potentially more meaningful land claims process.

For some, Asch and Zlotkin's position is too extreme (or idealized) because it assumes that Aboriginal peoples seek the same degree of autonomy as they possessed at contact and that original treaties occurred in an international context, that is, in a nation-to-nation context. But this is a misreading. Asch and Zlotkin claim only that Aboriginal peoples, through negotiations, seek to constantly define and redefine their relationships to newcomers:

> In sum, for Aboriginal people, the purpose of negotiations today is the same as it has always been, since the time of the first historic treaty: to shape a relationship between Aboriginal people and the newcomers based upon sharing, to come to an agreement that clarifies not only property rights but also how Aboriginal people and non-Aboriginal people will accommodate each other. (Asch and Zlotkin 1997: 218)

Aboriginal communities enter negotiations with the government with the full knowledge that they are redefining their relationships within the Canadian state. An evolving sense of Aboriginal rights is essential to the development of meaningful negotiations and is the only way that First Nations, who have signed treaties at different times across the country, can achieve relative equality in access to land and resources.

The difference between the neo-conservative and more liberal positions lies in their perception of the relative degree of autonomy sought by Aboriginal communities and how this autonomous position can be resolved with federal objectives and a national sense of identity. The perspectives are as complex as those that seek to parse the difference between Quebec sovereignty, distinct society, strong or weak federalism, and so forth. They are complex and critical to the future of the country. We must hope for a land claims process that allows Aboriginal peoples to speak of their aspirations for self-government and economic self-sufficiency within the context of a renewed federalism. This would allow them to affirm their commitment to Canada while identifying their right to self-determination. Both the federal government and the Aboriginal leadership need to educate the public about how land claims are constructive rather than destructive vehicles for change. Land claims are not about the loss of resources to the mainstream, they are about the investment of land and resources and the development of the economic potential of the Aboriginal population. If claims settlements enhance Aboriginal pride (or, rather, identity) and generate economic development, then they offer the potential for greater participation in the broader economy and in Canadian society generally (Cairns 2000: 200).

A constant refrain from the right is that the courts have become too powerful and are beginning to usurp the power of legislatures. This argument is often made in Charter cases, such as in the gay marriage issue, but also in reference to the interpretation of Aboriginal rights. Provincial and federal supreme courts advance Aboriginal rights as they interpret the relevance of historical treaties and the meaning of Aboriginal rights under the Charter. Most Canadians, in fact, are satisfied with the role of the courts. An Ipsos-Reid Poll held in the wake of the gay marriage controversy found that Canadians like the status quo. The majority (71 per cent) felt that "it should be up to Parliament and Provincial Legislatures, not the Courts, to make laws." This is the status quo: only legislatures can make laws, while courts are placed in the position of ruling on whether the legislation violates or contradicts the Charter and/or constitutionally protected rights. According to the same poll, a majority (54 per cent) believed that judges hold "too much power," but it also clearly demonstrated that mainstream Canadians feel "the courts have an important role to play in interpreting the Constitution." A clear majority (77 per cent) of those polled felt that courts are "within their rights to issue decisions that are based on constitutional grounds that become legally binding."[13]

Despite the poor wording of the survey questions, these results indicate that Canadians prefer what William Thorsell calls a "regulatory" role for the courts. Thorsell, also writing after the gay marriage ruling, draws attention to the difference between "activist" and "regulatory" courts. An activist court is prepared to "rewrite a law" (or, more accurately, interpret a law proactively in a court decision) that it deems unconstitutional, whereas a regulatory court will point out that a law is problematic and gives legislators a time frame in which to amend it. Thorsell argues that regulatory courts give legislators much more opportunity to revisit laws through public debate and to craft new legislation that appeals to the broad spectrum of Canadians (Thorsell 2003b: A13).

Is true equality the same as total equality under the law? A view of civil society that accepts — and respects — multiple value and belief systems should recognize that "equal but different" solutions may sacrifice equality under the letter of the law in order to achieve tolerance and respect for another culture's beliefs. Writing for the *Globe and Mail* on the "New Canada," Matthew Mendelsohn comments that there are a number of things policy-makers should take away from our understanding of the new generation of young adult Canadians. They are more tolerant of the role of the Supreme Court and trust its judgement more than legislatures. As Mendelsohn notes, the high courts have taken the Charter seriously and in the process have struck important decisions on same sex marriage, the legalization of marijuana for medical use, doctor-assisted suicide, stem cell research, and Aboriginal rights (Mendelsohn 2003: A13). In spite of the loud disclaimers of the right wing, these decisions reflect the values of a young generation of Canadians.

The relative importance of the courts and legislatures is subject to ongoing debate. In our recent history, the courts arguably have set the moral tone for much public policy and have forced the hands of politicians who wish to move slowly on issues that appear volatile to religious and conservative voters. Yet, in every case, we have seen Canadians react with nonchalance and accept the new status quo. We can hope that in the future, within the next generation, these decisions will produce mainstream attitudes that are not simply tolerant of diversity but that embrace difference.

The future role of the Supreme Court as arbitrator of difficult questions concerning Aboriginal rights seems certain. We can expect court challenges to be a continuing if not permanent feature of the political landscape. Specific rulings are shaped by treaty arrangements, a history of federal legislation and policy implementation, and the complex interplay of documentary and oral history. What the courts have done over the past two decades of Charter interpretations is to argue consistently for a liberal and inclusive view of Aboriginal rights and to recognize that the rights of collectives (minorities and Aboriginal peoples) can be rationalized in relation to individual rights. To date, the Supreme Court's interpretation of Aboriginal rights has shared much in common with the vision put forward by RCAP: Aboriginal rights must be seen as organic and evolving over time so that Aboriginal peoples' historic sacrifice of land is recognized and their special status affirmed.[14]

NOTES

1 See <http://www.laws.justice.gc.ca/en/const/annex_e.html#guarantee>.

2 The literature on treaties is complex, as is the modern interpretation of them by the courts. For an excellent introduction to the topic by Aboriginal and non-Aboriginal social scientists, the reader should consult Asch 1997.

3 Flanagan 2000: 134-35; see also 151-53, passim. I say "in theory" because Flanagan's starting point is the 1969 Vienna Convention on the Law of Treaties, which, of course, does not consider the history of settler societies or the political rights of Indigenous peoples as separate political entities.

4 For a description of comprehensive and special claims policies, go to <http://www.ainc-inac. gc.ca/pr/pub/ywtk/index_e.html#lc>.

5 In what is now central Ontario, the Robinson-Huron and the Robinson-Superior treaties were signed in 1850. Treaties were then numbered, Treaty 1 through 11, which was signed in 1921 in the Dene's western sub-Artic region of the Northwest Territories. The final treaty of the historic period, the William Treaty, was signed in 1923, again in East-Central Ontario.

6 Specifically the numbered treaties, which were signed.

7 Signed at Fort Carlton and Fort Pitt; see <http://www.ainc-inac.gc.ca/pr/trts/trty6/trty6a_e. html>.

8 The role of the provinces in Aboriginal health is complex. For the most part non-status Aboriginal people living off reserve are treated as regular citizens under provincial health plans. But the federal government reimburses provinces for prescription drugs, hospital care, and other forms of care for status Indians.

9 This statement drastically oversimplifies the complexity of these issues. In specific circumstances, for example in the *Corbiere* decision, the court has had to distinguish between status and non-sta-

tus voting rights. The rights of Métis and non-status Indians have, at least to date, been restricted in comparison to those of status Indians.

10 The Fraser Institute refers to von Gernet as Professor of Anthropology, University of Toronto at Mississauga. In fact, von Gernet is an adjunct professor who has been employed under contract by the Department of Indian Affairs and Northern Development and has testified on behalf of the government in numerous native rights/land claims court cases. See <http://ocap.ca/node/112>.

11 In fact, the First Nations-specific "pilot" fisheries on the Fraser River had been designated for a limited number of bands and were opposed by non-Native *and* Native commercial ocean fishers who argue that the Fraser should be open to all fishers or under the same conservation regime as ocean fisheries.

12 For details on the decision see <http://72.14.205.104/search?q=cache:ILPSWwrZYtUJ:www. fns.bc.ca/pdf/PR_reBCCADecision_KappJune06.pdf+Judge+Kitchen%27s+ decision+and+the+Supreme+Court&hl=en&gl=ca&ct=clnk&cd=2>.

13 The poll was reported by the *Globe and Mail* under the misleading headline "Public against judges making laws." Letters to the editors the following day pointed out that the headline revealed the *Globe*'s editorial agenda, as the poll actually supported the status quo. See Sallot 2003.

14 The political scientist Will Kymlicka (1995) notes that some Aboriginal leaders reject the notion that their First Nations should be subject to the Charter or that the European judges on the Supreme Court can render decisions that are culturally appropriate. This is, strictly speaking, logical given a philosophy of an inherent right to self-government. In practice, however, this is an extremist position, and we can expect Aboriginal leaders to follow Supreme Court decisions and to agree that First Nations citizens be subject to the Charter or to similar human rights standards.

CHAPTER 9 Sustainable Economic Development

The neo-conservative right suggests that Aboriginal economic practices are unsuited to the contemporary economy. As we have seen (Chapter 5), such views leave little room for an understanding of Aboriginal practices which, while distinct, have been adapted to fit the contemporary marketplace. My focus in this chapter is on reserve-based economies rather than urban businesses. We know next to nothing about the values and practices of Aboriginal entrepreneurs, who have not been the subject of much research or debate, although nearly 86 per cent of 27,195 self-employed Aboriginal people reside off reserve, with over 61 per cent in urban centres. Urban Aboriginal entrepreneurship needs to be more carefully researched, for it is quite likely that it is unique, incorporating collective goals and traditional values. To assume, as Kay and others do, that Aboriginal culture makes the promotion of economic development impossible is to mischaracterize and stereotype (Kay 2001).[1] Aboriginal peoples do not wish to transfer traditional economic practices from the trapline to the boardroom. But Aboriginal entrepreneurs may wish to bring Aboriginal values about decision-making, consensus-building, and economic collaboration or cooperation with them into their businesses. Empirical evidence is needed to demonstrate this.

Is there hope that First Nations can, over the long term, develop sustainable reserve-based economies?[2] The neo-conservative right answers a resounding "no," while Aboriginal peoples themselves, as well as many researchers who have studied both traditional economic activities and modern economic enterprises, answer a cautious and optimistic "yes." The diversity of Aboriginal communities means that there must be multiple paths to economic well-being and that no single solution is right for specific individuals or First Nations. A small percentage of Aboriginal entrepreneurs, about 14 per cent, currently reside on reserve. A considerable number of men work off reserve, sometimes seasonally, in forestry or other resource industries. Many workers commute to nearby towns and cities. First Nations are significant employers in health and social services, housing and construction, and service industries. And since the 1990s, with access to Aboriginal-specific development funds, First Nations are pursuing a range of collective businesses in order to address unemployment and foster economic growth. Even here, however, it is important to realize that their resources vary dramatically across the country — some bands, such as the Cree of Quebec and Nisga'a of British Columbia, have comprehensive claims (modern treaties) and so have access to huge territories with their forest and mineral resources. Some Western bands have access to oil and gas reserves. However, many reserves, particularly those in remote locations, are small and have few resources and extremely limited opportunities for economic growth. For these communities, the only hope is for treaty renovation that would expand land bases, new agreements to provide employment in existing resource industries, and so forth (Asch and Zlotkin 1997).

In order to gain a realistic perspective on economic development, we must again confront the stereotypes that suggest Aboriginal culture is incapable of adapting to the modern economy. One such stereotype is that Aboriginal peoples are welfare dependent and a drain on taxpayers' resources. Some mainstream Canadians are apt to blame the victim by suggesting that Aboriginal peoples lack self-reliance and wish to remain dependent on government hand-outs. John Cummins, the Conservative (and former Alliance Party) Member of Parliament, in a submission to the Select Standing Committee on Aboriginal Affairs, closely parallels arguments made by Smith (Chapter 2). He airs one of the central tenets of the assimilation argument: that the blame for Aboriginal underdevelopment lies squarely on the federal government's intervention into reserve life and the creation of a "cradle-to-grave" welfare system in Aboriginal communities, "a system of special benefits and rights that has sapped the aboriginal community of its life." He cites, among others, the historian James McDonald, who demonstrated that Aboriginal peoples, while engaging in some traditional economic activities, participated in major industries in the nineteenth century and were critical to the overall economic vitality of British Columbia. From this, Cummins claims that Aboriginal peoples were integrated in the business economies of the nineteenth century, but that federal welfare policies of the last century created a culture of dependency on reserves. He suggests that Aboriginal participation in fishing and other resource industries should be welcomed but in no way should Aboriginal peoples receive special protections or privileges to assist them in entering this industry on a level playing field. Aboriginal underdevelopment can be traced to "a mood developed in the middle part of the last century that aboriginals needed protecting, needed special assistance, that they could not and should not be asked to face the hardship and rigors of the rough and tumble industrial society that BC was becoming" (Cummins 2001).

Certainly, government policies of the last two centuries marginalized Aboriginal reserves and so created the conditions for welfare and dependency on state resources. But Cummins fails to see access to resources as an Aboriginal right and implies that Aboriginal peoples are ill-equipped to compete economically, that they are somehow taking a free ride on the Canadian taxpayer. He overlooks the fact that Aboriginal peoples have proven themselves capable in a wide range of economic activities — as farmers, fishers, cannery workers, ranch owners, and so on — a point made clearly by RCAP.[3] RCAP demonstrates, for example, that there is historical evidence that between 1930 and 1960 Aboriginal people were successfully making the transition from a traditional to a modern economy before dislocation and dispossession created dependency in various parts of the country.[4] This economic marginalization was exacerbated and entrenched by the Great Depression of the 1930s and by federal and provincial policies, which were adopted in response to economic distress and which disadvantaged Aboriginal peoples.

Cummins falsely links Aboriginal rights and dependency, blaming the victim for the economic marginalization that is the product of colonial policy. The implication here, once again, is that Aboriginal peoples need to regain the independence and self-reliance they once had and that this can only be accomplished by removing any protections or their special rights so that they may compete freely in the marketplace. Certainly, there are many Aboriginal people who move to the city to seek better employment opportunities, but there are also many who wish to remain on reserve (and have the right to live there) and who are dedicated to reserve-based economic development.

Numerous federal policies in both the historic and contemporary periods have economically disadvantaged Aboriginal peoples. For example, under the Indian Act, the Crown holds reserve land in trust. As a result, individual economic participation in the mainstream economy is difficult because, until very recently, it was next to impossible for individuals to sell land or to use their property as collateral to obtain loans. Until the 1990s when Aboriginal business and development banks were established, Aboriginal people could not leverage small business loans or other start-up funds because they had no collateral to offer to banks.

The neo-conservative position ignores the government's attempts to spark entrepreneurship through development loans, insisting that a sense of personal property and individual ownership is critical to entrepreneurship and economic competition. This argument is designed to reject traditional, cooperative, or communal economic activities as socialistic. American economists Terry Anderson (1995)[5] and Bruce Benson (1992) argue that Aboriginal property rights extend from traditional belief systems and that, as a result, contemporary economic practices can be based on past traditions. However, most neo-conservatives believe that any sense of private property was rare among hunters and gatherers and that only the Canadian Indian tribes on the West Coast had any real system of property values.[6] Thus, for Aboriginal people to succeed, they must abandon any cooperative economic activity and enter the free market to compete with mainstream Canadians. And they must compete on Western terms, accepting that private property is a mark of civilization. Then, the neo-conservative argument continues, any economic development based on such a system is a proof of abandonment of traditional ways and of integration into the mainstream (Flanagan 2000: 118).

Not surprisingly, a recent study by Flanagan for the Fraser Institute, a right-wing think tank, encourages the adoption of private ownership as a partial solution to Aboriginal underdevelopment. It points out that private ownership is possible under recent federal changes to land management policies. Private allotments already exist on many reserves (on a very small scale). In certain cases — for example, the Six Nations reserve — the majority of land is held by individuals in farm allotments. The study encourages the formation of trusts to monitor the sale and classification of land (Flanagan and Alcantara 2002). Although some experimentation and a mixture of land use practices that are capable of responding to the circumstances of particular reserves and that are controlled and planned by Aboriginal peoples are laudable aims, we must reject the neo-conservative assumptions on which they are based — that collective ownership somehow dampens responsibility, that private wealth is the key to entrepreneurship, and that collective economic activities are equivalent to socialism or communism. First Nations have collective property rights to reserves totaling more than 2.7 million hectares, and this land base is growing as Aboriginal and treaty claims are settled.[7] What is insidious in neo-conservative attitudes about property, and what Aboriginal critics object to, is the suggestion that private ownership encourages a responsibility for ones' property that, through the work ethic, will lead Aboriginal people out of poverty because of their new interest in personal wealth.

The basic misrepresentation here is that Aboriginal cultural values around sharing, egalitarianism, and economic cooperation are socialistic and that collective ownership smacks of socialism and prevents the development of entrepreneurialism. Neo-conservatives portray reserve-based economies as backward, collectivist (communistic), and unsustainable without heavy government subsidies. Right-wing commentators stereotype reserves as "islands of communism," thereby associating forms of Aboriginal collective ownership with failed soviet-style management. Kay cites the well-known neo-conservative writer Kenneth Minogue: "The idea of 'Aboriginal economies' is also preposterous ... Basically, what is being advocated is [North Korean-style] autarky. It's a sort of socialist fantasy — like the Israeli Kibbutzim or the kolkhozes in the Soviet Union. Except, in this case, the fantasy is based on the noble savage myth instead of socialism" (Kay 2001).

To compare soviet-style economies with the tribal, land-based cultures of Aboriginal communities is to defy logic and standards of social science research. It creates a bogus view of Aboriginal economic culture and is designed to taint deeply rooted Aboriginal notions of land, economy, and sustainability with the broad brush of communism. Not only does such a comparison reveal an ignorance of Aboriginal cultural values, it imputes a lack of self-sufficiency to members of an entire culture. The fact is that the values associated with hunting, fishing, and trapping have been proven to promote self-sufficiency and decreased reliance on government subsidies. Many studies have shown that wildlife harvesting greatly decreases the reliance of Aboriginal peoples on government welfare. Berkes and other researchers have clearly demonstrated that hunting and trapping provides literally millions of dollars in food and additional income to northern communities (Berkes *et al.* 1994; Cummins 2004: 110-25). This represents a significant portion of First Nations income and provides food that otherwise would need to be imported.

In all of this there is the suggestion that traditional land use practices are fixed in time, that Aboriginal economies are somehow separate and at odds with mainstream economic interests, or that Aboriginal values are somehow antiquated. These assumptions allow neo-conservatives to set up a false dichotomy between land-based and modern economic activities. Kay suggests that any sign of interest in material wealth is proof that Aboriginal peoples have rejected their traditional cultural values. But both on and off reserve, Aboriginal peoples seek culturally meaningful employment, an economic livelihood that allows them to be self-sufficient, and sustainable economic practices that show respect for human and animal life and the environment.[8] Indeed, as we will see, it is because Aboriginal leaders have so steadfastly privileged the protection of the environment over mainstream development interests that they are so feared by neo-conservative commentators.

Researchers who have studied remote and northern First Nations economies present a picture of Aboriginal peoples who make conscious choices to live on reserve in order to have access to the land and to the animals with whom they sustain important spiritual relations.[9] These northern mixed economies are integrated into wider regional economies as the wealth of Aboriginal communities partially supports non-Aboriginal businesses off reserve. Moreover, land-based economic activities, whether by full-time or recreational hunters, provide opportunities for Aboriginal peoples to sustain their spiritual relationship to the environment. The James Bay Agreement, for example, grants Cree hunters an Income Security Program that allows them to receive income supplements when they are engaged in traditional pursuits. For over three decades, Feit has documented how the Quebec Cree continue to sustain relationships with the animals they hunt and how the fight for the survival of this lifestyle is integral to their resistance to the development and destruction wrought by large-scale hydro development and resource industries (Feit 2004a, 2004b).

RCAP spends an entire volume on issues of land, resources, and economic development.[10] It begins by noting that colonial processes, including the Indian Act, are responsible for the current marginalization and continuing poverty faced by Aboriginal reserve populations. This marginalization occurred as the result of government failure to adhere to the terms of treaties and to protect Indian lands over time. RCAP emphasizes the need to develop reserve-based economies that are capable of sustaining self-government. These economies might be comprised of groups of reserves or Aboriginal territories obtained through land claims or other resource-sharing agreements, but they would have sufficient resources — including, for example, timber and mineral rights — so that Aboriginal-controlled and -operated businesses could develop.[11] RCAP also advocates the development of collective enterprises and greater co-management of resource industries, although it acknowledges that this type of economic development can occur only if there is negotiation of adequate land claims and the renovation of existing claims where reserves currently lack insufficient access to land and resources.

Flanagan acknowledges that there are some positive aspects to RCAP's economic recommendations: they are based on capitalist notions of economic competition and entrepreneurship and aim to eliminate, through long-term investment and land claims, Aboriginal welfare dependency. He notes, significantly, that the main reason this economic vision is doomed to failure is because the required $2 billion per year that RCAP suggests should be initially invested in economic strategies will not be forthcoming (Flanagan 2000: 183-84; see also Scott 2004: 307). On this point, experts from the left and right can agree: without significant, long-term economic investment, sustainable economic development will not be achieved, particularly for those First Nations that do not currently have access to resources gained through comprehensive claims.

Flanagan also notes that land and resource wealth does not necessarily automatically eliminate dependency or "attendant social pathologies." For instance, on the Morley and Hobbema reserves in Alberta oil and gas royalties have led some families to wealthy lifestyles, but welfare dependency, ill health, and other social problems remain for many residents (Flanagan 2000: 184). This contradiction is true and points to the fact that access to oil revenues is not always equally shared and that royalties or investment income are only meaningful if they can be used to develop business and industries that can employ community members. Short-term economic gains do not necessarily translate into sustainable economies. This realization also accounts for why RCAP argues that economic development must be accompanied by investments in health and cultural programs, because wealth alone will not resolve the intergenerational causes of many social problems like addictions or family violence.

The RCAP proposals for economic development are at times naïve, isolationist, and idealistic. Flanagan, for example, labels the RCAP approach "economic nationalism" and suggests that it accepts the "discredited idea" of import substitution — the idea that reserves lose economic resources to external business and must develop sufficient levels of businesses so that they can capture and contain dollars that come on to reserve through transfer payments. It is clear that any attempt at economic development that fails to see reserves as part of regional and national economies is doomed to failure.

Some neo-conservative commentators suggest that the RCAP recommendations are so severely flawed that they would lead to increased unemployment and welfare dependency (Flanagan 2000: 184-85). However, with the development of progressive claims policies and the creation of cooperative or co-managed resource agreements, economic development can occur on the majority of reserves. The quickest way to begin this economic development is to sign self-government agreements to allow self-defined collectivities of First Nations to manage and share resources. The government is now actively pursuing regional economic development strategies across the country.[12] Aboriginal economic development will require such collective efforts by groups of First Nations in concert with provincial governments, Aboriginal development corporations, and non-Native business and resource industries (see Scott 2004: 308-10). The realization of self-government offers sufficient reward to Aboriginal communities to encourage the creation of these necessary regional economic systems.

Another common critique of Aboriginal peoples points to corruption or financial mismanagement by band councils. While instances of financial mismanagement certainly occur (see Chapter 11), a separation of political powers from collective economic enterprises will address the problem. This is already happening. Neo-conservative critics also pick on the failure of Aboriginal enterprises that are funded or subsidized by federal money, such as the Canadian Aboriginal Economic Development Strategy, which provided loans and financing for commercial enterprises and joint ventures. Auditor general reports tend to support these accusations by detailing serious failures in Aboriginal businesses and little return on government investment. Although it is never a good idea to throw good money after bad, Aboriginal enterprises must be supported in the developmental period and given the opportunity to innovate and experiment in order for long-term economic development to occur. It is natural to expect a degree of failure, particularly given the limited resources available to Aboriginal communities and the difficulties associated with opening new markets.

Usually these failures are spoken of in isolation, as a problem of Aboriginal business or of Aboriginal ability, rather than as a feature of regular business practice. In Canada roughly 150,000 businesses fail every year, but when Aboriginal businesses fail, it is taken as a sign of incompetence or as evidence that they do not have the skills to compete in the marketplace.[13] And, although Aboriginal economic development is heavily subsidized by the government, there is a wide range of private mainstream enterprises that the government routinely subsidizes and supports to the tune of close to $4 billion annually. Aboriginal economic failures are normalized when placed alongside the routine failures and bankruptcies of mainstream companies but are made to seem exceptional when embedded in a critique of special rights.

The small size of reserves and the lack of access to mineral or forest resources are problems that must be overcome. Likewise, investment is needed in education, economic management, and other technical skills. But there are positive signs of economic development: the increased numbers of Aboriginal-owned small businesses, the improvements in transparency in First Nations governments, the efforts of Aboriginal development banks, and much more. These gains are often ignored by the media and neo-conservative critics, who fail to account for the time and effort needed for capacity building in order to end dependency — a process that can take decades, not years. As a result, Canadians are often oblivious to the signs that Aboriginal underdevelopment is slowly being addressed in many, if not all, First Nations.

The development of major resource industries is capital intensive. Although First Nations may sign partnership agreements with existing national or multinational companies to allow access to land or resources, it is unlikely that they will be able to compete on their own with major resource industries. Aboriginal employment in resource industries is easily encouraged through federal and provincial economic development policies. For example, the agreement between Inco Limited and the Province of Newfoundland and Labrador for the mining lease at Voisey's Bay includes provisions for employment and revenue-sharing with the Labrador Inuit Association and the Innu Nation. The project involves the development of the nickel deposit as well as construction of a hydrometallurgical processing plant on the Avalon Peninsula and includes training and development for Aboriginal people in mining-related jobs, employment of Aboriginal workers, and community consultations and partnerships concerning the use and stewardship of lands.[14] Such arrangements, even if falling short of true co-management relationships, are groundbreaking in protecting the environment while ensuring Aboriginal participation in major industries.

Aboriginal peoples have resisted development whenever it potentially endangers their land and way of life. In the 1970s and 1980s Aboriginal peoples in Quebec and the Northwest Territories opposed (along with environmental groups) major hydro or oil pipeline projects. For this reason, they are often portrayed by neo-conservatives as hindering mainstream economic interests. Flanagan, for example, lists many examples of Aboriginal opposition to small and large development projects, including the Cree opposition to the Great Whale hydroelectric development, that have cost taxpayers money or impacted mainstream business interests (2001: 1-3). Flanagan's other examples of the cost of "aboriginal orthodoxy" include the government's expenditures on RCAP and the Berger Inquiry (which led to a moratorium on the Mackenzie Valley pipeline), as well as the cost of the Oka confrontation. Thus, he sees both specific bands and

Aboriginal peoples in general as a liability to mainstream business interests and a threat to the economic well-being of the country.

A close reading of development literature refutes this view. A recent collection edited by Mario Blaser, Harvey Feit, and Glenn McRae, aptly named *In The Way Of Development* (2004), carefully illustrates Aboriginal understandings about sustainable economic development and traditional forms of environmental knowledge that are at the heart of collective approaches to economy. The numerous studies in this collection show how Indigenous leadership and communities in Canada, the United States, and South America have acted in concert with non-governmental organizations and governments to confront the growing influence of transnational corporations and to protect their traditional territories. These analyses make clear that, however strategically Indigenous peoples have acted, their aim has always been to assert their own values about economy and the environment and, increasingly, to participate in development projects — but on their own terms. RCAP, too, recognizes the interest of Aboriginal communities in sharing in meaningful and culturally appropriate forms of development.

Several of the studies in *In The Way Of Development* focus on the James Bay Cree's long struggle with Quebec Hydro over the development of dams in the region as a way of illustrating how Aboriginal peoples oppose the mainstream corporate mentality that pursues development even when it comes with a heavy cost to the wider environment. For Aboriginal peoples, the price of development is too high when it jeopardizes the health of humans, animals, and the land. They want sustainable development that can provide not only income and security for Aboriginal families but the long-term health of animal populations.

Several analysts contrast the economic goals of development projects with the life projects of Indigenous communities.[15] Put simply, they show how Indigenous ambitions are tied to their knowledge of place and environment and how, despite their willingness to share land and resources, Indigenous peoples are portrayed by corporations and government as being backward and therefore as obstacles to modernization, development, and state progress (Blaser 2004: 26-28). Quite the contrary, because their identity and culture is tied to the land, Indigenous peoples have fought to ensure that any development that occurs does not threaten the continuation of their culture or obscure the promise of their children's future.

In the remote north, multinational corporations have little civic or moral check on their actions. Many are consumed with the extraction of mineral and other resources and bent on maximizing their profit at every turn. Aboriginal communities, non-Aboriginal northerners, and to a lesser extent, environmental lobbyists, have drawn public attention to the plunder of northern lands and have, with constant resistance, forced corporations to adopt practices that are less harmful to northern environments and populations. Writing of his role as a political strategist for the Cree, Brian Craik shows how successful opposition to development projects requires Native peoples to form alliances with non-Native groups, develop astute public relations strategies, consult broadly with communities, and convince the public that there are real alternatives (such as energy conservation) to existing practices (Craik 2004: 166-85). In Mathew Coon Come's words, Indigenous peoples are often the "environmental and economic conscience" that governments or business do not have (Coon Come 2004: 159).[16] They have acted to protect the northern environment and to sustain their rights to land and to harvesting activities at great cost to both human and environmental health. Dawn Martin-Hill, a Mohawk scholar, documents the cost and suffering that the Lubicon Cree in Alberta, and Lubicon women in particular, have experienced as part of their longstanding fight to have their land claim recognized and to oppose the oil and forestry industries' destruction of their territories (Martin-Hill 2004). What is apparent in this instance, and in many others, is how Aboriginal peoples, despite the loss of life and constant attacks on their cultural existence, continue to hold fast to ethical values and actions aimed at sustaining their community and protecting the environment.

So different are Indigenous conceptions of land, resources, and the environment that Deborah McGregor, an Anishnabek writer from Whitefish River First Nation, suggests they transcend even the notion of sustainable development. She notes that there is no such concept in Aboriginal languages and stresses that traditional environmental knowledge (TEK) concerns itself with how humans can and must give back to the environment. She notes however, that TEK, when acknowledged and used in mainstream environmental and resource management, is often co-opted by the dominant society interests. That is, "because of the existing power structure, integration has translated into 'assimiliation' of Aboriginal TEK into dominant regimes" (McGregor 2004: 82-84). Yet, she remains hopeful that the sharing of TEK by Aboriginal peoples and the combination of Indigenous and Western environmental science hold the promise of building co-management and other relationships between Aboriginal peoples, industry, and government.

In another article in *In The Way Of Development*, Colin Scott, an anthropologist at McGill University, carefully examines the work of Flanagan and other neo-conservatives to illustrate how their ideas are rooted in European notions of civilization, progress, and private property (Scott 2004; see also Blaser *et al.* 2004: 19). Scott believes that Flanagan reasonably summarizes many of the views of Aboriginal and non-Aboriginal intellectuals in his description of the new (Aboriginal) orthodoxy but that he overstates the extent to which these tenets have penetrated state policy. While Flanagan is clearly fearful that the RCAP recommendations might be accepted over time, Scott notes that to this point those concerning ownership and control over land and resources have been ignored; for example, the rights of First Nations, even where recognized, have been curtailed by federal and provincial governments who insist on having veto power in co-management regimes.

Although neo-conservatives fear the implementation of RCAP development recommendations and warn of doom (increased unemployment, welfare dependency, and poverty) should they be implemented, Scott is cautiously optimistic about the prospects of sustainable Aboriginal economies. Although state and corporate control over northern lands has produced mainstream wealth along with Aboriginal poverty and marginalization, it is too early to tell whether Aboriginal self-government and control over autonomous territories will be able to correct this historical process, which has been accepted by mainstream Canadians as an "historically inevitable course of evolutionary progress." Scott is cautious in his reading of the evidence of Aboriginal economic development and unwilling to predict the future. He sees economic development, sustainability, and the building of new northern regional economies as an experimental and emerging process involving Native and non-Native communities, First Nations, and provincial and federal governments. He suggests that, based on the experience of the James Bay Cree, qualitative and quantitative studies suggest significant lifestyle improvements for those in control of their land and resources when compared to other Aboriginal communities who have not had access to comprehensive claims (Scott 2004: 307-08).

This pragmatic view of Aboriginal economic development emphasizes the need for mixed regional economies adapted to the particular historic, cultural, and economic circumstances of both Native and non-Native communities. The economic future seems brightest for communities that have signed modern treaties, such as those found among the James Bay Cree or Nisga'a. It seems more challenging for those smaller communities with limited land bases and resources. However, even in the absence of treaty renovation, smaller communities continue to experiment with a range of collective enterprises — wind farms, recycling ventures, ecotourism projects — that provide sustainable approaches to economy.

Like the Cree leader Mathew Coon Come, Stephen Kakfwi has been involved in the long-term fight for sustainable development. Now in his fifties, the Dene leader and premier of the Northwest Territories was first involved at the age of 23 in the fight against the building of the MacKenzie Valley pipeline (Campbell 2003). That resistance movement, which brought together a coalition of environmental groups and Aboriginal peoples, led to the Berger Inquiry and a ten-year moratorium on development. In fact, the moratorium lasted more than 20 years until 2000, when the Dene themselves proposed a new pipeline. In the interim, much of the political landscape changed. In the 1970s, the paternalism of Ottawa and multinational corporations lay behind the ill-conceived, environmentally unsound pipeline proposal that would have done little or nothing for the Dene's economic well-being. The moratorium allowed land claims to be settled and the

Dene to obtain increased powers to govern their territory. Aboriginal leaders came to participate in and control the territorial government assembly. Along with this increased political capacity came a voice for sustainable development.

Today, the Dene, with their claims to land and distinct governance recognized, are in a position to move forward on a natural gas pipeline which, with the aid of new technology, is more environmentally sustainable and which guarantees economic participation and a share in decision-making for the Dene people. As a *Globe and Mail* editorial noted, a key concession in the deal was the "creation of a large network of interconnected protected areas where no development will occur."[17] The pipeline development, with a projected value by TransCanada Corp of $5 billion, gives these Aboriginal people, through the formation of the Inuvik-based Aboriginal Pipeline Group, a one-third share and status as a full-fledged partner in the joint venture. The project holds the long-term potential for Aboriginal training and a share in over 2,300 jobs. These same principles of equal participation and sustainability have been applied in the development of the Northwest Territory's other major development initiative, the creation of a diamond industry, which has produced over $1 billion in rough-cut diamonds and which has already carved out a unique brand in international fashion circles (Jang 2003). In short, Aboriginal peoples have forced government and business to acknowledge their presence and their values. Although the process of development was delayed, there is now the opportunity for sustainable economic practices that enhance, rather than impede, Canada's economic growth.

Aboriginal resistance to mainstream economic development, particularly in the remote north, has led over time to better development — projects that remain profitable, limit environmental damage, train and employ Aboriginal workers, and build relationships between Aboriginal community leaders and international corporations. Aboriginal peoples are not opposed to development *per se*; they are opposed to development at any cost.

Is the promise of sustainable economic development reasonable, or is it a figment of the imagination of well-meaning but economically naïve do-gooders and left-leaning academics? Scott's cautious appraisal gives the clearest signal that Canadians should remain hopeful that a significant number of Aboriginal people can remain on the land and continue traditional land-based economic activities while participating as employees, entrepreneurs, and decision-makers in modern resource-based industries. What little truth exists in neo-conservative arguments can be summed up in this way: many Aboriginal reserves are very small and, given current policies and economic practices, lack sufficient resources to sustain economic development. But progress is being made through comprehensive claims, the signing of co-management and other agreements with resource industries, and the promotion of Aboriginal-specific start-up funds for small and medium businesses. Much more needs to be done, including the development of policies to enhance treaty renovation. However, there is little doubt that a future generation of Canadians will one day thank the current Aboriginal leadership for leading them to more sustainable environmental and economic practices.

NOTES

1   Kay contrasts contemporary economic practices with the values or behaviours of hunting and gathering societies in order to suggest that there is an "incompatibility between economic integration and cultural autonomy." He is puzzled by the fact that the Aboriginal experts he interviewed were "surprised or mildly offended" when he raised this line of thought.

2   For more information on urban Aboriginals, see the Aboriginal Business portal and the Statistics Canada 2004 Aboriginal Entrepreneurs Survey available at <http://strategis.ic.gc.ca/epic/inter net/inabc-eac.nsf/en/ab00335ehtml#factsheets>.

3   I would like to thank the anonymous reviewer of this book for this point.

4   See RCAP 1996b, "Economic Development" (RCAP Vol. 2: *Restructuring the Relationship*) Chapter 5.

5   Anderson is Executive Director of the Property and Environment Research Center, which advocates "free market environmentalism." See Anderson and Hill 2004; also see Flanagan 2000: 114.

6   See, for example, Flanagan's characterization of property rights in different early contact societies. In West Coast societies where a ceremonial complex known as the "potlatch" occurred, individual chiefs could accumulate wealth and manipulate it on behalf of the collectivity. But anthropologists have demonstrated that these and other economic systems underwent a period of rapid inflation and expansion in the early contact period, as a result of European and Russian trade. There seems little doubt that beliefs about property may have changed significantly at that time.

7   See the Turtle Island News discussion in response to the publication of the Flanagan and Alcantara report <http://www.turtleisland.org/discussion/viewtopic.php?p=7>.

8   Admittedly, in generalizing this way I am in danger of feeding the equally powerful stereotype of Aboriginal peoples as "natural" environmentalists. Of course Aboriginal people would like to have the same standard of living (and opportunity and health care, etc.), as mainstream Canadians. However, many Aboriginal leaders would sacrifice material wealth for the health of their people, community, and environment. Ideas of economic and environmental sustainability are deeply entrenched in the Aboriginal worldview.

9   Anthropologists have long studied Aboriginal peoples' relationship to animals, their hunting strategies, and the continuing importance of hunting and trapping for northern economies. A host of studies, all of which are ignored by conservatives, could be cited here. In addition to the works cited in the text, the reader might begin with Tanner 1979, Brody 1981, Wenzel 1991, Feit 2004b, and Blaser *et al.* 2004.

10 See RCAP 1996b, Vol. 2: *Restructuring the Relationship, Part One and Two*; and Vol. 5: *Renewal, A Twenty Year Commitment*, Section 2: "Economic Disparities, Government Expenditures and the Cost of the Status Quo."

11 RCAP 1996e, Vol. 5: especially, 826-28 and 970-92.

12 See for example the description of regional economic development programs by Indian Northern Affairs <http://www.ainc-inac.gc.ca/ps/nap/abo/abo13/11abo13_e.html> and <http://www.ainc-inac.gc.ca/ps/nap/circ/cirli_e.html>.

13 See the Industry Canada website at <http://strategis.ic.gc.ca/epic/internet/insbrp-rppe.nsf/en/rd01000e.html>.

14 Although it is easy to be skeptical about corporations' need for good public relations with respect to their approach to Aboriginal communities, these efforts must be viewed as groundbreaking in some ways; see the Inco website at <http://www.inco.com/development/community/partnerships/Aboriginal/default.aspx> and their "Social Responsibility Report" at <http://www.inco.com/development/reports/social/2004/default.asp>.

15 The term "life project" was apparently first used by Bruno Barras, a leader of the Yshiro-Ebitoso people of the Paraguayan Chaco, and has subsequently been adopted more widely; see Barras 2004: 47.

16 Coon Come is a former Mistassini Chief, Grand Chief of the Grand Council of the Cree, and National Chief of the Assembly of First Nations. He refers specifically to the Cree struggle against the Quebec government, but his remarks can be interpreted more generally to the role Indigenous peoples take as a conscience and moral opposition to unethical corporate practices.

17 *Globe and Mail* 2003a.

CHAPTER 10 Hopeful Signs: Capacity Building in Health

I n this chapter I examine Aboriginal health care as an example of capacity building.[1] This, the area that I know best, demonstrates the complexity of Aboriginal and non-Aboriginal efforts to improve the lives of individuals and communities in a slow, positive, and incremental process of change. The good news is that capacity has been developed in many fields during the modern Aboriginal rights era, despite the nay-saying of the neo-conservative right. As a result, many, perhaps most, First Nations are poised to assume control over a wide range of jurisdictions. These jurisdictions comprise something more than a municipal form of government and something less than federal powers; in short, they constitute a unique third order of government that will be discussed in the following chapter.

Neo-conservative arguments often begin by suggesting that the "poverty, misery and despair" of Aboriginal communities is evidence of failed government policies.[2] Aboriginal incidence rates — no matter what the disease or illness — are anywhere from three to five times the national average; this is as true of chronic illnesses, such as respiratory and heart disease, as it is of mental illness.[3] Though some gains have been made, Aboriginal children and youth continue to suffer from horrendous suicide rates; in some age categories, they are the highest rates in the world (Leenaars et al. 2001; Waldram et al. 2006). The neo-conservative right and the liberal left agree about one thing: the ill health of First Nations is proof positive that radical change is needed. The question is what type of policies should be pursued: those that promote self-government or integration into the mainstream.

The national media presents Aboriginal communities as ill, dysfunctional, and suffering from welfare reliance and social pathologies. There is a significant degree of truth behind these images. But what the media fails to write about, and what we must come to understand, is that First Nations are slowly building capacity in health and social services, despite the failure of the federal government to significantly invest in rural and remote care. There are hopeful signs that Aboriginal communities have turned the corner. Some government policies are working, and First Nations are moving forward, despite many obstacles, in their path toward self-determination in the field of health.

The recovery of Aboriginal communities is hard to see, partly because a nuanced understanding of Aboriginal identity and politics is necessary to appreciate the rationale for many approaches that they are taking. In order to see the improvements, we must have something to measure these changes against — a baseline. Unfortunately these social indicators are few and far between; it is difficult to demonstrate improvements in Aboriginal well-being because we have little longitudinal data. It is quite possible that, at least in terms of health status, things will get worse before they get better. For example, current smoking rates among youth on reserve are much higher than mainstream rates; in some communities as many as 60 per cent or more of youth smoke (national averages are roughly 18 per cent). This can only translate into increased risks for lung cancer in the future, and for that reason considerable efforts are being put into smoking prevention programs across the country.[4]

In the meantime, contra-indicators of positive change must not be misinterpreted and used as proof that policies of self-determination are failing. Aboriginal people now have greater control over health care decisions than they did ten years ago, and yet their health status has continued to decline during this period. For example, in Wikwemikong, one of the communities I work in, diabetes rates have increased by 5 per cent, chronic respiratory problems by 6 per cent, and obesity by 30 per cent during the last decade.[5] Why does health decline when Aboriginal people gain control over their services?

Qualitative research and first-hand experience with communities can help explain this situation. First, health providers are only now beginning to accurately measure community health. They are finding that many illnesses have been underestimated, under-diagnosed because of a lack of screening services, or under-reported. Second, there is a time-lag between when culturally appropriate health services are implemented and when improved health outcomes result (and then can be measured). Aboriginal control over health services has meant the beginning of culturally relevant health promotion and health education and improved access to services. As a result, more Aboriginal people are being screened for various illnesses. This increased awareness of health translates, at least temporarily, into increased incidence rates. Many more people are now aware that they have diabetes or cancer or other illness, and this in turn, at least in theory, allows for better treatment or management of these diseases. In the case of mental health, we are only now getting to the point where the stigma of seeking care is declining. As denial around issues of family abuse, physical and sexual violence, and the long-term impact of what in Indigenous health science models is being referred to as historical trauma — the personal and familial outcomes of residential schools, child welfare policies, and other colonial policies — is ending,[6] the numbers of people seeking mental health or addictions counselling has increased as have the incidence rates for various specific diagnoses (depression, etc.). Thus, an increase in specific reported illness rates can actually be taken as a positive sign that stigma has ended, knowledge has increased, and people — and communities — are beginning to heal. Because researchers are now helping communities to establish indicators of social and economic health that can be used to study increased community capacity in the future, the pay-off to current efforts at capacity building will not come for five, ten or 20 years from now.

Capacity building refers to individual and community efforts necessary for sustainable development. Most commonly the term refers to the need to improve education, infrastructure, and basic health and social services. The well-known physical infrastructure problems of First Nations illustrate the government's failure to provide for basic needs that are taken for granted by mainstream Canadians. The recent water and environmental health crisis at Kashechewan, which forced the evacuation of community members, is evidence of water systems that are poorly planned and maintained. Similarly, household mold, asbestos insulation, inadequate ventilation, and a lack of smoke detectors in homes are all preventable environmental health concerns that would simply not be tolerated by mainstream public health authorities.

RCAP captures the notion of capacity building in its third volume, titled *Gathering Strength* (1996c), which examines federal policy and suggests innovative initiatives in governmental relations, economic development, community healing, and education. Some of its ideas — for example, on how to heal communities in the wake of residential school abuses — have been implemented by the federal government. RCAP stresses the need for capacity building that places culture and traditional values at the centre of contemporary efforts to rebuild communities. What research exists on economic development, health, and governance in Indigenous communities within Canada, the United States, and Australia all supports this approach. Work by Cornell and Kalt, for example, through the Harvard Project on American Indian Economic Development, clearly links self-determination, sovereignty, and nation building to improved economic opportunities for Aboriginal peoples.[7] My own research suggests that health and self-determination are integrally related and that personal healing and cultural awareness translate more broadly into community empowerment and control (Warry 1998; Jacklin and Warry 2004a). However, numerous challenges to the delivery of health care in rural and remote locations remain. They include, among others, poorer access to specialist services and illness screening programs, the difficulty of providing training to existing community-based staff, and high nursing turnover that leads to poor continuity of care and follow-up with patients.[8] However, improvements in health care have occurred over the past two decades. Alcoholism rates are lower, the numbers of abstainers are greater, and the public use and abuse of alcohol has decreased (sadly, among youth, the use of drugs, as in mainstream society, has increased). As we noted above, Aboriginal people are more aware of many health concerns, including diabetes and obesity, and of the need for improved nutrition and fitness. Unfortunately, a range of geographic and environmental challenges — from a lack of recreational facilities to the high cost of nutritious foods — mitigate against the pursuit of healthy behaviours (Warry 1998; Waldram *et al.* 2006).

Given concerns about health care funding in Canada, taxpayers are interested in ensuring that Aboriginal health services are effective and efficient. In the late 1980s, an audit revealed that Health and Welfare Canada was incapable of providing any information about the effectiveness of Aboriginal health programs (Waldram *et al.* 2006). At the same time, the federal government put in place the Indian Health Transfer policy that allowed First Nations to assume administrative control and governance over their health programs. The policy called for community-based research and consultation leading to the development of Community Health Plans (CHPs). Once in place, First Nations were to use these CHPs to develop programs to address community needs. Jacklin and Warry (2004a) have argued that Indian Health Transfer is an "unhealthy health policy" and have critiqued its professed claims for enhancing self-determination in health care. In short, we argue that the federal government has used the rhetoric of self-determination to disguise a policy of cost containment while sustaining the status quo with regard to health services delivered to First Nations.[9]

Under the Indian Health Transfer policy, Aboriginal health programs must be evaluated every five years prior to the renewal of transfer agreements.[10] This requirement is both good and bad. On the one hand, it ensures that Health Canada has an ongoing sense of the key issues in program delivery and can, at least to some degree, assess the efficiency and effectiveness of services. On the other hand, it can be seen as a type of accountability surveillance of First Nations by a mistrustful government — few other federal programs are under such scrutiny. Indeed, few mainstream health or social services programs are so closely evaluated.

I have been involved in Indian Health Transfer training, planning, research, and evaluation for over a decade, primarily in the North Shore-Manitoulin region of Ontario.[11] Such evaluation research is one of the basic aims of social science. As Dawson and Tilley note, "social programs are undeniably, unequivocally, unexceptionally social systems, and they are composed, as in any social system, of the interplay of individual and institution, of agency and structure, of micro and macro social processes" (1997: 406). Evaluation findings in Aboriginal communities need to formally recognize what Dawson and Tilley call the context of social programs and their embeddedness in larger social systems and policy contexts.[12] We cannot blame First Nations for delivering poor quality services if the blame is more accurately to be put on inadequate funding and inappropriate government policies.

Participatory evaluation is designed to help health boards and managers critically assess how they can change their roles or programs and better document the effectiveness, or inefficiencies, of their work.[13] It encourages program participants to be reflexive[14] about their work and to think of the information they require to better accomplish their objectives. Participatory evaluation, or what Fetterman has called empowerment evaluation, is a process whereby the evaluator assumes the role of facilitator or trainer rather than external critic.[15] It is a staged approach that ends with empowerment when participants have acquired all the skills necessary to conduct ongoing self-evaluations.[16] In my work I have attempted to strike a balance between, on the one hand, work that builds capacity and engages participants in program change and, on the other, research that provides an objective outsider's read on issues of accountability and program effectiveness.

So what is the current status of First Nations health care systems? My evaluation research clearly demonstrates that, at least in northeastern Ontario, First Nations are providing quality service to their community members and that, particularly given the degree of change that has occurred through the layering of federal and provincial services over the past decade, health services are well interfaced with local and regional health systems (Jacklin and Warry 2004a, 2005; Warry and Sunday 2000; Warry and Jacklin 2000). In Ontario, recently developed Aboriginal-specific services have included mental health treatment and long-term care facilities. Community members are happy with the fact that health services are now directly administered by committees, boards, or incorporated health bodies. They are satisfied with the quality of service provided by health care professionals, including physicians and nurses. Health care professionals are respected by the community at large. There is some concern about the biomedical orientation of services, and many Aboriginal people would like to see a greater emphasis on traditional approaches. Community members and service providers have also voiced concern about governance issues, specifically about political interference by chiefs or councillors that leads to poor morale and confusion over roles and responsibilities. However, the communities with which I have worked have all taken steps to incorporate health services or separate them organizationally from First Nations or tribal councils. Overall, my evaluations clearly demonstrate that health services are carefully and efficiently administered, that there is ongoing concern for the evaluation and professional upgrading of workers, and so forth. All the programs operate with small surpluses; external financial audits have all been positive.

A decade ago it was possible to find communities without written health policies and procedures in place. Now First Nations not only have adopted formal policies concerning hiring, promotion, and evaluation, but some have also adapted standard industry procedures to fit the specific cultural and organizational needs of their communities. In the late 1980s, for example, complaints about poor hiring processes were common. Important jobs were not advertised, and chiefs or councillors were said to select relatives for band jobs. These practices led to the charges of nepotism and organizational mismanagement that neo-conservative commentators continue to use to taint First Nations governance to the present.

But First Nations have responded to community demands for open and transparent hiring processes and, to a lesser extent, for regular staff performance evaluations.[17] Now jobs are routinely advertised in regional newspapers, and specialized or executive level positions are the subject of national searches. Considerable time and effort have been expended on health board development, and a generation of community volunteers has come to demand the highest possible standards from their leadership and community workers. Certainly, instances of mismanagement continue to occur, and, where they do, they seem invariably to make good press, but they are the exception rather than the rule. In my experience, First Nations councils and Aboriginal health organizations are working very hard to govern in open, transparent, and equitable ways.

What is lacking is the ability of organizations to self-evaluate best practices and develop coherent health information systems. That is, there remains very little accurate data on health status and no way to track individual or community health over time. The federal government has been unwilling to fund First Nations technology and staff or to promote the development of local health information systems. Despite considerable work on a national health information system during the late 1990s, a system that was never effectively implemented or evaluated, the development of Aboriginal health information systems remains a low priority for the government. Health Canada seems only concerned with gathering data on mandatory programs (immunizations and communicable disease reporting), which in many communities is cost-inefficient. In a nutshell, then, the government wants to ensure that Aboriginal health programs are having an impact, but they are not prepared to invest time or resources in programs that would allow communities to self-monitor community health status.

In my experience, volunteers, managers, and frontline workers have been extremely dedicated to improving organizational policies and practices. They have actively sought constructive criticism and have been very open in discussing the strengths and weaknesses in their organizations and in criticizing management or political leadership. In short, there is nothing hidden in these First Nations. There is always an honest willingness to improve health care, professional practice, and the governance of health organizations.

Health boards and managers have also worked efficiently to develop services in an environment of fiscal restraint caused by the federal government's refusal to enhance funding of transferred services. Take, for example, Mnaamodzawin and Wikwemikong Health Services on Manitoulin Island.[18] Mnaamodzawin, whose primary focus is on health promotion and primary care, delivers health services to five smaller First Nations (populations range from roughly 50 to 350 individuals). Its staff includes nurses and nurse practitioners, CHRs and NNADAP workers,[19] and a mental health case manager. Nursing services are offered in smaller communities only one or two days a week, and doctors' clinics may occur only once a month. Only three of the five communities have clinic or counselling space available, and the majority of clients have a family physician whom they visit off reserve. Mnaamodzawin workers must constantly balance consistent delivery of regional programs with the unique needs of its member First Nations. Regional staff, who travel to all the reserves, must respect individual needs while working hard to develop team approaches and regional referral networks (to nurse practitioners, physicians, and specialists) in order to develop a well-rationalized regional health care system. Health care workers, who often serve family members or friends, have gone to great lengths to explain practice patterns to their communities and to reassure their clients about the need for confidential recording and sharing of client information.

In 1999, an evaluation pointed to conflict and occasional conflict of interests between UCCM tribal council and the health services. Shortly after, Mnaamodzawin Health Services incorporated, while maintaining a reporting relationship with the UCCM tribal council. As a result, the health services are now building a distinct reputation, separate from the tribal council.

In recent years Mnaamodzawin has done a remarkable job at piecing together funding from multiple sources to meet community needs. To date, it has lacked sufficient resources to invest in Indigenous medicine and so relies on the expertise of a traditional coordinator funded through another organization, Noojmowin Teg Health Access Centre. Mnaamodzawin's Mental Health Program has been recognized for its innovative team approaches to treatment. The mental health case management program, for example, integrates Indigenous and Western assessments into the intake and treatment process.[20] The Northeastern Mental Health Centre in Sudbury has acknowledged that this team is the most efficient in managing case loads in the area. Suicide rates in Mnaamodzawin have been very low in comparison to other Aboriginal communities, and innovative work is being done with regard to historical trauma and residential school experiences. Even a decade ago Aboriginal peoples were in denial about many personal and family problems and were reluctant to seek help. Over recent years, self-referrals and referrals by health care providers to counsellors, psychologists, and traditional healers have continued to increase. This is a sign that community members are beginning to end the denial that used to exist around personal and family problems, but it also means that current resources and referral networks are strained to the limit.

Diabetes rates for Aboriginal populations are roughly three to five times the national average. The Mnaamodzawin Diabetes Program is another example of a well-respected program that pieces together patchwork funding from three diabetes funding agencies.[21] The health board decided to enhance programming by dedicating one part-time nurse as a diabetes educator. This program is just one of many examples of how culturally appropriate services are important. Diabetes

Educator Eleanor Debassige is fluent in the Anishnabe language, and one of the clear strengths of the program is that assessments and education can be done in that language with older clients. She can also translate health concepts and bio-medical terms, such as instructions concerning doses for prescriptions, which are written in English and not easily understood by all clients. More generally, the program is based on the understanding that Aboriginal patients perceive and experience diabetes in unique ways. Aboriginal clients' ideas about body image and weight gain, and attitudes toward maintaining healthy lifestyles while living with diabetes, differ in comparison to those of mainstream clients who have diabetes.[22] This is just one of many examples of how a disease is transformed into a distinct illness that needs to be understood and treated in culturally specific ways.[23]

Wikwemikong First Nation illustrates two other issues. In contrast to Mnaamodzawin, Wikwemikong health services includes a full service health clinic for roughly 3,000 clients both on and off reserve. Wikwemikong Health Clinic has four attending physicians (on a daily rotation), nurse practitioners, and nurses. The clinic is open five days a week. A health committee manages the health services and reports directly to the First Nations band council. The Wikwemikong population is large enough to support a clinic, physician services, a dentist, and some specialist services.

Wikwemikong has long dedicated itself to ensuring Indigenous medicine is central to health care practices. As well as having a full-time traditional healer on staff, the architecture of the clinic itself signals its commitment to culturally appropriate services: it is shaped as a Thunderbird, with the healing lodge, attached to the main building, as its head. Referrals and consultations between Western physicians and the traditional healer, Ron Wakegejig, are common, and the traditional program is particularly active in diabetes care and prevention. Mr. Wakegejig estimates that about half of the clients use traditional medicine to manage their diabetes. He views Indigenous medicine as complementary to Western biomedical approaches; it is not intended to replace Western treatments.

More generally, where provincial or other funding opportunities for traditional medicine exist, local control over health services has also led to greater promotion of Indigenous medicine. In Ontario, the Aboriginal Healing and Wellness Strategy has provided funds for nutritionists and/or traditional medicine coordinators (through health access centres). Thus, while federal health transfer has not provided for direct support (or recognition) of traditional practices, it has, through enhancing local control over health administration, allowed community members to reorient existing services so that new funds (and human resources) can be used to support traditional medicine activities.

Wikwemikong provides another lesson in the politics of health care. In 2004 the nursing clinic was temporarily closed by First Nations Inuit Health Branch as the result of a chart audit that questioned the scope of practice of the nurses.

The nurse supervisor visited the reserve and noted that the health centre nurses were handing out over-the-counter medications or otherwise treating clients who had not been seen by physicians. These concerns were subsequently clarified and found unwarranted, and the supervising nurse responsible for the audit apologized formally to community leaders. Following meetings between staff, health board, and Health Canada officials, the clinic was reopened. However, the closure damaged its reputation in the eyes of some community members and affected staff morale. For example, even though physicians continued to see patients throughout the closure, and other services remained available, many community members thought the entire clinic had been closed.

This situation reveals that Aboriginal health organizations have only limited administrative and management control over health services and that the federal government retains effective control over health care. What is equally problematic in such cases is the paternalism of government officials, who have little contact with the reserve but who assume they know better than local staff and act, unilaterally, as if First Nations managers are incapable of understanding issues around supervision, referral, and scope of practice.

These Aboriginal health organizations are still in their formative period. Evaluations of them reveal many issues concerning policy, practice, communication, and role definition that are common to any service organization, whether mainstream or Aboriginal. Many challenges remain. There is a critical shortage of skilled Aboriginal health care managers and other professionals. Culturally appropriate policies need to be developed or refined. For example, "progressive discipline" policies are difficult to implement, in part because direct discussion of poor behaviour runs contrary to Aboriginal cultural norms, which tend to emphasize the avoidance of conflict or confrontation. Much more work needs to be done to build measurable outcome indicators into programs. Nonetheless, Aboriginal managers and staff are clearly concerned with professionalism and quality of service.

Significantly, these evaluations also demonstrate that having local health care services available sharply reduces the use of emergency services offered at the local regional hospital, thus producing better, more cost-effective health services overall. And, significantly, they show clearly how culturally appropriate care, health promotion, and Indigenous healing programs benefit Aboriginal clients.

Given my 15-year experience in health research, I argue that what is required is not more surveillance, monitoring, and evaluation designed to reassure the government about service delivery, but rather an investment in organizational capacity building that includes dollars dedicated to health management, administrative training, and the development of health information programs. While taxpayers may be reassured by the knowledge that the government is closely monitoring Aboriginal programs, there seems to be a paternalistic double standard at work here. There is the continuing assumption that Aboriginal programs are somehow at risk or not up to mainstream standards. A more productive attitude and policy on the part of the government would accept that Aboriginal health boards and directors understand community needs and are competent to make decisions. It would provide more funds for culturally appropriate programs and invest in health information systems. This would enable Aboriginal communities to more quickly get on with the business of planning systems of health care and documenting the changing health status of their communities. As critics of the Indian Health Transfer policy point out, the initiative is itself in need of serious renovation and reform. Current dollars in support of health governance within the transfer envelope and in support of training are inadequate. Frontline workers, particularly NNADAPs or CHRs, are often underpaid and undereducated for the complex roles they must fill. New monies are required to support Indigenous medicine and mental health initiatives, among many other priorities. Additional funding is also needed to support training programs to build human resource capacity in health delivery.

However flawed the Indian Health Transfer policy is, it has resulted in slow improvement to health programs that are designed and delivered by Aboriginal people to meet the health needs found in First Nations. There are positive signs that individual and community health are improving — from the reduction in addictions, to improved diabetes care, to increased awareness of healthy lifestyles. Frontline workers are struggling to improve the health of their communities despite an overwhelming disease burden. They are concerned with professionalism and with quality service, even where they sometimes lack the education, training, or professional credentials of mainstream providers. Health managers are concerned with the creation and delivery of efficient and cost-effective culturally appropriate services, even while they work within an environment of severely restricted budgets that have not been significantly enhanced for over a decade.

Hill *et al.* (2001) have explored some of the issues facing Aboriginal health care managers in Australia, who must confront the differences between Aboriginal and non-Aboriginal cultures on a daily basis.[24] Aboriginal managers, for example, place importance on kinship and see power within organizational settings as more dependent on personal rather than organizational structure. Everything from the style of meetings to organizational leadership through to the dynamics of service delivery within a historical context make for unique challenges and distinguish Aboriginal organizations from their mainstream counterparts. The authors make it clear that Aboriginal health managers continue to face unrealistic expectations from governments and that even where government policy recognizes "the imperatives for self-determination in health policy and program development, interactions with other units or individuals may be colored by prejudice and misunderstanding" (Hill *et al.* 2001: 475).

In Canada, to date, most Aboriginal health programs are staffed by a combination of Native and non-Native staff. Unfortunately, the majority of senior or specialist positions, including mental health counsellors, consulting psychologists or psychiatrists, physicians, and nurse practitioners are non-Native, as are many health managers. This means that at the local level there is a need for mentoring programs and other human resource strategies through which educated, non-Native staff can pass on their skills to Native workers who lack professional diplomas or post-graduate qualifications. Even when such recommendations have been made, these strategies are difficult to implement because they are not financially supported by the federal government. Similarly, it is hard for health organizations to afford to support educational leaves when qualified local staff wish to return to school for professional development.

Ultimately, local capacity building is linked to improvements in professional programs, human resource training, and tertiary education. In particular, capacity for culturally specific and appropriate health care practices will only be accomplished by the next generation of Aboriginal health care workers and by developing and disseminating culturally appropriate models of health care practice. This is perhaps where the greatest evidence of enhanced Aboriginal capacity lies. Aboriginal education has improved immensely over the past two decades, and Indigenous knowledge production is increasingly a concern of Aboriginal scholars in community colleges and universities.

At the local level, Aboriginal schools and cultural curriculums, including Native language programs, are producing a generation of students who are proud of their heritage. The textbooks that contained negative images of Aboriginal peoples as savages have, for the most part, disappeared, and in their place are educational resources celebrating the contributions of Aboriginal peoples and the vibrancy of their contemporary culture. Although Aboriginal drop-out rates continue to be too high, more Aboriginal people are attending community colleges and universities than ever before. Special pre-medicine courses are available, and medical schools are slowly beginning to accept mature students with community-based experience in lieu of university degrees. These advances have been hard fought. For example, it took considerable advocacy over several years from Aboriginal leaders, including Dawn Martin-Hill, Director of the Indigenous Studies Program, before McMaster Medical School finally agreed to reserve as many as five admissions per year for Aboriginal students.

First Nations are also developing special outreach and advocacy programs to attract students into key occupational categories and induce them to practice on reserve. For example, the Six Nations' 2020 Vision initiative aims to have 20 Native physicians (as well as other health care workers) graduate by the year 2020. The Northern Ontario School of Medicine, the first new Canadian medical school in over 30 years, has made Aboriginal health a key priority area and is seeking to attract Aboriginal students to its programs.[25] Aboriginal-specific programs in Native studies, human services, social work, law, and other fields exist throughout the country. And in each of these fields Aboriginal academics and students are developing culturally specific forms of social and health care practice.

Aboriginal people have also assumed greater control over research in their communities and, as a result, over the production of knowledge. Aboriginal culture has long been the subject of interest for academic researchers, most notably anthropologists. But for years Aboriginal people complained that they were "researched to death." An enormous amount of academic research — the vast majority — was conducted to further the careers of academics and was of little practical benefit to Aboriginal communities.[26] This type of research was both colonial and paternalistic. However, over the past 20 years, researchers have turned to new methods that are both more participatory and more action or policy-related. These participatory action research (PAR) methods have slowly taken hold and are now commonplace. Today students work with communities from the very beginning of their research. As Jacklin and Kinoshameg (2005) show, they conduct research "only if it's going to mean something" and do so in a way that is respectful of Aboriginal ways and attuned to Indigenous knowledge, values, and ethics. This type of research requires more time, energy, and commitment because researchers must constantly negotiate and renegotiate their objectives and produce reports that are approved by the community, as well as by their academic peers. It is the only methodology that can contribute to the decolonization of Aboriginal research.

Aboriginal researchers are also developing Indigenous research practices based on their cultural values rather than on Western scientific assumptions. These changes at the local level have forced academics and major government agencies to transform their policies and procedures. The Social Sciences and Humanities Research Council, the largest funder of social science research, now has an Aboriginal research initiative that ensures greater involvement of Aboriginal scholars and community members in the review of research proposals and that channels monies into community-based applied research. The Institute of Aboriginal Peoples' Health (IAPH) is one of 13 Canadian institutes for health research. Under the direction of Jeff Reading, an Aboriginal epidemiologist, the IAPH has developed the Aboriginal Capacity and Developmental Research Environments (ACADRE) initiative. Eight of these research and training networks have been created across the country, including the Indigenous Health Research Development Program (IHRDP), a partnership between Grand River Polytechnic (Six Nations), McMaster University, and the University of Toronto.[27] This program, like other ACADRE centres, supports the next generation of Aboriginal health researchers. It provides special scholarship supports at the MA, Ph.D., and post-doctoral level and more closely links university-based researchers with community health practitioners. Along with other organizations such as the National Aboriginal Health Organization,[28] the ACADRE centres have promoted the study of Indigenous medicine, the development of Aboriginal codes of ethics for health research, and Indigenous models for health research and knowledge transfer.[29]

Capacity building, therefore, is also about improved control over knowledge production and the determination of research agendas. Aboriginal people have begun to assume control not only over health services, economic development, education, child and family services, and governance but also over the production of the knowledge and information systems that were formerly dominated by mainstream academic and government researchers.

The health of Aboriginal communities remains poorer than that of mainstream society. But there is ample evidence that Aboriginal communities have turned the corner and that their capacity to control and deliver services, in health and other jurisdictions, is being demonstrated on a daily basis. The Aboriginal vision of healthy revitalized cultural communities is a long-term one, and it will be several generations before it is realized. The first step is to end the post-colonial discourse and paternalism that assumes that Aboriginal people are not capable of managing their own affairs. This stereotype only blinds us to the hard work that is being done and undermines Aboriginal capacity building by suggesting that Aboriginal efforts are somehow antithetical to the interests of the dominant society.

NOTES

1   The definitive source for Aboriginal Health issues is Waldram, Herring, and Young's *Aboriginal Health in Canada* (2006). This book traces the impact of colonialism on Aboriginal community health and outlines the jurisdictional issues associated with contemporary health care delivery.

2   This phrase is Smith's 1996: 229-30.

3   The exception to this statement is the incidence of cancer, which has been lower than average in certain cancers or equal to mainstream rates. However, over the past 30 years, Aboriginal cancer rates have dramatically increased and are now surpassing mainstream rates in some categories; see Marrett and Chaudhry 2003. Aboriginal people are also diagnosed later, and their cancer survival rates are much lower than other Canadians.

4   The Aboriginal Unit of Cancer Care Ontario, for example, has put great effort into developing an Aboriginal tobacco strategy that aims to distinguish between traditional (ceremonial) uses of tobacco and the misuse of commercial tobacco and to make Aboriginal communities "tobacco wise." For more information, go to <http://www.cancercare.on.ca>.

5   Health status indicators are drawn from self-reported data in the 1988 and 2000 community members' needs assessments; see Jacklin and Warry 2004b.

6   Waldram 2004 provides a comprehensive review of Aboriginal mental health issues.

7 See, for example, Cornell 2002 and Cornell and Kalt 2006 on institutional capacity, economic development, and nation-building; Wien 1999 on economic development and good governance; Mondak 1998 on social capita; Fawcett *et al.* 1995 and Perkins and Zimmerman 1995 on empowerment approaches.

8 See Minore *et al.* 2005 for a discussion of the effects of nursing turnover in remote First Nations.

9 Although exceptionally difficult to calculate, per capita spending on Aboriginal health, according to the Romanow Report, is higher than that for mainstream Canadians; data from Saskatchewan suggests spending may be roughly double that of mainstream Canadians because Aboriginal peoples access both federal and provincial (physician and hospital) services (Romanow 2002: 217). This difference may be easily explained by the overall poorer burden of health and need for care faced by Aboriginal people.

10 For a discussion of research and program planning associated with transfer, see Warry 1998.

11 M'Chigeeng First Nation, Wikwemikong Unceded First Nation, and Mnaamodzawin Health Services, the latter representing five small First Nations (Whitefish River, Aundeck Omni Kaning, Sheguiandah , Zhiibaahaasing, Sheshegwaning); see Warry and Jacklin 2000, Warry and Sunday 2000, Warry and Beckett 1999).

12 Dawson and Tilley advance what they term a "scientific realist evaluation" perspective that "avoids the traditional epistemological poles of positivism and relativism" (1997: 405-06). They outline four aspects of an evaluation situation: embeddedness, mechanisms, context, and outcomes. Their approach is compatible with anthropological analysis which stresses the nature of interventions within a holistic view that takes into account how outcomes vary according to environment and other factors.

13 Clark and Cove examine participatory evaluation within the context of Aboriginal research. They note that researchers have responsibilities to the communities in which they work, to the agencies funding the research, and ultimately to the broader discipline of anthropology or academia, but they state unequivocally that the nature of participatory evaluation is such that the researcher's primary responsibility is to those most directly affected by the project and that it is the responsibility of the evaluator to "give voice" to their concerns (1998: 45).

14 As Hart and Bond (1995) note, the term reflexive, which is derived from critical theory, tends to be used in academic literature, and the term reflective in organizational and professional literature, even though the terms are not strictly interchangeable.

15 Fetterman 1996, see also Fetterman *et al.* 1996. For a discussion of some aspects of Indigenous evaluation approaches, see Robertson *et al.* 2004.

16 Jackson and Kassam utilize a relatively unknown paper by Reibens (1995), who makes the point that the rhetoric of empowerment in participatory evaluations "far exceeds the reality achieved on the ground" and who argues that participatory evaluation should incorporate the methods and framework of Guba and Lincoln's (1995) "fourth generation evaluation." The point is that issues are defined by stakeholders, and where objectivity is impossible, the evaluation "emerges out of interaction" between evaluator and evaluee. See Riebens 1995: 9, cited in Jackson and Kassam 1998: 5.

17 The lack of yearly performance evaluations is a concern for some workers, who would invite more frequent peer-reviewed assessments of their work. Certain aspects of performance appraisals are also seen as culturally inappropriate. The lack of regular evaluations is also a common concern in many non-Native organizations.

18 Mnaamodzawin translates as "healthy life (styles)" in Anishnabek.

19 The acronyms stand for the Community Health Representative Program and the National Native Alcohol and Drug Abuse Program, two long-standing community programs offered on all reserves and funded by the federal government. These programs have undergone several evaluations and are essential in providing community members with addictions and health promotion services. At the same time they are classic examples of programs that suffer from a lack of focus, attempt to be "all things to all people," and are often staffed by workers with poor educational backgrounds.

20 The Ontario Aboriginal Healing and Wellness Strategy is unique in providing funding for health services, including Aboriginal health access centres both on and off reserve, and in having a provincial health policy that recognizes and values Indigenous medicine. See Ontario 1992 and the AHWS Website <http://www.ahwsontario.ca/about/about_top.html>.

21 The diabetes program is funded through the Northern Diabetes Network, Ministry of Health and Long Term Care; the Aboriginal Diabetes Initiative from the Union of Ontario Indians; and with some transfer dollars from First Nations Inuit Health Branch. See Jacklin and Warry 2005.

22 See for example, Sunday and Eyles (2001) for a discussion of diagnosis and the management of diabetes risk in the Manitoulin community of Whitefish River and Speilmann (1998) on Aboriginal language and body image.

23 Medical anthropology commonly distinguishes between disease — the underlying biological process — and illness — the way the disease is culturally constructed and interpreted.

24 Once again, there are a great many similarities between the Australian and Canadian cases. The language of Hill et al.'s analysis is somewhat inaccessible and concerns strategic political decision-making by Australian managers. Nonetheless, many of their observations apply equally to First Nations health care.

25 Formally known as the Northern Ontario Medical School. For the school's vision and statement on Aboriginal health, see Kerr and Ashby 2004.

26 For readings on the philosophy and practice of participatory action research, see Reasons and Bradbury 2001.

27 For more information on these centres, go to <http://www.ihrdp.ca>. The Ontario ACADRE co-investigators include Kue Young and Cornelia Wieman, Public Health Sciences, University of Toronto; Harriet MacMillan, Psychiatry and Behavioural Neurosciences and Pediatrics, McMaster University; Dawn Martin-Hill, the Academic Director of Indigenous Studies at McMaster; and myself.

28 See the National Aboriginal Health Organization website at <http://www.naho.ca>.

29 For three interesting articles on Indigenous knowledge and its application to human resources, research, and policy see Nabigon and Mawhiney 1996; Nabigon et al. 1999; and Kenny 2004.

CHAPTER 11 The Third Order: Accountable Aboriginal Governments

In order to improve the conditions facing Aboriginal peoples on reserve, Aboriginal leaders must have the ability to control their own affairs and develop culturally appropriate political institutions. Self-government is the political mechanism through which a broad variety of Aboriginal rights to self-determination — from the implementation of Indigenous forms of law and medicine through to spiritual practices — will be implemented and protected. Currently, the vast majority of First Nations operate within jurisdictions normally associated with municipalities and with their authority delegated by the federal government according to the Indian Act. What Aboriginal leaders want is real authority, without having to resort to government approval for their decision-making.

Roughly half of the Canadian public seem to be in favour of the idea of self-government. Opinion is divided because of a continuing lack of clarity about just what jurisdictions might be involved.[1] In 1986 the federal government adopted a Hawthorn-style municipal approach in its Community-Based Self-Government Policy; however, this policy, favoured by neo-conservatives, has not been successful and has been rejected by First Nations leadership.[2] The 1992 Charlottetown Accord, had it been adopted, would have seen constitutional recognition of Aboriginal governments as a "third order" within the Canadian federation.[3] RCAP makes it clear that Aboriginal governments would not be mini nation-states but rather governments that would be distinct jurisdictionally within a Canadian framework of the provinces and federal government. It argued, for example, that Aboriginal nations could collectively form governments on a regional or tribal basis and should have an opportunity to aggregate their interests on fiscal matters (RCAP 1996b). This would require a fiscal framework negotiated by representatives of the federal and provincial governments and national Aboriginal peoples' organizations. The position of the AFN, however, is clear in stating that Aboriginal governments must have the right to define, in their own terms, the form as well as the content of laws and that a third order of government would entail the right to develop culturally appropriate political institutions.

Neo-conservative critics warn that a third order of governance will be politically divisive, institutionally unwieldy, costly, and potentially damaging to the Canadian state (Flanagan 2000: 5, 89-112; see also Cairns 2000: 136-46). Contained in most of these attacks on the idea of self-government is a deep paternalism that infers Aboriginal peoples are incapable of managing their own affairs. As we have seen, some Canadians continue to see social problems, poor infrastructure, and poverty as the fault of current First Nations councils and, in so doing, blame Aboriginal leadership, rather than colonialism, for the conditions found on reserve.

Neo-conservative arguments against self-government often begin with "evidence" that First Nations governments are mismanaged. Flanagan states:

> Almost everyday, Canadian newspapers publish stories about the waste and corruption on Indian reserves. Patronage and nepotism flourish; standards of fiscal accountability are lax, large deficits are common, and federal oversight weak. (2001: 15)

This association between waste of taxpayers' money, mismanagement, and incompetence is a powerful stereotype that blinds Canadians to the benefits of self-government.

The Centre for Aboriginal Policy Change (CAPC), a conservative advocacy organization funded by the Canadian Taxpayers Federation, places accountability at the centre of its research. Their website states: "billions of tax dollars are spent each year of which little seems to be properly accounted for or find its way to people it is intended to help." The CAPC suggests that First Nations councils are to blame, that monies given to councils should instead be given to individuals and taxed back to councils, that the reserve system should be abandoned, and that Aboriginal peoples be encouraged to assimilate into mainstream society.[4] This is propaganda that masks as policy research. These common sense solutions are offered as suggestions for policy change, but they ignore the fact that constitutional protection of collective treaty and other rights already exists in the 1982 Constitution Act.

CAPC reaches back to 1999 for evidence of mismanagement, noting that in that year "the Department of Indian Affairs received 300 allegations ranging from nepotism to mismanagement in 108 Indian Bands."[5] But this is weak evidence of poor management. Political accountability is built into reserve political processes. Indian and Northern Affairs Canada (INAC) has ongoing accountability requirements that include yearly financial audits of First Nations. The department intervenes when a band's auditor gives an adverse opinion with respect to the financial statements of the council, when the health or welfare of community members is compromised, or when councils have a cumulative deficit equivalent to 8 per cent of total annual revenues.[6] INAC's intervention policy differentiates three levels of financial concern and different remedies in each case. In the most severe cases, the government appoints third-party managers to balance the books and restore financial accountability.

Unethical and immoral behaviour is not culture-bound, and a quick look at Canadian history reveals that it is not confined to one political party or another. Consider, for instance, the Gomery Inquiry, which demonstrated corrupt or unethical financial and political practice at the highest levels of former Prime Minister Jean Chrétien's Liberal government. Nepotism too, is common in the public service, most obviously in the hiring of friends and family members for summer student positions, a practice condemned by the Canadian Federation of Students. However, nepotism is excused when practiced in private sector businesses, because taxpayers' monies are not involved (Galt 2003). In short, these critiques once again place Aboriginal leaders on the wrong side of a double standard.

The Indian Act is silent on the subject of financial accountability. Other governments in Canada operate with accountability frameworks set out in legislation. In 2002, the Chrétien government attempted to introduce accountability requirements as part of the First Nations Governance Act, Bill C-7. The result: not since the White Paper in 1969 was a piece of legislation met with such widespread opposition. The AFN argued that the accountability provisions maintained INAC's existing paternalism and that what was required was bilateral accountability; that is, it was time the government was held accountable to First Nations. Significantly, they also charged that the act was developed without sufficient consultation and that no consideration was given to culturally specific forms of governance. In the end, the Chrétien government withdrew the bill after extensive public opposition on several fronts.

One of the Auditor General's Reports in 2004 — the same year the auditor's report sparked the Gomery Inquiry — focused not on First Nations mismanagement but on the inappropriateness of the government's third-party manager policy.[7] Aboriginal leadership has long complained about this policy, which they regard as paternalistic and ineffective.[8] Third-party managers, who are non-Aboriginal outsiders, are paid between $195,000 and $312,000 per year by the band's INAC budget; moreover, the selection process is not open and transparent. The auditor concluded that INAC did not adequately monitor and assess the performance of third-party managers, even though they are responsible for administering up to $50 million per year of the department's budget for reserve financing. She also noted that in 2002, 32 of 608 First Nations had third-party managers and that First Nations had no say in the selection of these managers.[9] If ever there were an indicator of poor management, this perhaps is it: 5.3 per cent of First Nations councils had significant financial problems.

So, should we view First Nations governments as financially irresponsible? The same Auditor General's Report noted that in 2002 First Nations across the country collectively were $300 million in debt. I have had numerous discussions with chiefs, councillors, and band administrators who argue that small ongoing deficits are inevitable given the demands for social programs aimed at addressing the many needs of First Nations residents. Meaningful comparisons to mainstream governments are difficult to make, but to put this issue in rough perspective, consider that municipalities are not allowed to run deficits. The result, according to the Federation of Canadian Municipalities, is an estimated $60 to $125 billion infrastructure deficit that includes deteriorating water, sewage, and road systems.[10] Prince Edward Island, with a population of about 140,000 people (less than one-third of the First Nations total population), has recently run an annual deficit of $55 million and has a cumulative debt of over $1 billion dollars. First Nations governments seem no more or less troubled than other governments in dealing with the financial constraints they face.

Financial management is another area where capacity is being built. The numbers of Aboriginal financial managers are increasing, and an Aboriginal Financial Officers Association has been formed in conjunction with Certified General Accountants to establish standards and certification procedures. To date, some 350 individuals hold this certification. Many First Nations and tribal councils have also taken the initiative to develop their own financial codes and by-laws related to financial management and accountability, reflecting the widespread concern in Aboriginal communities over the development of open and transparent fiscal policies.

The fact that status Indians do not pay tax to support their governments is seen as an unwarranted perk by many Canadians and, as we have seen previously, is a constant irritant to neo-conservatives (Flanagan 2001: 15). Neo-conservatives assume that only when Aboriginal people pay taxes will they begin to hold their own governments accountable. Quite aside from the fact that mismanagement or overspending in mainstream governments does not seem to unduly concern taxpayers, this argument neglects the complex treaty relationship between the Crown and First Nations. Status Indians who work on reserve do not pay income tax.[11] Non-status Indians and those status Indians working in urban centres do. For example, income tax by Saskatchewan urban Aboriginal teachers amounts to $6 million annually.[12] Such taxes paid by off-reserve Aboriginal people are never mentioned when federal expenditures on Indian Affairs are questioned. It should also be noted that pay scales on reserve are often below national averages, so that the net effect of tax-free income is negligible in many cases.[13]

From a First Nations perspective, tax exemption is a clear acknowledgment of sovereignty — citizens cannot be taxed, according to international law, by a foreign power. Their tax exempt status was upheld in 2002 in a careful decision by Justice Douglas Campbell, who found clear assurances by the commissioners in Treaty 8 (Cree and Dene in Northern Alberta) that the treaty "would not lead to any forced interference with their mode of life, that it did not open the way to the imposition of any tax."[14] Tax exemptions flow from treaty rights; to deny or disparage them is another example of how neo-conservatives reject Aboriginal peoples' special status. Whether Aboriginal governments in future, once truly sovereign, choose to raise revenue through various taxes is a matter that will be debated by First Nations leadership. Although forms of individual income tax would currently seem to be unlikely or inappropriate, the AFN has acknowledged the need for First Nations governments to obtain powers to tax and to be able to tax economic activities occurring on reserve land.

What is imbedded in neo-conservative perspectives is the suggestion that Aboriginal community members do not care about good governance because they are getting a free ride at Canadians' expense. A more informed view points to the growing evidence that First Nations have already assumed responsibility for open and transparent political processes. Roberta Jamieson, former Chief of Six Nations and former Ombudsman of Ontario, states the matter rather succinctly:

> Outside observers point out that hopelessness, substance abuse and poverty are rife on some Native reserves, and that in some instances, bad government is a factor. Corruption, mismanagement, and undemocratic conduct are totally unacceptable to First Nations. Accountability and transparency are just as much goals for us as they are for Canadians. Hardly a model of accountability, Indian Affairs itself is very much involved in setting up situations in which bad government can flourish. (Jamieson 2003)

Aboriginal people, just like other Canadians, want good governance and are appalled by waste and corruption. Aboriginal leaders seek accountability systems that make their leaders responsible to First Nations members, or to Aboriginal organizations, rather than to the federal government. They want an end to paternalism that allows the government to watch over Aboriginal communities and an end to bureaucracy that disables, rather than enables, good governance and decision-making.

The AFN believes that accountability is bi-directional and reciprocal and that reconciliation can only occur if the paternalism of the Indian Act is left behind. They propose a broad accountability framework that would "provide meaningful assessments and track real progress in addressing the shameful conditions facing First Nations communities" (AFN 2005a, 2005b). In order to accomplish this, the AFN proposes the development of supporting institutions including a First Nation's Auditor General, Ombudsman, and Office of Fiscal Relations.

It is perhaps significant that Paul Martin, as a candidate for the Liberal leadership, announced his opposition to the First Nations Governance Act and promised to place Aboriginal issues higher on the Liberal Party's agenda. On becoming prime minister, he announced that he had no intention to revise the Governance Act. In April 2004, more than 70 Indigenous leaders met with Martin and several other ministers in the first Canada-Aboriginal Peoples Roundtable, where the prime minister seemed to signal a new era in Aboriginal affairs. He stressed the bilateral nature of First Nations-Canadian state relations and promised Aboriginal leaders "a full seat at the table" and the end of the era of policies that were developed first and discussed with Aboriginal leaders later.[15]

2005 might have been regarded as a benchmark year in the Indigenous rights movement. Following the roundtable, the Martin government took the important step of signing a First Nations-Federal Crown Political Accord (the Accord).[16] It reaffirmed a partnership model between First Nations and the federal government and recognized the Supreme Court view that reconciliation with Aboriginal peoples is the basic purpose of Section 35 of the Constitution Act. The Accord advanced a partnership model to promote meaningful processes and policies that would lead to new and enhanced opportunities for First Nations governance and capacity building. Significantly, it noted that collaborative discussions for these new policies and processes should draw, in part, on the Penner Report,[17] the RCAP reports, and on the AFN's recent report on self-government, *Our Nations, Our Governments: Choosing our Own Paths* (AFN 2005a).

Shortly after, the AFN released its agenda for change, titled simply *Getting from the Roundtable to Results* (AFN 2005b). A review of its proposals for changes in education, housing, economic development, health, and governance quickly reveals ideas that are consistent and at times derivative of the RCAP recommendations.[18] Clearly, in the last decade, the AFN has carefully mapped out — and in many cases scaled down — ideas for implementing self-government and advancing Aboriginal social and economic development. These ideas are budgeted in an admittedly costly, but realistic, financial framework that sees the federal government investing in Aboriginal communities in order to reach sustainability over time.

The AFN put forward a ten-year financial agenda with specific allocations in different jurisdictions and called for $774 million immediately and $2.3 billion in new monies over five years. The budget included an escalator clause to keep pace with inflation and noted:

> The resources are there. The Government of Canada has a well-established track record of significantly underestimating budget surpluses with the additional funds paying off the federal debt. Given the crisis in First Nations communities, the AFN is asking that some of this money be used to pay off the "debt" that the government owes First Nations communities. (AFN 2005c)

In the fall of 2005, the actions of Prime Minister Martin seemed to match the Liberal government's political rhetoric on self-determination. In the aftermath of the Kashechewan water crisis, a crisis that would alone require millions of dollars in federal and provincial expenditures to correct, Martin chose the First Ministers

Conference on Aboriginal Issues to announce over $5 billion in new money to invest in education, health, housing, and economic opportunities. These funds were in addition to the federal government's commitments to residential school compensation. As well, the First Ministers Conference committed its members to developing increased opportunities for self-government.

The convergence of the Accord with significant investment in capacity building and recognition of the AFN's governance agenda held the promise — a temporary glimmer of hope — for meaningful self-government. As the AFN notes, what is required is the principle of Aboriginal control over change — from the development of policy to the implementation of programs — that will allow for the provision of culturally appropriate forms of governance and social and economic development.

After all, current Aboriginal government is imposed government. First Nations councils, based on "first-past-the-post" voting systems, have been imposed on small, family, and clan-based communities. Neo-conservatives imply that Aboriginal social and cultural practices are responsible for inappropriate conduct or incompetence and that kin groups contest band government elections in order to win favours for family and friends, thus blaming the socio-political structure of reserves for mismanagement (Flanagan 2001: 14-15; Kay 2001). They attack culture rather than the imposed or colonial political order mandated under the Indian Act. Corruption is not the product of family or clan groupings but is the result of unethical conduct by individual politicians. Nonetheless, there is a distinct political culture on reserve, and it is this distinctiveness that requires the revitalization or creation of culturally relevant forms of governance that are suited to their small, kinship-based nature.

Many Canadians will have difficulty with the proposal that non-Western forms of governance should be allowed within Canada. But as testimony to the Standing Committee on Aboriginal Affairs shows, many Aboriginal leaders view Indian Act councils as inappropriate for their communities.[19] Traditional clan systems had different ways of identifying leaders — sometimes through merit, sometimes through hereditary systems. These traditional systems placed authority in the hands of leaders who had demonstrated their fairness and concern for the welfare of the entire group over the course of their lives. In certain areas, clans assigned duties, responsibilities, and political roles; for example, in the case of the Anishnabek, a particular clan leader might have responsibility for solving disputes or for particular ceremonies. Today, many communities would like to move to some version of their traditional system or to other innovative forms of representational government. In Anishnabek territory, clan systems remain very much alive, and communities are beginning to discuss what customary forms of governance might ensue, once they can be freed from the Indian Act. It has been suggested, for instance, that clan mothers be given a greater role in acting as a check on the authority of chiefs. Other forms of governance will emerge in Cree, Haudenausaunee, and other cultures.

In mainstream discourse, Indigenous political systems are denigrated and Western democratic forms elevated, because it is assumed that only European institutions can protect the rights of individuals. There is fear that the rights of Aboriginal women would be threatened under traditional political systems and the suggestion that Christians would see Indigenous forms of spirituality enforced by First Nations councils. But the Accord states clearly that First Nations governments would acknowledge applicable international human rights instruments and that they "will respect the inherent dignity of all their people, whether elders, women, youth or people living on or away from reserves." Suggesting that Aboriginal culture, in its emphasis on the collective, egalitarianism, and Indigenous political forms, is somehow philosophically opposed to the protection of individual rights demonstrates ignorance of Aboriginal cultural values, which respect individual diversity even while emphasizing collective goals.

Signa Daum Shanks, an Aboriginal lawyer and historian, notes that the term self-government is itself a Western invention, with no real equivalent in Aboriginal culture:

Whenever I hear someone use this term, I get a little nervous. Throughout Canada's history Aboriginals' life patterns have not been considered valuable enough to be accepted and nurtured. Whether it was an Indigenous harvesting technique, or scientific knowledge or even a governance method, non-Indigenous administrations thought most Aboriginal ways were not worth protecting. I wonder if some government people today who promote this idea of self-government really recall this history.

Daum Shanks adds that self-government should stand for "policies that stop the damage of the past and prove that Indigenous values are respected now and in the future."[20] It is perhaps unfortunate that the term self-government is so entrenched in Canadian discourse. It often implies some form of delegated authority and European-style institutions. We would be better to talk about accountable Aboriginal governments that will develop according to the principles and logic of Aboriginal cultural ways.

The Accord held the promise of such governments, agreeing with the AFN suggestion that Aboriginal governments may take many shapes and "may not fit the value of 'majority rule,' preferring instead values like consensus, unity, harmony, and respect" (AFN 2005a: Section 3.3). The AFN has similarly stated the need for the development of First Nations constitutions built on Indigenous law, local customs, traditions, and values. Such a perspective lays open the possibility of the re-emergence of traditional systems of law, medicine, and other forms of Indigenous knowledge (Borrows 2002). Until very recently, these homegrown solutions were not even contemplated by the federal government.[21]

Key aspects of liberalism, the dominant political tradition in Canada, include a privileging of the rights of individuals, a concern for justice and human rights, a broad concern for the welfare of the community, and a respect for minorities and other types of collectivities.[22] Many policy issues hinge on weighing the value of collective versus individual rights. In Canada we have increasingly come to value collective rights, at some expense to the rights of individuals; the rights of smokers, for example, have been drastically curtailed as an awareness of collective public health rights increased. The rights of minorities, including gays and lesbians, have been enhanced by Supreme Court decisions based on the Charter of Rights and Freedoms. The protection of the rights of Aboriginal peoples is a defining characteristic of the Charter.

As Niezen notes, Indigenous claims to self-determination do not fit comfortably into any of major paradigms of liberalism:

> ...one of the most important challenges for the human rights project is creating conditions favorable to the protection of distinct societies without sacrificing too many of the rights and protections of individuals. (Niezen 2003: 136-37)

At the heart of this issue is whether or not Aboriginal claims to their own culturally appropriate forms of governance and social institutions somehow undermine the rights and responsibility of citizenship as experienced by mainstream Canadians.

Kymlicka[23] contributes to this debate by arguing that we must recognize the difference between a society's external protections against domination and its internal restrictions of its own members (Kymlicka 1995: 37, cited in Niezen 2003: 137). He believes that liberals should endorse those political relationships that promote equality and fairness between groups and should reject restrictions (or at least resist enforcing dominant-society views) that would limit a group's right to sustain — or to challenge — traditional values and practices. He also makes the important point that "generally speaking, the demand for representation rights by disadvantaged groups is a demand for *inclusion*" in the larger society, thus suggesting that most ethnic and minority claims for representations imply a desire to fully participate in the state (Kymlicka 1995: 38-39, 120, passim).[24] In contrast, both self-government and separatism, at least potentially, reflect a desire to weaken the state:

> Self-government rights, therefore, are the most complete case of differentiated citizenship, since they divide the people into separate "peoples," each with its own historic rights, territories, and powers of self-government; and each, therefore, with

its own political community. They may view their own political community as primary, and the value and authority of the larger federation as derivative. (Kymlicka
1995: 182)

For this reason Kymlicka suggests that "it seems unlikely that according self-
government rights to a national minority can serve an integrative function." He
notes, however, that the long-term impact of Aboriginal self-government claims
are far from clear. Some ideas, such as the designation of special Aboriginal representation in the Senate or in other intergovernmental processes, "clearly serve
a *unifying* function" and help "reduce the threat of self-government" (Kymlicka
1995: 237, notes 9 and 10; emphasis mine).

Kymlicka sees self-government as, at least potentially, a threat to the status of
the nation-state. He perceives a logical contradiction in the nature of different
citizenship rights and from citizens' natural allegiance and identity to their primary political nation. Thus, the state's denial of self-government rights can itself
become destabilizing by encouraging resentment or secession. When minority
claims — such as in the Aboriginal case — are seen as undermining national sta-
bility and solidarity, this is often based on "underlying ignorance or intolerance."
He suggests that the fundamental challenge to liberalism and liberal theorists is
to "identify the sources of unity in a multination state" (Kymlicka 1995: 192).

In contrast, writers such as James Tully, and Taiaiake Alfred[25] argue that
Aboriginal peoples have the potential to transform the nation-state from within
by challenging Eurocentric notions of liberalism. In the Aboriginal context, Tully
refers not to multiculturalism but to interculturalism. He notes how many writers, including Kymlicka, who argue for the reworking of liberalism or nationalism, continue to deny the legitimacy of Aboriginal traditions and institutions and
to see them as "subordinate to the European-derived traditions and institutions."
Tully's interculturalism "challenges modern constitutionalism by starting from
the three features of cultural diversity: citizens are in cultural relations that overlap, interact and are negotiated and reimagined" (Tully 2001: 53-54).[26] His view
respects Aboriginal cultural institutions and opens the door to a Canadian state
in which alternative and culturally appropriate cultural institutions, Aboriginal
and European, can co-exist.

For this to happen, however, Canadians need to understand the social and
political values that are inherent in Aboriginal culture. Alfred suggests that
Aboriginal notions of respect can be used to build a concept of nationhood that
is more inclusive of diverse cultural ways and that would allow for alternative
and multiple political and legal structures. He argues that greater appreciation of
Indigenous political philosophy can help us escape the "intellectual violence" of
the dominant society's nation-state model. He prefers to see a relationship between

mainstream and Aboriginal peoples modelled on the Two Row Wampum—a theme I return to in the Conclusion (Alfred 1999: 62-65).

Neo-conservatives are fearful of the consequences of self-government. They conjure up images of islands of independence within a larger Canada and raise the prospect of ethnonationalism, itself a term that suggests war-torn countries where ethnic rivalry has lead to the break-up of nation-states. Even in the more moderate views of writers such as Cairns, we find the assertion that a sovereign right to self-government will undermine collective Canadian goals or a shared sense of Canadian identity.

But Indigeneity and ethnonationalism, at least as expressed in Quebec sovereignty claims or the ethnic secession movements in Eastern Europe and elsewhere, are different orders of phenomenon than Aboriginal self-government. Any attempt to link them are mistaken, and the attempt itself is divisive. Likewise, at the collective level, Aboriginal-federal relationships are a different order than those of the provinces and territories. Niezen makes it clear that Indigenous peoples "do not as a rule aspire to independent statehood" and that they should not be lumped as secessionists with ethnic minorities who have such aspirations (Neizen 2003: 203-04). As he notes, the size and scale of Indigenous populations makes secession an unreasonable and unworkable option and that secession would jeopardize the legal (and sometimes fiduciary) responsibilities formed through treaties and other formal relationships with the state which give Indigenous peoples a distinctive and elevated political status in comparison to other types of ethnic minorities. These observations are true in the case of Canadian, American, Australian, and New Zealand Aboriginal populations.

Cockerill and Gibbins also argue that self-government need not be seen as a threat to mainstream political institutions. They acknowledge that the implementation of self-government will require the development of interface mechanisms and relations between Aboriginal and non-Aboriginal governments. They note that the majority of First Nations have not argued for a totally independent nationhood but rather for the development of a third order of government within Canada, as part of existing liberal-democratic institutions (Cockerill and Gibbins 1997: 384-87). In fact, interface mechanisms already exist everywhere, though, in many instances, they are still in need of refinement. Because Aboriginal people move from reserves to nearby towns and cities on a weekly or daily basis, they insist that their institutions, however different, be complementary to and harmonious with those of mainstream society. First Nations negotiate regularly with provincial and federal governments to obtain funding for health, education, and other services. Traditional healers refer patients to family physicians, and vice versa. Provincial Crown attorneys participate in alternative justice programs on reserve and attend Aboriginal healing circles. Provincial police have different standards of intervention for certain offences on and off reserve. Mainstream investors team with First Nations in joint ventures located on reserve — and on and on. None of these interrelationships threaten the social order or undermine mainstream values.

Are Aboriginal and Canadian citizenship rights reconcilable? Cockerill and Gibbins aptly capture the complexity of this issue when they refer to Aboriginal peoples as "reluctant" citizens of the Canadian state. Aboriginal identity, as Kymlicka recognizes, is the principal identity for many individuals: a person feels first Aboriginal and only secondarily Canadian. This clearly offends some neo-conservatives, who would prefer Aboriginal peoples to adhere to the melting pot identity of Canadian immigrants and who attempt to denigrate special status by referring to Aboriginal peoples as immigrants or an ethnic minority.

Aboriginal and settler (Canadian) identities are historically and forever connected and affirmed in treaties and in existing federal-Aboriginal trust relationships. We may question (or simply find curious) the ethnic and political allegiance of those who hold dual citizenship; we do not see, at least at the individual level, these rights and status as problematic in any way. Aboriginal citizenship, like biculturalism, is best articulated by individuals in their participation in various political arenas. To repeat, Indigenous political identity does not undermine Canadian citizenship rights.

With the exception of a small number of Aboriginal people who claim international standing for First Nations, Aboriginal claims for self-determination and self-government are commonly put forward as a solution that would enhance Aboriginal peoples' participation in the Canadian state and ensure their potential as full citizens. Mathew Coon Come, Phil Fontaine, Ovid Mercredi, and other national leaders have been consistent in stressing, in both national and international forums, their desire to participate in a new Canada and in denying any claims to secession or nationalism as used in reference to Quebec claims for sovereignty (see Niezen 2003). The majority of Aboriginal peoples value the trust relationship that is invested in the Crown and are mistrustful of any changes to policy or agreements that might see this relationship weakened. Aboriginal leaders suggest that rather than seeing self-government claims as inherently destabilizing, we consider them part of a new and diverse political order (AFN 2005a).

Arguments that First Nations wield power "like" a province or that their powers be confined to those of municipalities miss the point. First Nations already act in a range of jurisdictions that do not easily fit any of the existing orders of government. For example, they maintain roads and infrastructure; set health and educational policy; and, with other Indigenous peoples, engage in United Nations and international forums concerned with their rights. As a different order of government, Aboriginal powers and jurisdictions will emerge over time to suit the needs and best interests of local and regional Aboriginal citizens.

The test of liberalism is in the development of political forms that seek accommodation between different and sometimes incommensurable cultural values. The search for Aboriginal governments that are built on Indigenous, rather than Western, values is the key to the survival of Indigenous cultures, not just in Canada, but worldwide. The development of a workable third order of government, one that recognizes political and cultural difference, will re-create, rather than undermine, the Canadian nation-state.

The struggles of Canadian Aboriginal peoples are linked to larger international processes that threaten the death of tribal peoples and cultures. As Niezen notes:

> Indigenous peoples are increasingly viewed as canaries in the iron cage of modernity. There is nothing equivocal, metaphorical, or too terribly mysterious about the demise of an Indigenous society when it occurs. Sociohistorical autopsies reveal consistent patterns of conquest, genocide, ethnocide, and political marginalization. Indigenism is an identity, like that which unifies survivors of the Holocaust, grounded in evidence, testimony and collective memory. (Niezen 2003: 15)

The peoples and cultures in the Amazon basin are under threat from major developments and deforestation. Australian Aboriginal peoples remain excluded from any type of constitutional framework and unprotected by human rights legislation. In the same week that Prime Minister Martin met with Aboriginal leaders to reaffirm Aboriginal rights and reconstitute federal-Aboriginal relationships in Canada, Prime Minister Howard of Australia unilaterally announced the abolition of Australia's representative Indigenous body, the Aboriginal and Torres Strait Islander Commission (Bradfield 2005).[27]

In 2005 First Ministers met with the federal government to discuss Aboriginal issues. The resulting Kelowna Agreement pledged an additional $5.1 billion in new monies to Aboriginal programs. In reflecting many of the principles of the AFN-Federal Government Accord, the Kelowna Agreement also represented the first real opportunity to develop culturally appropriate First Nations governments over the long term. But, by 2006, the promise of the Accord and Kelowna Agreement seemed lost. This giant step forward in the quest for Indigenous rights to self-determination seems easily reversed by a Conservative government bent on returning to the paternalism of the previous Governance Act. As John Ibbitson noted prior to the 2006 election, Tom Flanagan remains a key advisor to Stephen Harper and the neo-conservative wing of the Conservative Party (Ibbitson 2005). Despite Harper's assurances that he does not take Flanagan's counsel on Aboriginal affairs, integrationist and assimilationist attitudes run deep in the Conservative Party, making the Liberal government's recognition of a unique path to self-government and enhanced funding to First Nations unpalatable to it. The Conservative government's first budget did nothing to advance the

Kelowna Agreement's objectives, reduced a promised spending commitment of $5 billion by 91 per cent, and failed to uphold the previous government's commitment of additional monies to improve Aboriginal health care.[28] Clearly, early actions by the Conservative government ignore both the Accord and the earlier RCAP reports and place defence, policing, and a range of other issues ahead of the needs of Aboriginal peoples. These actions serve to entrench existing poverty and dependency rather than to offer the glimmer of hope offered by the Kelowna Agreement — a plan on which Aboriginal leadership, provincial governments, and the federal New Democratic Party, the Liberal Party, and the Bloc Québécois had reached consensus.[29]

Canada, despite the sad state and ill health of First Nations, is well ahead of the curve on Indigenous rights. For this reason, our actions can have an immense long-term impact on emerging global political processes, which are attempting to reclaim an Indigenous political space within the nation-state and to reconcile the needs of Indigenous nations within a structure of national and international relations. Canada, in its search for a consensus approach to understanding Aboriginal issues, can and should be a leader in Indigenous rights and can help define the place of Indigenous peoples on the world stage. But this cannot and will not occur unless politicians and voters educate themselves about Aboriginal cultures and learn to reject the politics of assimilation and integration.

NOTES

1   As I note elsewhere in this volume, Aboriginal issues are generally marginalized, and I have been unable to locate opinion polls dealing directly with the issue of self-government. Cockerill and Gibbins note that at the time of the Charlottetown Accord in 1992, 47 per cent of adult Canadians thought Aboriginal governments should exercise powers similar to provincial governments but 59 per cent supported the constitutional designation of First Nations as a "Distinct Society" (1997: 400, n.1).

2   For a more detailed review of Government approaches to Aboriginal government see Chapter 9 of RCAP (1996b) available at <http://www.ainc-inac.gc.ca/ch/rcap/sg/sg27_e.html>.

3   The 1983 Penner Committee, which examined Aboriginal self-government, saw First Nations as equivalent to provinces and suggested that First Nations laws and provincial laws would have no effect on each other (see Canada 1983). The report was ignored, but came to shape later ideas of self-government, including those of RCAP.

4   "The Centre for Aboriginal Policy Change is dedicated solely to examining current Aboriginal policy and court decisions from the perspective of those — Native and non-Native — who will pay the bill: the taxpayers." Quoted on the website, available at <http://www.taxpayer.com/pdf/Road_to_Prosperity_September_2005.pdf>.

5 The Centre's "policy paper" also argues for the creation of individual property rights (Fiss 2005: 3). Tanis Fiss is Director of the CTF's Centre for Aboriginal Policy Change. See "The Road To Prosperity" available at <http://www.taxpayer.com/pdf/Road_to_Prosperity_September_2005.pdf>.

6 The INAC's financial intervention policy can be found at: <http://www.ainc-inac.gc.ca/pr/info/int_e.html>.

7 These problems with the third-party manager process had still not been corrected in 2006. See <http://www.oag-bvg.gc.ca/domino/reports.nsf/html/20060505ce.html> and <http://www.oag-bvg.gc.ca/domino/reports.nsf/a1b15d892a1f761a852565c40068a492/958b22c311e95159852571650053c468?OpenDocument&Highlight=0,2004>.

8 *Windspeaker* 2004, Vol. 21/12 (March) available at <http://www.ammsa.com/windspeaker/topnews-March-2004.html>.

9 Auditor General Sheila Fraser examined ten cases in four regions; she found that in some instances third-party managers were operating from offices far from First Nations and rarely visited the communities for which they were responsible.

10 See Federation of Canadian Municipalities 2006. The estimates range from $60 billion by the Canadian Council of Professional Engineers to $125 billion by the Conference Board of Canada.

11 The Federal Court of Canada has also ruled that Native workers employed by reserve-based companies do not have to pay income tax, even if they live and work off reserve.

12 City of Saskatoon, "Building Bridges with The Aboriginal Community," available at <http://www.city.saskatoon.sk.ca/org/leisure/race_relations/buildingbridges.pdf>.

13 Status Indians, who carry an identity card, do not pay sales tax and receive other drug, medical, dental, and other benefits, estimated to be as much as $8,000 per person per year. Many of these benefits, however, are available to other Canadians through employer benefit plans. For those status Indians who are unemployed or living below the poverty line, these benefits are an important subsidy.

14 *Globe and Mail* 2002a.

15 See the introduction to AFN and Government of Canada 2005. Paul Martin stated "It is now time for us to renew and strengthen the covenant between us" and committed that "No longer will we in Ottawa develop policies first and discuss them with you later. The principle of collaboration will be the cornerstone of our new partnership."

16 AFN and Government of Canada 2005: 1-9.

17 See note 2 in this chapter.

18 The AFN perspective, reports, and policies referred to in this section are listed in the bibliography and can all be found on-line at <http://www.afn.ca/article.asp?id=3>.

19 For an interesting dialogue of the First Nations Governance Act, see the testimony of Chief Earl Commanda, Chairman, Serpent River First Nation, North Shore Tribal Council; Chief Patrick Madahbee, Aundeck Omni Kaning, and Terry Debassige of the M'Chigeeng First Nation; and Chief Franklin Paibomsai, Whitefish River First Nation, United Chiefs and Councils of Manitoulin, before the Standing Committee on Aboriginal Affairs, Northern Development and

Natural Resources, 37th Parliament, 2nd Session, 17 March 2003, available at <http://www.parl.
gc.ca/infocomdoc/37/2/AANR/Meetings/Evidence/AANREV42-E.HTM#Int-452854>.

20 CBC Commentary, 6 February 04 available at <http://www.cbc.ca/insite/COMMENTARY/2004/
2/6.html>. See also Shanks 2004.

21 As previously noted, one reason the 2002 First Nations Governance Act introduced by the Liberal
Party and supported by the Progressive Conservative Party because of its accountability provisions, was so vehemently opposed by First Nations was that it continued to promote Western
forms of representational democracy for Aboriginal communities and was mute on the issue of
culturally appropriate political institutions.

22 The relative emphasis on individual versus collective rights varies across parties. The New
Democratic Party values collective rights and public ownership of essential services, whereas the
Conservative Party privileges individual rights and advocates reduced government presence in
both the public and private sector. For most Canadians, however, these key liberal values are
played out differently according to specific issues. The Liberal Party of Canada has succeeded by
being able to gauge public opinion and move slightly left or right from the centre, issue by issue.

23 Will Kymlicka is a political scientist at Queen's University, Ontario.

24 My discussion here cannot do justice to Kymlicka's writing, which illuminates many complex
relationships between the nation-state and Indigenous self-government claims.

25 James Tully is Distinguished Professor of Political Science, Law, Indigenous Governance and
Philosophy at the University of Victoria; Taiaiake Alfred is Director of the Indigenous Governance
Program at the same university.

26 Tully's book argues for a form of constitutionalism that would allow for the aspirations of Quebec
as well as Aboriginal peoples' claims.

27 Bradfield states: "Once again in Indigenous affairs, Australia comes up badly in comparison with
Canada. While in recent times Australian and Canadian approaches have been very different, the
two countries share essentially the same status as settler societies dealing with the existence of a
distinct and vocal Indigenous minority."

28 The only Accord commitment the Harper government met was for $300 million in support of
off-reserve housing, which it then off-loaded to provincial governments for implementation. In
a CBC National interview with Peter Mansbridge following the budget, Finance Minister Jim
Flaherty responded to questions about the Kelowna Agreement by emphasizing that the government was already spending $9 billion dollars on Aboriginal peoples.

29 For CBC coverage of the failure of the Conservative government to uphold the Kelowna Agreement
see <http://www.cbc.ca/news/background/aboriginals/undoing-kelowna.html>. The conservative
position statement on Kelowna can be found at <http://www.conservative.ca/EN/1091/38552>.

CONCLUSION The River

During the early contact period, the Haudenosaunee and Dutch made treaties of peace and friendship. These treaties were marked symbolically by the gifts of wampum belts.[1] One of these, the Gus-Wen-Tah or Two Row Wampum, has become an important symbol in the debate over Aboriginal issues, largely as a metaphor for distinct status and self-government.

The Two Row Wampum is comprised of two rows of purple wampum on a white background. The white represents the purity of the agreement and the purple the spirits of European and Aboriginal ancestors. Between the two rows are three threads of wampum that symbolize peace, friendship, and respect. According to one common Aboriginal explanation:

> The concept of the Two Row was developed by our ancestors so they could peacefully co-exist, conduct trade and share resources with the European Nations. The Two Row embodies the principles of sharing, mutual recognition, respect and partnership and is based on a nation-to-nation relationship which respects the autonomy, authority and jurisdiction of each nation.[2]

In short, the wampum signals respect for European and Aboriginal cultures, laws, and customs. In Haudenosaunee oral tradition, the two purple rows symbolize ships, canoes, or vessels travelling down the same river. Accordingly, this means that the two peoples "will travel the river together, but each in our own boat. And neither will try to steer the other's vessel."[3] More recently, interpretations of the Two Row Wampum — as in the nation-to-nation reference above — have taken on more specific political references in order to re-emphasize the status of equals between the Crown and First Nations during the early contact period.

Wampum belts signified political and diplomatic relationships not only between tribes but also between First Nations and Europeans. The Two Row Wampum was one of several that signified the latter relationship. The Friendship Wampum shows stylized human figures, Aboriginal and European, holding hands in friendship, linked in common purpose. The Covenant Wampum presents Europeans and Aboriginal peoples as links in a chain, thus binding together through treaty relations. Taken together, these three wampum belts symbolize cultural respect, political independence, and mutual reliance between Haudenosaunee and European nations.

But the Two Row Wampum especially has come to have symbolic weight. Cairns makes much of the image, emphasizing that it was designed to symbolize mainstream and Aboriginal (Iroquoian) peoples on separate and parallel paths (Cairns 2000: 92, 203; see also 70-71 and 206). He notes that this interpretation of the wampum is supported by former Grand Chief Ovid Mercredi and Aboriginal lawyer Mary Ellen Turpel, who also see it as a sign of respect for cultural difference and a recognition that different orders of government can peacefully co-exist (Cairns 2000: 70-71). However, for Cairns, and many others, the Two Row Wampum is a red flag — a danger sign that the recognition of contemporary Aboriginal rights could lead to multiple mini-states within Canada and which raises the spectre of separation, not unlike the divisive debates over Quebec. Cairns argues that too great a degree of autonomy leads to separatist thinking and undermines a group's commitment to Canada; for example, he cites the Old Order Amish, who choose to live as a community apart from the mainstream. For Cairns, the future of Canada cannot lie in the separation of Aboriginal and Canadian peoples or governments; thus, he resists any suggestion of self-government that would increase Aboriginal autonomy at the expense of a shared commitment to common political institutions and a national agenda.

The Two Row Wampum signalled political understanding, at least from the perspective of the givers; it is arguable whether the receivers fully understood this import. So the interpretation of wampum, like the wording of many legal contracts, is subject to dispute. Those, like Cairns, who see it as a sign of parallel paths, forget to mention that a common river surrounds the two vessels: the Two Row Wampum reflects the presence of shared environment and country. The oral history speaks of two vessels moving in the same direction and so expresses common purpose: that Aboriginal and mainstream Canadians exist within a shared geography and life course. Thus, the Two Row Wampum is best thought of as representing a river of common ideas or mutual intentions in a magnificent environment that Aboriginal peoples allowed Europeans to share. It might even be interpreted as a future vision for our country — a common path that would allow Aboriginals and newcomers to proceed together, autonomously, toward goals while sustaining their unique cultural ways.

Borrows has interpreted the Two Row Wampum in just this way — as a symbol of "mutuality" and "interconnectedness" that is sufficiently broad to allow for shared citizenship:

> The ecology of contemporary politics teaches us that the rivers on which we sail our ships of state share the same waters. There is no river or boat that is not linked in a

fundamental way to the others; that is, there is no land or government in the world today that is not connected to and influenced by others. (Borrows 2002: 149)[4]

This is a liberal, kind-spirited, and Aboriginal view, one that is in keeping with the concept of friendship and mutual dependency (also symbolized by the two other wampum belts) that so characterized the early settler period when Whites and Aboriginal peoples were true allies.

This type of progressive thinking is needed today. If we are to understand Aboriginal peoples, we must decolonize our thinking and translate culture into action by way of progressive social and political policy. There are positive signs that this has begun to occur in many parts of the country. However, the national media continues to support a radically conservative agenda on Aboriginal rights. In speaking of Paul Martin's ascension to prime minister, the *Globe and Mail* acknowledged that the "plight of Canada's Natives should shame every Canadian" and called on the government to respect rights guaranteed in the Constitution. Yet, in the same breath, the editors called existing financial support for Aboriginal programs "generous" and argued that the chief problem confronting Aboriginal peoples was their inability to "integrate into the mainstream." Their solution was for Martin to "steer native policy away from its obsession with exhaustive native rights and status toward a model that fosters integration through prosperity" (Globe and Mail 2003b). And therein lies the central assumption so deeply embedded in neo-conservative thought—the need for integration and the belief that Aboriginal peoples should embrace European values rather than their own. The challenge for the Canadian government is to pursue a relationship with First Nations that is in keeping with the 2005 AFN-Liberal Government Accord and that is respectful of culturally appropriate institutions.

First Nations are not Canada's Palestine, and Aboriginal self-government will not and cannot lead to Quebec-style separation. Aboriginal peoples long ago embraced European settlers and welcomed them on their land. Some Aboriginal people do not think of themselves as Canadian citizens. Others think of themselves as Aboriginal first and Canadian second. But contrary to neo-conservative warnings, Aboriginal political identity is in no way a threat to Canada or Canadian political institutions. It is true that Aboriginal self-government raises difficult questions concerning incommensurable beliefs, values, and behaviours. We have seen and survived early examples of these cross-cultural collisions. Some of the most interesting challenges have been dealt with in criminal courts—Indigenous healers have been charged with malpractice; defendants have escaped punishment through appeals to Indigenous beliefs; convicted offenders have been banished to the woods, rather than jail. We are living in a time when Aboriginal institutions—health organizations, child welfare services, etc.—will reshape social practice and policy for Aboriginal peoples. These new forms of social practice will need to interface and harmonize with mainstream institutions, but they cannot be integrated.

Whether on reserve or in cities and towns, virtually every indicator — from education to conflict with the law, from health status to welfare rates — points to the misery of Aboriginal peoples when compared to mainstream Canadians. I have purposefully ignored the many challenges Aboriginal peoples face — urban gangs, warehousing in correctional institutions, high drop-out rates, and much more — because these issues will only be addressed once true reconciliation between mainstream and Aboriginal Canadians occurs. For this to happen, we need to accept the distinctiveness of Aboriginal cultures and the unique processes and institutions that they will create to solve their own problems.

Canadians need to demand more of our media, educate ourselves, and seek out information that is based on solid research and first-hand understandings of Aboriginal communities. But we must also think creatively and, as Aboriginal people would suggest, with our hearts as well as our minds. The trick in seeking consensus on social policy is to balance reason and emotion. The dominant characteristics of neo-conservative political commentary, aside from its rejection or neglect of social science research, are self-interest and protection of the privileged and the status quo. As Elie Wiesel suggests, "the opposite of love is not hate, it is indifference."[5] Indifference allows us to turn the other way and retreat to the sanctuary of our small worlds, untouched and untouchable by those less privileged than we are. The continuing poverty and marginalization of Aboriginal peoples in a country where wealth abounds is incomprehensible unless we understand our indifference. There is no rational reason for failing to solve Aboriginal issues. We understand intellectually — or are at least beginning to understand — the policies and political strategies required to realize Aboriginal self-government. What we now require are emotional responses: personal and collective ways to overcome our indifference and place Aboriginal issues at the forefront of the Canadian social and political agenda.

The next time you encounter media opinion about Canadian politics, political identity, social change, or Canadian values, look for the Aboriginal content. Nine times out of ten, Aboriginal voices are not heard, and Aboriginal issues are invisible. We need to learn how to see Aboriginal people in everyday life. This will be achieved only through educating people about the significance of culture and building diversity into our public policy-making.[6] We must constantly demonstrate the value of diversity thinking and confront the fears associated with alternative lifestyles and cultures. We should protect diversity at every turn and resist the temptation to homogenize Canadian culture.

In the case of Aboriginal peoples, the process of decolonization has required constant resistance to the state, court battles, behind-the-scenes negotiations, demonstrations, and outright confrontation. The direction of change points only one way—toward self-determination. As Aboriginal leaders map out a more certain pathway for their communities, Canadians will more fully appreciate the meaning of Aboriginal culture and find it unthreatening. Diversity thinking, which promotes a deeper understanding of cultures, will lead to a new vision of the nation-state and to new forms of alliances or coalitions between Aboriginal peoples and mainstream Canadians. The discourse on Aboriginal rights in Canada is misinformed because it fails to take account of the nature of culture, identity, colonialism, and ongoing structural racism. This understanding is essential to an informed citizenship in any society, but it is critical in a country where descendants of a settler society intermix with first-generation immigrants and First Nations.

The New Age philosopher Ken Wilber[7] suggests that contemporary social movements (including anti-globalization efforts) have arisen through a complex series of intellectual and political contestations about the nature of the status quo. According to him, most people remain trapped in antiquated mindsets that include an attachment to conventional and scientific thinking associated with traditional and fundamentalist religions, colonialism, and corporate states.[8] However, he sees signs of a new type of consciousness evident in several types of thinking, including deep ecology, diversity thinking, liberation theology, and cooperative inquiry, as practiced by perhaps 10 per cent of the world's population. He believes that we must embrace spiritual and emotional, as well as rational, ways of knowing in order to develop new styles of thinking capable of freeing the human spirit from divisiveness (Wilber 2000: 9-12, 41-45).

Wilber's theory (if it deserves that label; it is largely non-empirical) has been criticized on several grounds, including, for example, the inadequacy of his evolutionary framework and his speculative faith in transcendental consciousness. But he is a hopeful and inspirational writer who is unafraid to argue that certain ways of thinking are more preferred, and progressive, for both individuals and communities. His argument for thinking that embraces diversity, sustainability, and cooperative approaches to social problems borrows from Aboriginal worldviews. Interestingly, he cites both the Canadian health care system and the Indigenous rights movements as evidence of social thinking that embraces spiritual and emotional understanding along with objective-rational knowledge.

Wilber sees the possibility of new forms of thinking and knowing the world that blend Western and non-Western worldviews. But his writing does not clearly articulate the complexities of cultural relativism and seems poorly constructed for working through the difficulties that must be faced when developing interface mechanisms between diverse cultures. Contemporary philosophers such as Jurgen Habermas (1998: 205-07, 211-12; 1990; 1984), Richard Rorty (1999: 32, 272-77), and Clifford Geertz (2000: 218-30) have expended considerable energy and ink pondering the ways in which people with diverse and incommensurable value systems can live together in a degree of harmony. Rorty, a "philosophical pluralist," warns against "mindless and stupid" cultural relativism that would see archaic values perpetuated in contemporary society; he believes in a "pragmatically justified tolerance" that can lead to pluralistic societies (Rorty 1999: 276). Habermas suggests the need for open, consensual, and rational dialogue aimed at establishing truths that can be agreed upon and move us past the clash of incommensurable beliefs. Geertz, an anthropologist, seems more open to non-Western, non-rational, and non-European approaches in calling for a politics of diversity that treats ethnic, religious, or cultural claims like any other social problem to be "dealt with, modulated, and brought to terms" (cited in Rorty 1999: 275; see also Geertz 2000).

These writers are struggling with the essential postmodern problem: how can liberalism be reshaped to equip us for a multicultural world where different groups offer different claims to truth? This intellectual debate is useful in pointing to new ways of thinking and acting that would bring diversity politics within our reach. A more obvious approach is to open ourselves to Indigenous knowledge and philosophy. Those who work closely with Aboriginal peoples know that, if we do so, the search for common consensus can easily be found. Indigenous philosophy is built around core values, including respect — for other humans of all cultures and for animals and the wider environment[9] — and sharing. Sharing is so central to Indigenous cultures that egalitarianism has become an important contemporary ethic. And, of course, it was their desire to share the land that so integrally connects us to Aboriginal peoples through treaty rights.

Niezen argues that the Indigenous rights movement promises not simply new forms of citizenship, but "the fulfillment of self-determination goals of Indigenous peoples (that) would constitute a completion of the process of decolonization." The recognition of Indigeneity does not require the creation of new nation-states or ethnonational states but constitutional recognition of the autonomy of Indigenous forms of self-governance and the implementation of treaties and agreements between Aboriginal peoples and state governments. Arguments that "Indigenous self-determination is the thin end of the wedge leading inexorably to global secessions" confuse ethnonationalist sentiments with Aboriginal ambitions and ignore United Nations' sanctioned dialogue and reforms that recognize the rights of Indigenous peoples to self-identify and to exist with distinctive forms of governance within pluralistic states. Niezen states:

> Indigenism is a transnational phenomenon, and as such it represents a process some
> might see as corrosive of nation-state authority and stability. In fact, Indigenous organizations are a form of transnational solidarity invading the institutional space of
> sites from two directions, both internationally and locally. (Niezen 2003: 194-99)

This understanding speaks of the re-creation and renovation of the modern nation-state into one where alternative forms of Indigenous governance are embraced in a pluralistic society and where international and transnational identities serve as a check on traditional jingoism. It recognizes the relationship between the local and the global and understands that citizenship rights can be muted or expansive depending on the political interests and inclinations of minority groups. It attempts to reconcile Indigenous desires for collective expressions with the need for individual human rights protections.

Such thinking is totally different from, and contrary to, the views of neo-conservative writers who see Aboriginal self-government as a parallel government or as creating a sea of micro-states that will be potentially divisive for the Canadian identity and state. This view of enclaves — the political equivalent of gated communities — comes from misunderstanding as well as privilege. It encourages fear by suggesting that political divisiveness might lead to violence. It promotes sameness or, rather, the continuing superiority of European institutions as an alternative to plurality.

When it comes to social, rather than economic change, society often moves to the left. The elimination of slavery, the rise of unions and workers' rights, the feminist movement, the uncloseting of gays and lesbians, and the recognition of the rights of the mentally challenged and disabled all occurred through the acceptance of ideologies championed by left-wing social activists. And in each case, social policy changes, from pay equity to ramping sidewalks, were met with resistance by business and government and accepted only when a failure to change was shown to be more costly than the change itself. Economic change occurs in conjunction with social policy only when it can be shown to be cost-effective or when the cost of prior practice becomes unsustainable in the marketplace.

RCAP offered a social policy agenda that Indian Affairs bureaucrats at both the federal and provincial levels ignore at their peril. Many RCAP recommendations have been pragmatically renovated or adopted in policies by the AFN, along with other Aboriginal organizations representing non-status and Métis peoples. These policies continue to represent an Aboriginal map that points forward toward self-determination. Strategies of capacity building and long-term investment hold the promise that healthy and productive First Nations and urban communities can fully participate in the Canadian economy while sustaining their cultural values and institutions. Where these culturally appropriate institutions have been created and embraced, they have been shown to be effective, cost-efficient, and non-threatening to the status quo. When the original RCAP recommendations were released, the federal government was running a deficit; nonetheless, RCAP made a case for investment spending in Aboriginal communities. Today, in an era when billion dollar budget surpluses are the norm, there is no excuse for the government's failure to substantially invest in such capacity building.

Indigenous scholars are central to the creation of new institutions and to the discourse on Aboriginal culture that must be created. Aboriginal writers like Taiaiake Alfred (1999: 142-43), John Borrows (2002), and Dawn Martin-Hill (2003) reveal to us forms of Indigenous knowledge that force us to rethink the logic of mainstream practices. They are attempting to define models of Indigenous science (from medicine to law and political science) that challenge existing natural and social science paradigms. Their work and ways of thinking are already informing our understanding of health, law, and governance systems that will be required to harmonize Indigenous systems within mainstream social systems. Aboriginal leaders are already using their insights, as well as the teachings of Elders, to forge new approaches to social policies.

Non-Native people who have seriously engaged with Aboriginal people as part of volunteer or work-related activities have told me how enriched they have been by Aboriginal approaches to activism and social change. Most Aboriginal people imbue their social activism with patience, tolerance, kindness, and respect. This is why the history of Native and non-Native relations in Canada has been characterized less by confrontation or violence and more by progressive attempts to assist Whites in understanding the inherent justice of Aboriginal rights positions.

We must elevate Aboriginal issues on the national agenda and place them alongside health care, education, and child poverty as key priorities. Why are Canadians reluctant to invest billions of dollars to correct Aboriginal conditions? We are prepared to invest in health care and desire a strong social safety net. Are we willing to see Aboriginal peoples languish in poverty and ill health? If so, is this because of racism, indifference, or ignorance? My argument has been that this indifference is largely the product of ignorance, or a lack of understanding of Aboriginal rights, and of a failure to see the progress that has occurred over the past 40 years. I believe that if Canadians better understand Aboriginal culture and aspirations, they will be able to confront misinformed arguments and stereotypes that continue to act as obstacles to Aboriginal ambitions. Most Canadians see Aboriginal affairs as a continuing drain on the taxpayer. Many believe that, given the poverty of communities and the poor economic location of reserves, to invest in development is really to throw good money after bad. These and other stereotypes must be replaced with a more sophisticated understanding of Aboriginal culture and capacity building.

Several changes must occur in order to deconstruct the assimilationist arguments of the neo-conservative right and advance the cause of Indigenous rights. First and foremost, we must come to grips with our history and with the fact that the settlement of Canada came at an enormous cost to Aboriginal peoples. We must understand and accept the oppression of past and current policies. We cannot whitewash the past. We must stop thinking of colonialism in the past tense and consider how ongoing colonialism impacts Aboriginal peoples.[10] We must recognize such current (post)colonial practices and decolonize our thinking. Above all else, we must recognize the double standards and paternalistic thinking that continue to exist.

Aboriginal peoples are ending the denial about problems that exist in their communities, problems such as depression, suicide, family violence, and abuse that are, to a great extent, the product of colonial history. But for reconciliation with Aboriginal peoples to occur, we must end our own denial about the role of systemic racism that perpetuates these conditions.[11] We also need to see the progress that has been made in First Nations, understanding that, despite some bureaucratic waste, most Aboriginal communities are spending provincial and federal monies wisely, effectively, and efficiently. First Nations are moving forward with meagre resources to improve the health and economic well-being of their population and are capable of managing these resources without interference from other levels of government.

In his introduction to the LaFontaine-Baldwin Essays, John Ralston Saul says, "much of the past 150 years of our history has been troubled — indeed, hobbled — by an almost childlike, head-under-the-blanket approach toward the central role of Aboriginals in the ongoing shape of Canadian Society" (Saul 2002). Saul, an advocate of diversity thinking, considers the Canadian approach to the nation-state to be revolutionary because it is non-monolithic. He and others, such as social critic Michael Ignatieff (2000), anthropologist Michael Asch (2002), and political scientist James Tully (2001), have written about how the mixture of three founding pillars of our country — Aboriginal, English, and French — has infused Canadian cultural identity with complexity and hybridity and has contributed to fundamentally Canadian attributes — respect and tolerance of diversity, environmental awareness, an appreciation for non-violence and consensus-building — that are recognized by other nations around the world.

Saul believes that the state, mainly through the courts, has done much to recognize the Aboriginal pillar of the Canadian state. But he believes that in everyday life Aboriginal peoples and their contributions are "almost automatically brushed aside." Although he hopes for a Canada in which the Aboriginal point of view becomes part of our everyday reality, he sheds little light on the individual or group processes that to date have fostered the process of marginalization. The process by which Canadians ignore, consciously neglect, and sometimes demean Aboriginal peoples and their role in our history, is difficult to fathom because it is subtle and, even when obvious, appears unintentional.[12] We do not like to believe that the plight of Aboriginal peoples is the result of any specific conscious effort, for that would require us to admit to systemic racism. And even when an understanding of our history reveals to us that the process of marginalization was direct and conscious — for example, through the terms of the Indian Act — few people are prepared to suggest that state colonialism was (and perhaps is) intentionally racist.

Neo-conservative arguments about Aboriginal issues are the latest in a long string of assimilationist arguments that have led to and supported discrimination of Indigenous peoples within our nation-state. The failure of these arguments, both philosophically and logically, stems at least in part from their inability to understand the meaning of culture and their unwillingness to encounter the politics of diversity or entertain notions of social and political institutions built on non-European values. We need to develop a vision of different orders of government that appeals to metaphors of seamless connectivity rather than social divides. It has been the continued Indigenous resistance to assimilation and integration that has forced contemporary nation-states to seek policies of accommodation and self-determination. Canadians are now poised to demonstrate to the world how diversity politics can be embraced and fostered. A deep appreciation and understanding of the nature of culture is essential if this new, national, and international aspiration is to be realized.

The promise of the Indigenous rights movement is not simply the ending of the marginalization of Indigenous minorities in Canada and elsewhere around the world. It is about the beginning of a new energy and intellectual growth that will result from the equal participation of Indigenous peoples in revitalized nation-states. There are high expectations, created by Indigenous leaders themselves, that the efforts of Indigenous peoples represent improved standards of environmental sustainability, better forms of governance built on consensus and the politics of inclusion, and even newer ways of thinking about intra- and international relations (Niezen 2003: 214).

Rather than asking whether Aboriginal peoples can ever truly be citizens of Canada, we should be asking how inclusion of Aboriginal peoples in Canadian political processes will transform our ideas of citizenship and our national identity. Indeed, it is through an infusion of Aboriginal values and a reinvention of the place of Aboriginal culture in the Canadian identity, that we will realize the potential of the river we travel together.

NOTES

1 Wampum are polished cylindrical beads, usually white or purple, made from whelks or quahog shell. The shells were rounded, pierced, and woven in designs. Precontact wampum was used as currency.
2 Presentations to the Special Committee on Indian Self-Government by the Haudenosaunee Confederacy and from Wampum Belts by Tehanetorens <http://www.kahnawake.com/ckr/two_row.html>.

3   There are countless references to the meaning of the Two Row Wampum, each with slight differences in wording or emphasis. This quote comes from the Native American Center for Living Arts, Quarterly Edition Newspaper (Winter 1980), translated by Huron Miller, available at <http://hometown.aol.com/miketben/miketben.htm>.

4   Prior to this statement, Borrows writes: "The Gus-Wen-Tah contains more than two purple rows. The three rows of white beads represent a counter-balancing message that signifies the importance of sharing and independence. These white rows, referred to as the bed of the agreement, stand for peace, friendship and respect. When these principles are read together with those depicted in the purple rows it becomes clear that ideas of citizenship also have to be rooted in notions of mutuality and interconnectedness" (2002: 149; see also Borrows 1997).

5   These words came to my attention while rereading the article by Nancy Scheper-Hughes (1991: 1145) concerning societal indifference to child death in Brazil. In a world where hunger and deprivation are common, child death takes on a "natural" quality. Death, like all else, is socially constructed, and, as Scheper-Hughes argues, in Brazil, socially responsible physicians must fight the tendency to see the lives of very young children as somehow more expendable than the lives of others.

6   For a discussion of the uses of diversity, of its analysis and its comprehension, see Geertz 2000: 68-88.

7   I wish to thank my colleague James Rice for drawing my attention to this admittedly controversial figure. Ken Wilber is a New Age philosopher, who has been described as the "Einstein of Consciousness." He is author of numerous best-selling books including *A Theory of Everything* and is reputed to be the world's most widely published philosopher. His theories, based on transpersonal and developmental psychology, attempt to integrate Western psychology and science with Eastern spirituality.

8   Wilber has proposed that humanity is moving in non-linear waves of existence (or "memes") toward new forms of consciousness. He believes (or hopes) that humanity is poised at a point where human consciousness will take a quantum leap into "second tier thinking" that will lead to the integration of pluralities and, eventually, toward holistic systems that will transform our society.

9   In Anishnabe culture, these values are referred to as the seven teachings of our Grandfathers or more simply as the grandfathers: Wisdom, Love, Respect, Bravery, Honesty, Humility, and Truth.

10 Postmodern analysis often refers to "post-colonial" processes, which describe the continuing impact of power and privilege in the creation of social inequity. But students often find the use of the term "post-colonial" in Indigenous studies confusing, taking it to mean that colonialism has somehow ended. See Proulx 2003 for a discussion of the terms colonialism and post-colonialism in the Aboriginal context.

11 "It is virtually impossible to separate individual and community healing... first and foremost, people need to 'end the denial' about problems that exist in the communities and that, to a great extent, are a product of colonial history" (Warry 1998: 207).

12　The process of marginalization, the "power-discourse" of mainstream society, makes Aboriginal peoples invisible in our history. Over the past two decades, there have been attempts to redress this wrong. Textbooks have been rewritten; most of the offensive and outright racist characterizations of Aboriginal peoples have been expunged from advertising and other visual media; and television series, such as the CBC's serialized history "Canada: A People's History" have attempted to write Aboriginal people back into our history.

REFERENCES

Aboriginal Healing Foundation. 2005. *Reclaiming Connections: Understanding Residential School Trauma Among Aboriginal People, A Resource Manual.* Anishinabe Printing. <http://www.ahf.ca>.

Adelson, Naomi. 2004 [2002]. *"Being Alive Well": Health and Politics of Cree Well-Being.* Toronto: University of Toronto Press.

AFN (Assembly of First Nations) and the Government of Canada. 2005. *A First Nations-Federal Crown Political Accord on the Recognition and Implementation of First Nations Governments.* <http://www.afn.ca/article.asp?id=1218>.

AFN. 2005a. *Our Nations Our Governments: Choosing Our Own Paths.* Report of the Joint Committee of Chiefs and Advisors On the Recognition and Implementation of First Nations Governments. <http://www.afn.ca/article.asp?id=558>.

AFN. 2005b. *Getting from the Roundtable to Results: Canada-Aboriginal People Roundtable Process, April 2004-March 2005, Executive Summary and Summary Report.* <http://www.afn.ca/cmslib/general/Round-Table1-2.pdf#search=%22Getting%20from%20the%20Roundtable%20to%20Results%3A%20Canada-Aboriginal%20People%20Roundtable%20Process%22>.

AFN. 2005c. *The First Nations Agenda for the 2005 Federal Budget: A Submission To The House Of Commons Standing Committee on Finance.* Ottawa: Assembly of First Nations.

Alfred, Taiaiake. 1999. *Peace, Power, Righteousness.* Don Mills, ON: Oxford University Press.

Alfred, Taiaiake. 2005. *Wasáse: Indigenous Pathways of Action and Freedom.* Peterborough, ON: Broadview Press.

Anderson, Terry L. 1995. *Sovereign Nations or Reservations? An Economic History of American Indians.* San Francisco: Pacific Research Institute.

Anderson, Terry L. (Ed.). 1992. *Property Rights and Indian Economies: The Political Economy Forum.* Lanham, MD: Rowman and Littlefield.

Anderson, T., and P.J. Hill. 2004. *The Not So Wild, Wild West: Property Rights on the Frontier.* Stanford, CA: Stanford University Press.

Asch, Michael. 2001. Aboriginal rights. In P. Baltes and N. Smelser (Eds.), *International Encyclopedia of Social and Behavioural Sciences* and in M. Galanter and L. Edelman (Eds.), *Law and Discipline.* Oxford: Pergamon. <http://www.sciencedirect.com/science/referenceworks/0080430767>.

Asch, Michael. 2002. From terra nullius to affirmation: reconciling Aboriginal rights with the Canadian Constitution. *Canadian Journal of Law and Society*, 17(2): 23-29.

Asch, Michael (Ed.). 1997. *Aboriginal and Treaty Rights in Canada: Essays on Law, Equality, and Respect for Difference.* Vancouver, BC: University of British Columbia Press.

Asch, Michael, and Norman Zlotkin. 1997. Affirming Aboriginal title: a new basis for comprehensive claims negotiations. In Asch 1997: 209-29.

Bagshaw, Geoffrey. 2001. Anthropology and objectivity in Native title proceedings. Paper delivered to the Adelaide Native Title Conference, Expert Evidence in Native Title Court Cases. 6-7 July.

Barnard, H. Russel (Ed.). 1998. *Handbook of Methods in Cultural Anthropology.* Walnut Creek, CA: AltaMira.

Barnsley, Paul. 2002. Tax-free status travels with new COO. *Windspeaker*, December. <http://www. ammsa.com/windspeaker/topnews-Dec-2002.html>.

Barras, Bruno. 2004. Life projects: development our way. In Blaser *et al.* 2004: 47-51.

Battiste, M., and J.S. Youngblood Henderson. 2000. *Protecting Indigenous Knowledge and Heritage.* Saskatoon: Purich Publishing.

Behiels, Michael (Ed.). 1999. *Aboriginal Peoples in Canada: Futures and Identities.* Canadian Issues 21. Montreal: Association for Canadian Studies.

Bennett, Marlyn, Cindy Blackstock, and Richard De La Ronde. 2005. *A Literature Review and Annotated Bibliography on Aspects of Aboriginal Child Welfare in Canada.* 2nd ed. First Nations Research Site of the Centre of Excellence for Child Welfare and The First Nations Child and Family Caring Society of Canada. <http://www.fncfcs.com/projects/FNRS.html>.

Benson, Bruce L. 1992. Customary Indian law: two case studies. In Anderson 1992: 27-39.

Berkes, F., P.J. George, R.J. Preston, A. Hughes, J. Turner, and B.D. Cummins. 1994. Wildlife harvesting and sustainable regional native economy in the Hudson and James Bay Lowland, Ontario. *Arctic* 47,4: 350-60.

Berry, J.W. 1999. Aboriginal cultural identity. *Canadian Journal of Native Studies* 19,1: 1-36.

Blaser, Mario. 2004. Life projects: Indigenous peoples' agency and development. In Blaser *et al.* 2004: 26-46.

Blaser, Mario, Harvey A. Feit, and Glenn McRae. 2004. Indigenous peoples and development processes: new terrains of struggle. In Blaser *et al.* 2004: 1-25.

Blaser, Mario, Harvey A. Feit, and Glenn McRae (Eds.). 2004. *In The Way of Development: Indigenous Peoples, Life Projects, and Globalization.* International Development Research Centre. London: Zed Books.

Boldt, Menno. 1993. *Surviving As Indians: The Challenge of Self-Government.* Toronto: University of Toronto Press.

Borrows, John. 1997. Wampum at Niagara: the Royal Proclamation, Canadian legal history, and self-government. In Asch 1997: 155-72.

Borrows, John. 2000. "Landed" citizenship: narratives of Aboriginal political participation. In Will Kymlicka and Wayne Norman (Eds.), *Citizenship in Diverse Societies.* Oxford: Oxford University Press. 326-44.

Borrows, John. 2001. Listening for a change: the courts and oral tradition. *Osgoode Hall Law Journal* 39: 1-38.

Borrows, John. 2002. *Recovering Canada: The Resurgence of Indigenous Law.* Toronto: University of Toronto Press.

Bradfield, Stuart. 2005. Indigenous affairs: post ATSIC, not post-colonial. *Australian Review of Public Affairs* (June). <http://www.australianreview.net>.

Brascoupe, S., and H. Mann. 2001. *A Community Guide to Protecting Indigenous Knowledge.* Ottawa: Research and Analysis Directorate, Department of Indian and Northern Affairs Canada.

Braveheart, Maria Yellow Horse, and Lemyra M. DeBruyn. 1998. The American Indian holocaust: healing historical unresolved grief. *American Indian and Alaska Native Mental Health Research* 8,2: 60-82.

Brody, Hugh. 1971. *Indians on Skid Row*. Ottawa: Northern Science Research Group, Department of Indian Affairs and Northern Development.

Brody, Hugh. 1981. *Maps and Dreams*. London: Penguin Books.

Bruner, Edward M. 1993. Introduction: the ethnographic self and the personal self. In Paul Benson (Ed.), *Anthropology and Literature*. Urbana, IL: University of Illinois Press. 1-26.

Brunton, Ron, Inga Clendinnen, Michael Duffy, Rod Moran, and Robert Manne. 2001. In denial correspondence. *Quarterly Essay* 2: 88-130.

Buddle-Crowe, Kathleen. 2001. From birchbark talk to digital dreamspeaking: a history of Aboriginal media activism in Canada. Ph.D. Dissertation. McMaster University.

Cairns, Alan C. 2000. *Citizens Plus: Aboriginal Peoples and the Canadian State*. Vancouver, BC: University of British Columbia Press.

Campbell, Murray. 2003. NWT leader's gem of an idea grabs attention. *Globe and Mail*, 11 July: A4.

Canada. 1983. *Indian Self-Government in Canada*. Report of the Special House of Commons Committee on Indian Self-Government (Penner Report). Ottawa: Supply and Services Canada.

Canada. 1997. *Gathering Strength, Canada's Aboriginal Action Plan*. Minister of Indian Affairs and Northern Development. Ottawa: Minister of Public Works and Government Services Canada.

Canadian Dictionary. 1999. Toronto: ITP Nelson.

CAUT. 2003. Canadian Association of University Teachers *Bulletin*. McMaster Senate Passes Restrictive Policy, 50, 5. A10.

Churchill, Ward. 1994. *Indians Are Us? Culture and Genocide in Native North America*. Toronto: Between the Lines.

Churchill, Ward. 1998. *A Little Matter of Genocide: Holocaust and Denial in the Americas 1492 to the Present*. San Francisco, CA: City Lights.

Chwialkowska, Luiza. 2002. Bands must make audits public. *National Post*, 15 June: A14.

Clark, Scott, and John Cove. 1988. Questions of ethics in participatory evaluation: a view from anthropology. In Jackson and Kassam 1988: 36-49.

Coates, Kenneth. 1999. Being Aboriginal: the cultural politics of identity, membership, and belonging among First Nations in Canada. In Behiels 1999: 23-43.

Cockerill, Jodi, and Roger Gibbins. 1997. Reluctant citizens? First Nations in the Canadian federal state. In Ponting 1997: 383-402.

Coon Come, Mathew. 2004. Survival in the context of mega-resource development: experiences of the James Bay Crees and the First Nations of Canada. In Blaser *et al.* 2004: 153-65.

Cornell, Stephen. 2002. What is institutional capacity and how can it help American Indian nations meet the welfare challenge? Paper prepared for the Symposium on "Capacity Building and Sustainability of Tribal Governments." Washington University, St.Louis. May 21-23. <http://udall center.arizona.edu/publications/pdf/inst_cap.pdf>.

Cornell, Stephen, and Joseph P. Kalt. 2006. Two approaches to economic development on American Indian reservations: one works, the other doesn't. The Harvard Project on American Indian

Economic Development and the Native Nations Institute for Leadership, Management, and Policy on Behalf of the Arizona Board of Regents. <http://www.jopna.net/pubs/jopna_2005-02_ Approaches.<pdf#search=%22Cornell%20and%20Kalt%201997%20Harvard%20Project%20on %20American%20Indian%20Economic%20Development%22>.

Craik, Brian. 2004. The importance of working together: exclusions, conflicts, and participation in James Bay, Quebec. In Blaser *et al.* 2004: 166-86.

Crawford, Tiffany. 2003. Aboriginal sisters win battle to stay with foster parents. *Globe and Mail*, 25 October: A5.

Cummins, Bryan D. 2004. *"Only God Can Own the Land": The Attawapiskat Cree*. Canadian Ethnography Series, Vol. 1. Toronto: Pearson Education Canada.

Cummins, John. 2001. Select Standing Committee on Aboriginal Affairs, 18 October. Vancouver. 2001 Legislative Session: 2nd Session, 37th Parliament. <http://www.legis.gov.bc.ca/cmt/37thparl/ session-2/aaf/hansard/a11018a.htm>.

D'Andrade, Roy, and Nancy Scheper-Hughes. 1995. Objectivity and militancy: a debate. *Current Anthropology* 36, 5: 399-40.

Dawson, Ray, and Nick Tilley. 1997. An introduction to scientific realist evaluation. In E. Chelimsky and W.R. Shadish (Eds.), *Evaluation for the 21st Century: a Handbook*. Thousand Oaks, CA: Sage Publications. 405-18.

Dennie, Roger. 2001. The drunken Indian. The Aboriginal Healing Foundation. *Healing Words* 2,3: 14-17.

Dickson-Gilmore, E.J. 1999. "More Mohawk than my blood": citizenship, membership, and the struggle over identity in Kahanawake. In Behiels *et al.* 1999: 44-62.

Dosman, Edgar J. 1972. *Indians: The Urban Dilemma*. Toronto: McClelland and Stewart.

Duran, Eduardo, and Bonnie Duran. 1995. *Native American Postcolonial Psychology*. Albany, NY: State University of New York Press.

Erwin, Steve. 2005. Ontario defends relocation from Kashechewan. *Globe and Mail*, 5 November: A15.

Evans, Raymond, and Bill Thorpe. 2001. The massacre of Aboriginal history. *Overland* (Winter): 21-40.

Fawcett, S.B., A. Paine-Andrews, V. Francisco, J. Schulz, K. Richter, R. Lewis, E. Williams, K. Harris, J. Berkley, J. Fisher, and C. Lopez. 1995. Using empowerment theory in collaborative partnership for community health and development. *American Journal of Community Psychology* 23,5: 677-98.

Federation of Canadian Municipalities. 2006. Shaping Our Future Advocacy Kit. Available at <http:// www.fcm.ca/english/advocacy/advocacy.html>.

Feit, Harvey, A. 2004a. James Bay life projects and politics: histories of place, animal partners, and enduring relationships. In Blaser *et al.* 2004: 92-110.

Feit, Harvey, A. 2004b. Hunting and the quest for power: James Bay Cree and Whiteman Development. In R. Bruce Morrison and C. Roderick Wilson (Eds.), *Native Peoples: The Canadian Experience*. 3rd ed. Don Mills, ON: Oxford University Press. 101-28.

Fetterman, D.M. 1996. Empowerment evaluation: an introduction to theory and practice. In Fetterman *et al.* 1996: 3-46.

Fetterman, D.M., S.J. Kaftarian, and A. Wandersman. 1996. *Empowerment Evaluation: Knowledge and Tools for Self-Assessment and Accountability.* Thousand Oaks, CA: Sage.

Fiss, Tanis 2005. The Road To Prosperity: Five Steps to Change Aboriginal Policy. Canadian Taxpayers Federation, Centre For Aboriginal Policy Change. <http://www.taxpayer.com/pdf/Road_to_Prosperity_September_2005.pdf>.

Flanagan, Tom. 1998. The last immigrants: Aboriginal self-government will likely solve nothing. Joining Canada's mainstream will. The Next City Discussion Group. <http://www.urban-renaissance.org/urbanren/index.cfm?DSP=content&ContentID=11628>.

Flanagan, Tom. 2000. *First Nations? Second Thoughts.* Montreal and Kingston: McGill-Queen's University Press.

Flanagan, Tom. 2001. Aboriginal orthodoxy in Canada. In Johns 2001a: 1-19.

Flanagan, Tom, and Christopher Alcantara. 2002. *Individual Property Rights on Canadian Indian Reserves.* The Fraser Institute. <http://www.fraserinstitute.ca/admin/books/files/property-rights.pdf>.

Fleras, Augie, and Jean Leonard Elliot. 1992. *The Nations Within: Aboriginal-State Relations in Canada, the United States, and New Zealand.* Toronto: Oxford University Press.

Galt, Virginia. 2003. Nepotism targeted in public sector. *Globe and Mail*, 6 August: C1.

Geertz, Clifford. 2000. *Available Light: Anthropological Reflections on Philosophical Topics.* Princeton, NJ: Princeton University Press.

Globe and Mail. 2002a. The assurance they gave. Editorial. 9 March: A16.

Globe and Mail. 2002b. For more transparency on Canada's reserves. June 22: A18.

Globe and Mail. 2003a. The pipeline handshake. 20 June: A16.

Globe and Mail. 2003b. Where Paul Martin should lead Canada.(2). 15 December: A16.

Globe and Mail. 2005. Moving Kashechewan. 29 October: A28.

Gualtieri, Antonio R. 1984. *Christianity and Native Traditions.* Notre Dame, IN: Cross Cultural Publications.

Guba, Egon G., and Yvonna S. Lincoln. 1995. *Fourth Generation Evaluation.* Newbury Park, CA: Sage.

Habermas, Jurgen. 1984. *The Theory of Communicative Action. Volume One: Reason and the Rationalization of Society.* Trans. Thomas McCarthy. Boston, MA: Beacon Press.

Habermas, Jurgen. 1990. *Moral Consciousness and Communicative Action.* Trans. Christian Lenhardt and Shierry Weber Nicholsen. Cambridge, MA: MIT Press.

Habermas, Jurgen. 1998. *The Inclusion of the Other: Studies in Political Theory.* Ed. Ciaran Cronin and Pablo De Greiff. Cambridge, MA: MIT Press.

Hart, E., and M. Bond. 1995. *Action Research for Health and Social Care: A Guide to Practice.* Buckingham: Open University Press.

Henry, F., and C. Tator. 2002. *Discourses of Domination: Racial Bias in the Canadian English Canadian Press.* Toronto: University of Toronto Press.

Hill, Peter S., John Wakerman, Sally Mathews, and Odette Gibson. 2001. Tactics at the interfaces: Australian Aboriginal and Torres Strait Islander health managers. *Social Science and Medicine* 52: 467-80.

Hobsbawm, Eric, and Terence Ranger (Eds.). 1983. *The Invention of Tradition*. Cambridge: Cambridge University Press.

Huggins, Jackie. 2002. Big ideas and small steps: Australia's approaches to reconciliation and Indigenous self-government. Paper delivered to A Just and Lasting Reconciliation: First Nations Government Conference. Vancouver (March): 1-12.

Ibbitson, John. 2005. Will Harper make summit's goals an election issue? *Globe and Mail*, 25 November: A4.

Ignatieff, Michael. 2000. *The Rights Revolution*. Toronto: Anansi Press.

Jacklin, Kristen, and Phyllis Kinoshameg. 2005. "Only if it's going to mean something:" Toward a Participatory Paradigm in First Nations Health Research. *The Canadian Journal of Native Studies* (in press).

Jacklin, Kristen, and Wayne Warry. 2004a. The Indian Health Transfer Policy: toward self-determination or cost containment? In Arachu Castro and Merrill Singer (Eds.), *Unhealthy Health Policy: A Critical Anthropological Examination*. Walnut Creek, CA: AltaMira Press. 215-34.

Jacklin, Kristen, and Wayne Warry. 2004b. *Wikwemikong Health Transfer Evaluation, Final Report*. Wikwemikong Unceded and the First Nations and Inuit Health Branch. Northwind Consultants.

Jacklin, Kristen, and Wayne Warry (with Agnes Mandamin and Tracy Farmer). 2005. *Mnaadmodzawin Health Services Inc. Evaluation Report*. Mnaadmodzawin Health Board and First Nations Inuit Health Branch. Northwind Consultants.

Jackson, Edward T., and Yussuf Kassam (Eds.). 1998. *Knowledge Shared: Participatory Evaluation in Development Cooperation*. Ottawa and Bloomfield, CT: IDRC/Kumarian Press.

Jamieson, Roberta. 2003. What do you mean "we," white man? *Globe and Mail*, 26 May: A11.

Jang, Brent. 2003. Landmark Arctic gas pipeline deal reached. *Globe and Mail*, 19 June: B1.

Johns, Gary (Ed.). 2001a. *Waking Up to Dreamtime: The Illusion of Aboriginal Self-Determination*. Singapore: Media Masters.

Johns, Gary. 2001b. The poverty of Aboriginal self-determination. In Johns 2001a: 20-45.

Kay, Jonathan. 2001. A case for native assimilation. *The National Post*, 8 December. <http://www.omnivore.org/jon/orwell/2001/Native_Assimilation/NA3.htm>.

Keesing, Roger M., and Robert Tonkinson (Eds.). 1982. Reinventing Traditional Culture: The Politics of Kastom in Island Melanesia. Special issue. *Mankind* 13,4: 297-398.

Kenny, Carolyn. 2004. *A Holistic Framework for Aboriginal Policy Research*. Ottawa: Status of Women Canada's Policy Research Fund and Government of Canada.

Kerr, Jonathan, and Linda C. Ashby. 2004. The new kid on the block: the Northern Ontario Medical School. *Medical Education* 81,2: 151-54.

Koenig, Edwin C. 2005. *Cultures and Ecologies: A Native Fishing Conflict on the Saugeen-Bruce Peninsula*. Toronto: University of Toronto Press.

Kymlicka, W. 1995. *Multicultural Citizenship: A Liberal Theory of Minority Rights*. Oxford: Oxford University Press.

Leenaars, Antoon A., Susanne Wenckstern, Isaac Sakinofsky, Ronald J. Dyck, Michael J. Kral, and Roger C. Bland (Eds.). 2001. *Suicide in Canada*. Toronto: University of Toronto Press.

Lucashenko, Melissa, John McLaren, and Jennifer Rose. Three Responses to Robert Manne's *In Denial. Overland* (Winter): 15-20.

Maar, Marion, Claudette Chase, Laurie C. McLeod, and Margaret Munro. 2005. Aboriginal families: healthy child development for First Nations, Métis and Inuit People. In *Facing the Challenges: Healthy Child Development.* Toronto: Ontario College of Family Physicians.

Manne, Robert. 2001. *In Denial: The Stolen Generations and the Right.* [First published in *Quarterly Essay* 1.] Melbourne: Black.

Marrett, Loraine D., and Munaza Chaudhry. 2003. Cancer incidence and mortality in Ontario First Nations, 1968-1991 (Canada). *Cancer Incidences and Control* 14,3 (April): 259-68.

Martin-Hill, Dawn. 2003. *Traditional Medicine in Contemporary Contexts: Protecting and Respecting Indigenous Knowledge and Medicine.* Ottawa: National Aboriginal Health Organization.

Martin-Hill, Dawn 2004. Resistance, determination, and perseverance of the Lubicon Cree women. In Blaser *et al.* 2004: 313-31.

McCaskill, Don. 1981. Migration, adjustment, integration of Indians in Toronto, Winnipeg, Edmonton and Vancouver: A comparative analysis. Culture 1,1: 82-89.

McGregor, Deborah. 2004. Traditional ecological knowledge and sustainable development: towards coexistence. In Blaser *et al.* 2004: 72-91.

Media Awareness Network. 2006. <http://www.media-awareness.ca/english/issues/stereotyping/ Aboriginal_people/Aboriginal_education.cfm>.

Mendelsohn, Matthew. 2003. Listen Up Canada. The New Canada Series. *Globe and Mail,* 2 July: A13.

Merry, Sally Engle. 2003. Human rights law and the demonization of culture. *Anthropological News* (February): 4-5.

Mickleburgh, Rod. 2003. Judge declares native fisheries invalid. *Globe and Mail,* 29 July: A1.

Minore, Bruce, Margaret Boone, Mae Katt, Peggy Kinch, Stephen Birch, and Christopher Mushquash. 2005. The effects of nursing turnover on continuity of care in isolated First Nations communities. *Canadian Journal of Nursing Research* 37,1: 86-100.

Mondak, J.J. (Ed.). 1998. Special issue: Psychological approaches to social capital. *Political Psychology* 19,3.

Morris, Mary Jane, Martin Cooke, and Stewart Clatworthy. 2004. Aboriginal mobility and migration patterns and policy implications. In Jerry P. White, Dan Beavon, and Paul S. Maxim (Eds.), *Aboriginal Conditions.* Vancouver: University of British Columbia Press. 108-30.

Nabigon, H., and A-M. Mawhiney. 1996. Aboriginal theory: a Cree medicine wheel guide for healing First Nations. *Social Work Treatment* 4: 18-38.

Nabigon, Herbert, Rebecca Hagey, Schuyler Webster, and Robert MacKay. 1999. The learning circle as a research method: the Trickster and Windigo in research. *Native Social Work Journal* 2,1: 113-37.

Naglar, Mark. 1973. *Indians in the City.* Ottawa: Canadian Research Centre for Anthropology, Saint Paul University.

Narayan, Kirin. 1993. How native is a "Native" anthropologist? *American Anthropologist* 95: 671-86.

Niezen, Ronald. 2003. *The Origins of Indigenism, Human Rights, and the Politics of Identity.* Berkeley, CA: University of California Press.

Ontario. 1992. *New Directions, Aboriginal Health Policy for Ontario*. Ministry of Health. Aboriginal Health Office.

OFIFC (Ontario Federation of Indian Friendship Centres). 2002. *Tenuous Connections: Urban Aboriginal Youth Sexual Health and Pregnancy*. Toronto: OFIFC. <http://www.ofifc.org/ofifc home/page/index.htm>.

Perkins, D., and M. Zimmerman. 1995. Empowerment theory, research, and application. *American Journal of Community Psychology* 23,5: 569-81.

Pocklington, Tom, and Allan Tupper. 2002. *No Place to Learn, Why Universities Aren't Working*. Vancouver: University of British Columbia Press.

Ponting, Rick J. 1997. *First Nations in Canada: Perspectives on Opportunity, Empowerment, and Self-Determination*. Toronto: McGraw-Hill Ryerson.

Proulx, Craig, 2003. *Reclaiming Aboriginal Justice, Identity, and Community*. Saskatoon, SK: Purich Publishing.

RCAP. 1993. *Aboriginal Peoples in Urban Centres*. Report of the Round Table on Urban Aboriginal Issues, Royal Commission on Aboriginal Peoples. Ottawa: Ministry of Supply and Services. <http://www.ainc-inac.gc.ca/gs/rec_e.html>.

RCAP. 1996a. *Looking Forward, Looking Back*. Volume 1. Report of the Royal Commission on Aboriginal Peoples. Ottawa: Canada Communications Group.

RCAP. 1996b. *Restructuring the Relationship*. Volume 2. Report of the Royal Commission on Aboriginal Peoples. Ottawa: Canada Communications Group.

RCAP. 1996c. *Gathering Strength*. Volume 3. Report of the Royal Commission on Aboriginal Peoples. Ottawa: Canada Communications Group.

RCAP. 1996d. *Perspectives and Realities*. Volume 4. Report of the Royal Commission on Aboriginal Peoples. Ottawa: Canada Communications Group.

RCAP. 1996e. *Renewal, A Twenty Year Commitment*. Volume 5. Report of the Royal Commission on Aboriginal Peoples. Ottawa: Canada Communications Group.

Reading, Jeff (with Brenda Elias). 1999. An examination of residential schools and Elder health. *First Nations and Inuit Regional Health Surveys*. Ottawa: First Nations and Inuit Regional Health Survey National Steering Committee. 29-54.

Reasons, Peter, and Hilary Bradbury (Eds.). 2001. *Handbook of Action Research: Participative Inquiry and Practice*. London: Sage.

Rebiens, C. 1995. Participatory evaluation of development interventions: the concept and its practice. Working Paper No. 4. Department of Intercultural Communication and Management, Copenhagen Business School, Denmark.

Restoule, Jean-Paul. 1999. Making movies, changing lives: Aboriginal film and identity. In Behiels 1999: 180-207.

Richards, John. 2001. Let's get past our reservations. *Globe and Mail*, 19 December: A19.

Richards, John. 2003. A better way to grasp the future. *Globe and Mail*, 10 February: A11.

Rigsby, Bruce. 2001. Representations of culture and the expert knowledge and opinions of anthropologists. Opening address, Adelaide Native Title Conference, Expert Evidence in Native Title Court Cases: Issues of Truth, Objectivity and expertise. 6-7 July.

Robertson, P., M. Jorgensen, and C. Garrow. 2004. Indigenous evaluation research. *American Indian Quarterly* 28,3 and 4: 499-527.

Romanow, Roy. 2002. *Commission on the Future of Health Care in Canada. Final Report.* Ottawa: Queens Printer. <http://www.hc-sc.gc.ca/english/care/romanow/hcc0086.html>.

Rorty, Richard. 1999. *Philosophy and Social Hope.* New York: Penguin Books.

Ross, Rupert. 1992. *Dancing With a Ghost.* London: Octopus Publishing.

Ryan, Joan. 1995. *Doing Things the Right Way: Dene Traditional Justice in Lac La Martre, NWT.* Calgary, AB: University of Calgary Press and Arctic Institute of North America.

Said, Edward. 1979. *Orientalism.* New York: Random House.

Sallot, Jeff. 2003. Public against judges making laws, poll says. *Globe and Mail*, 11 August: A1, 5.

Saul, John Ralston. 2002. Rooted in the power of three. The LaFontaine-Baldwin Essays. *Globe and Mail*, 8 March: A15.

Scheper-Hughes, Nancy. 1991. Social indifference to child death. *The Lancet, Culture and Medicine Series* 337 (May): 1144-47.

Scott, Colin. 2004. Conflicting discourses of property, governance, and development in the Indigenous North. In Blaser *et al.* 2004: 299-312.

Scott, James C. 1985. *Weapons of the Weak: Everyday Forms of Peasant Resistance.* Hartford, CT: Yale University Press.

Seidle, Leslie. 2005. Exploring Canadians' views on Aboriginal issues. *Portraits of Canada 2004*: Part 4. Centre for Research and Information on Canada. <http://www.cric.ca>.

Shanks, Signa Daum. 2004. Mamiskotamaw: "Oral history," "Indigenous method," and Canadian law in three books. *Indigenous Law Journal* 3,1: 181-92.

Simpson, Jeffrey. 2002. When they poll the know-nothings. *Globe and Mail*, 11 December: A21.

Simpson, Jeffrey. 2003. Trolling for trouble on fishery rights — again. *Globe and Mail*, 30 July: A13.

Simpson, Jeffrey. 2005. Aboriginals are voting with their feet for a third way. *Globe and Mail*, 26 November: A27.

Simpson, L.R. 2004. Anticolonial strategies for the recovery and maintenance of Indigenous knowledge. *American Indian Quarterly* 28,3 and 4: 373-84.

Skye, Jairus. 2006. Aboriginal healing and identity in the urban Aboriginal context. MA thesis. McMaster University.

Smith, Melvin H. 1996 (1995). *Our Home OR Native Land: What Government's Aboriginal Policy Is Doing To Canada.* Toronto: Stoddard.

Smylie, J., C.M. Martin, N. Kaplan-Myrth, L. Steele, C. Tait, and W. Hogg. 2003. Knowledge translation and Indigenous knowledge. *Circumpolar Health* 63, suppl. 2: 139-43.

Spielmann, Roger. 1998. *You're So Fat!: Exploring Ojibwe Discourse.* Toronto: University of Toronto Press.

Stackhouse, John. 2001. Canada's apartheid. *Globe and Mail*, 5 November-19 December.

Steckley, John L., and Bryan D. Cummins. 2001. *Full Circle: Canada's First Nations.* Toronto: Prentice Hall.

Stymeist, David H. 1975. *Ethnics and Indians: Social Relations in a Northwestern Ontario Town.* Toronto: Peter Martin Associates.

Sunday, Julie, and John Eyles. 2001. Managing and treating risk and uncertainty for health: a case study among First Nation's Peoples in Ontario, Canada. *Social Science and Medicine* 52: 635-50.

Tanner, Adrian. 1979. *Bringing Home Animals*. Social and Economic Studies No. 23. Institute of Social and Economic Research. Memorial University of Newfoundland.

Thorsell, William. 2003a. Canadian democracy's spare tires. *Globe and Mail*, 20 October: A15.

Thorsell, William. 2003b. Good law, but bad process. *Globe and Mail*, 11 August: A13.

Treat, James (Ed.). 1996. *Native and Christian: Indigenous Voices on Religious Identity in the United States and Canada*. New York, NY: Routledge.

Tuhiwai Smith, L. 2001. *Decolonizing Methodologies: Research and Indigenous Peoples*. London: Zed Books.

Tully, James H. 2001 [1995]. *Strange Multiplicity: Constitutionalism in an Age of Diversity*. Cambridge: Cambridge University Press.

Venne, Sharon. 1997a. Honour bound: Onion Lake and the spirit of Treaty Six: the international validity of treaties with Indigenous peoples. Copenhagen, Denmark: International Work Group for Indigenous Affairs.

Venne, Sharon. 1997b. Understanding Treaty 6: an Indigenous perspective. In Asch 1997: 173-207.

Venne, Sharon. 2001. Treaty making and its potential for conflict resolution between Indigenous Nations and the Canadian State. In *Blind Spots: An Examination of the Federal Government's Response to the Report of the Royal Commission on Aboriginal Peoples*. Ottawa, Canada: Aboriginal Rights Coalition.

von Gernet, Alexander. 1996. Oral narratives and aboriginal pasts: an interdisciplinary review of the literature on oral traditions and oral histories. Ottawa: Research and Analysis Directorate, Indian and Northern Affairs Canada.

von Gernet, Alexander. 2000. What my elders taught me: oral traditions as evidence in aboriginal litigation. In Owen Lippert (Ed.), *Beyond the Nass Valley; National Implications of the Supreme Court's Delgamuukw Decision*. Vancouver, BC: The Fraser Institute.

Wagamese, Richard. 2005. The stain of Kashechewan's dirty water. *Globe and Mail*, 29 October: A29.

Waldram, James B. 1997. *The Way of the Pipe: Aboriginal Spirituality and Symbolic Healing in Canadian Prisons*. Peterborough, ON: Broadview Press.

Waldram, James B. 2004. *Revenge of the Windigo: The Construction of the Mind and Mental Health of North American Aboriginal Peoples*. Toronto: University of Toronto Press.

Waldram, James B., Pat Berringer, and Wayne Warry. 1992. "Nasty, brutish, and short": anthropology and the Gitksan-Wet'sewet'en Decision. *The Canadian Journal of Native Studies* 12,2: 309-16.

Waldram, James B., D. Ann Herring, and T. Kue Young. 2006 [1995]. *Aboriginal Health in Canada*. 2nd ed. Toronto: University of Toronto Press.

Wallace, Anthony. 1972. *The Death and Rebirth of the Seneca*. New York: Random House/Vintage.

Warry, W. 1992. The Eleventh Thesis: Applied Anthropology as Praxis. *Human Organization* 51, 2: 1-13.

Warry, W. 1998. *Unfinished Dreams: Community Healing and the Reality of Aboriginal Self-Government*. Toronto: University of Toronto Press.

Warry, W., and K. Beckett. 1999. *Wikwemikong Health Transfer Evaluation Report*. Wikwemikong Unceded First Nation, Health Board and Medical Services Branch. Northwind Consultants.

Warry, W., and K. Jacklin. 2000. *Mnaadmodzawin/UCCM Health Transfer Evaluation Report*. Mnaadmodzawin Health Board and Medical Services Branch. Northwind Consultants.

Warry, W., and J. Sunday. 2000. M'Chigeeng Health Transfer Evaluation. M'Chigeeng Health Services and Medical Services Branch. Northwind Consultants.

Weaver, Sally. 1990. A new paradigm in Canadian Indian policy for the 1990s. *Canadian Ethnic Studies* 22,3.

Wente, Margaret. 2003a. Race politics and Emma's fate. *Globe and Mail*, 15 July: A15.

Wente, Margaret. 2003b. What Lisa wants. *Globe and Mail*, 14 August: A15.

Wente, Margaret. 2004. Blood and the bonds of belonging. *Globe and Mail*, 5 June: A21.

Wente, Margaret. 2005. All because of a broken $30 part. *Globe and Mail*, 15 November: A27.

Wenzel, George. 1991. *Animal Rights, Human Rights*. Toronto: University of Toronto Press.

Wien, F. 1999. The Royal Commission report: Nine steps to rebuild Aboriginal economies. *Journal of Aboriginal Economic Development* 1(1): 102-19.

Wilber, Ken. 2000. *A Theory of Everything, An Integral Vision for Business, Politics, Science and Spirituality*. Boston: Shambhala.

Windshuttle, Keith. 2000. The myths of frontier massacres in Australian history. *Quadrant* 44: 10-12.

INDEX

Aboriginal academics. *See* Aboriginal scholars
Aboriginal Action Plan, 120
Aboriginal affairs funding
    "Indian Industry," 29–30, 39
    media criticism, 72–73
Aboriginal and Torres Strait Islander
    Commission, 179
Aboriginal and Treaty Rights (Asch), 42
Aboriginal Capacity and Developmental
    Research Environments (ACADRE),
    162–63
Aboriginal Child and Family Services, 78
Aboriginal child welfare policy, 77–79, 102, 115
    removal of children from white foster
    parents, 104
Aboriginal children, 72
    "adopted out" to white parents, 58, 77–78,
    102
    extended families, 80
    higher risks in life, 79
    illegitimate, 79
    removal from families and reserves, 15,
    57–60, 77–78, 102–03 (*See also* resi-
    dential schools; "Sixties Scoop"; Stolen
    Generations report)
    suicide rates, 151
Aboriginal Christianity, 90–91
Aboriginal citizenship, 34, 108, 178. *See also*
    Canadian citizenship
    citizens plus, 35, 46–47
    shared citizenship, 184
"Aboriginal Commercial Fishery in B.C., The"
    (Smith), 39
Aboriginal communities. *See* First Nations;
    reserves; urban Aboriginal population
Aboriginal Council of Toronto (ACT), 116,
    120–21
Aboriginal cultural revitalization movement,
    14, 111–12
Aboriginal culture, 28, 95, 106
    balance with human rights, 28
    civilization evaluation, 43, 54
    contemporary Aboriginal cultures, 49, 91
    continuing integrity, 96
    cultural norms, 159
    diversity, 11, 17, 89, 117
    ignorance of, 15
    as inferior, 43
    loss of, 146
    norms, 159
    part of Canadian national identity, 92, 192
    pre-contact, 89
    resistance to assimilation (*See* assimilation)

    seen as tied to reserve, 111
Aboriginal development corporations, 139,
    143–44
Aboriginal economic development, 75–76
    Aboriginal entrepreneurs, 116, 137
    Aboriginal-specific development funds,
    137, 148
    collective approaches to economy, 140, 145,
    147
    conflict with mainstream economic inter-
    ests, 141, 148
    cooperative economic activities, 139
    importance of land claims, 123, 133
    land-based economic activities, 141
    need for mixed regional economies, 147
    positive signs of, 144
    reserve-based, 137, 139, 142–43
    small business, 139, 144
    sustainable economic development, 14, 137,
    142, 145–48, 153
Aboriginal economic failures, 61, 143
Aboriginal education, 161–62. *See also*
    Indigenous knowledge; traditional
    environmental knowledge (TEK); university
    education (or community college)
    improvements in, 161
    Indigenous research practices, 162
    in journalism and broadcasting, 81
    medical students, 161
    Native language programs, 115, 161
Aboriginal elites. *See* Aboriginal leadership
Aboriginal Financial Officers Association, 170
Aboriginal Fisheries Strategy (AFS), 128, 130
Aboriginal Friendship Centres Program
    (AFCP), 113
Aboriginal government as third order. *See* third
    order of government
Aboriginal Healing and Wellness Strategy
    (AHWS), 120, 158
Aboriginal Healing Foundation (AHF), 61–62
Aboriginal health care, 36–37, 48, 117, 152, 159
    Aboriginal healers, 118, 158
    Aboriginal medical students, 161
    Aboriginal medicine, 27–28, 91, 157–58,
    163, 167, 174
    Australia, 160
    and awareness of healthy lifestyles, 160
    complementary to Western practices, 158
    culturally appropriate services, 103, 152,
    157, 160, 162
    Friendship Centres, 114
    funding, 154, 157–58, 160
    health care in rural and remote areas, 153

health clinics, 36, 115
ill health, 17, 40, 142, 151–52, 160
improvements to programs, 153, 160
Indian status and, 126
Institute of Aboriginal Peoples' Health, 103,
  162
link to self-determination, 153
mental health, 155, 157, 160
residential school syndrome, 103
smoking prevention programs, 152
staffing, 161
transparency, 156
Aboriginal health information systems, 156,
  159–60
Aboriginal identity, 77, 99, 107, 119, 151, 178
artificial identity divisions, 103–04
colonialism and, 101–02
cultural, 95, 106
defined by the state, 102–04
diversity, 106
hybridized, 18
identity formation, 100
need for self-identification, 105, 108, 118
political, 185
Aboriginal identity politics, 101
Aboriginal issues, 26
Canadian public on, 16–17, 19
debates or "culture war" in Australia, 16
ignorance concerning, 14
low on electorate agenda, 80
Aboriginal language programs, 115, 161
Aboriginal languages, 10, 99, 158
Aboriginal leadership, 16, 30, 35, 40, 42, 79, 180,
  190. *See also* First Nations councils
asserting collective rights on reserves and
  cities, 17, 113
blamed for poor conditions, 168
environmental protection (*See*
  environment)
on extinguishment, 132
hereditary leadership systems, 34, 47, 173
role in Territorial government assembly, 148
seen as incapable of good government, 76
Aboriginal Legal Services of Toronto, 117
Aboriginal media, 80–81
and identity formation, 100–01
newspapers, 80–81
Aboriginal off-reserve population. *See also*
  urban Aboriginal population
labour force participation rate, 116
Aboriginal oral history, 125, 129, 183
"aboriginal orthodoxy." *See* "new Aboriginal
  orthodoxy"
Aboriginal participation in mainstream institutions, 36, 91

Aboriginal peoples, 10–11. *See also* First
  Nations; Indigenous peoples
adapting Western practices, 35, 95
assimilation arguments (*See* assimilation)
avoidance of conflict or confrontation, 159
biculturalism, 106
blamed for problems (blaming the victim),
  55, 70, 72, 76, 138–39
as citizens plus, 35, 46–47
citizenship (*See* Aboriginal citizenship;
  Canadian citizenship; enfranchisement)
debates in Canada, 26
defined as Indian, Inuit, and Métis, 123
economic development (*See* Aboriginal
  economic development)
as entrepreneurs, 91, 116, 137
environmental issues (*See* environment)
guilt concerning, 41
higher education (*See* Aboriginal education)
historic claims (*See* land claims; treaties)
hybridized identity (*See* Aboriginal identity)
ignorance of, 13, 17
importance to Canadian identity, 14–15, 17,
  48, 92, 101, 106, 191–92
"in the way" of mainstream economic prosperity, 17, 71, 73, 141, 144–45, 148
integrated in business economies in 19th
  century, 138
integration, 17, 37, 44, 46, 76, 140, 185
as just immigrants, 43–44, 178
leaders (*See* Aboriginal leadership)
linked to larger international processes, 179
marginalization and poverty (*See* poverty)
Métis, 45, 103–04, 121, 123
middle-class, 116
non-status Indians, 9, 34, 45, 80, 103–07,
  117–18, 121, 127, 170, 189
as one of three founding pillars, 191
political division (status and non-status,
  etc.), 102–04
professionals, 116–17
reinvention of nation-state, 18
right to self-identify, 105, 108, 188
scholars (*See* Aboriginal scholars)
state-created dependency, 17
state-sponsored violence against, 56, 58
status Indians, 34, 42, 47, 103, 117, 126
stereotypes, 14, 88, 100–01, 115–16, 137–38,
  168
as threat to Canadian social fabric, 47, 71
turned the corner, 15–16, 191 (*See also*
  capacity building)
welfare dependency, 45, 101, 138, 141–43
Aboriginal Peoples Television Network
  (APTN), 81, 89
Aboriginal Pipeline Group, 148

Gen 5/16 TD